LENT TO MARION NEXT

REMEMBERING WOOLWORTH'S

Frank Winfield Woolworth:
April 13, 1852–April 8, 1919

R E M E M B E R I N G

WOOLWORTH'S

A Nostalgic History of the World's

Most Famous Five-and-Dime

Karen Plunkett-Powell

ST. MARTIN'S PRESS / NEW YORK

To the memory of

Frank Winfield Woolworth, and to that of the other founding fathers: Charles S. Woolworth, Earle P. Charlton, Seymour H. Knox, Fred M. Kirby, William H. Moore and Carson C. Peck. Although the name "Woolworth" has been removed from the company masthead, the contributions of the pioneers of the world's most famous five-and-dime will persevere.

Library of Congress Cataloging-in-Publication Data

Plunkett-Powell, Karen.
    Remembering Woolworth's : a nostalgic history of the world's most famous five-and-dime / Karen Plunkett-Powell.—1st U.S. ed.
        p.   cm.
    Includes bibliographical references and index.
    ISBN 0-312-20670-4
    1. Woolworth Corporation. 2. Variety stores—History.
3. Woolworth, Frank Winfield. 1852-1919. I. Title.
HF5465.U6W864   1999
381'.12'06573—dc21   99-15918
                                                                        CIP

Book design by Richard Oriolo

10   9   8   7   6   5   4   3   2

CONTENTS

PART ONE

REMEMBERING FRANK WINFIELD WOOLWORTH:
THE MERCHANT PRINCE

PART TWO

REMEMBERING WOOLWORTH'S . . .
AROUND THE WORLD

ACKNOWLEDGMENTS

Many of the individuals I want to acknowledge are people I have grown to know very well, even though I have never met them in person. Due to the magic of today's technology, I was able to communicate with people in big cities and rural towns all over the United States, and across Europe. This was a wonderful experience, and I appreciate the way you all took time out of your busy schedules to answer my e-mails, faxes, and phone calls. Others among my acknowledgment list are those who have been in my life for years, and I continue to value their friendship.

First, I want to extend my heartfelt appreciation to the Woolworth's "boys" who shared their valuable business insights and personal experiences about ye olde Red-Fronts: Chuck Wilkerson, John Compton, Tom Biglin, and the ever-entertaining and knowledgeable "El Verde"—as well as those legal beagles and former Woolworth's execs, employees, and "Z" message board posters who prefer not to be mentioned by name. You helped me locate primary source materials, copies of Frank Woolworth's "General Letters", hard-to-find company brochures, photographs, and vital reports. Without these contributions, this book would not have been possible.

To Sue Woolley and Mike Frankel, who have enriched my life with their goodness and have made the road to finishing this book a road filled with joy; and to author Helen C. Pike for her inspiration and ideas.

For editing assistance, I salute my critique partners, Donna Steinhorn, Lois Simon Rosenthal and Johnnie Ryan Evans.

Deep appreciation to my talented editors, Andrew Miller and Marian Lizzi, to my agent and dear friend, Alice Orr, to copy editor, Nancy Hanger, to Anikah McLaren, and to the outstanding art and design team at St. Martin's Press.

Kudos to those incredible researchers who always managed to find the most obscure data in record time: Joel Gaines, and the Three Wise Men: Charlie Boyle, Art Jenssen, and Dr. Ed Buckley.

Hats off to Ginger Shelley, Jim Stokes, Anne Adams, and the rest of the staff of the Lancaster Historical Society in Pennsylvania, as well as to the Jefferson County Historical Society of Watertown, New York. Both organizations have made an important commitment to preserving the Woolworth legacy.

Special thanks are in order for those of you who so generously shared your time, knowledge, memories, special skills, photos, documents, five-and-dime collectibles and/or much-needed support and encouragement: John W. Adams, Sandy Biggs, Joe Bilby, Mary Blatnik, The Book Haven of Lancaster, Victoria Broadhurst, Joel Cadbury, Ellen Childs, Barbara Comerford, Chris Cormier, Charles Correll, Veronique Daganaud, Nick, Elaine & Gail De Risi, Dorn's Photo, John Dylla, Sandy Fergesun, Bob Finnan, Melodie Francis, Olga Freeman, Bill Ignizio, Eric Jung, Andrea Kane, Shannon Kelly, Annie A. Kruger, Marie Lance, Geoffrey S. Lapin, Liz Larabee, Pat Leary, Joan McAfee, Lois McDonald, Stacey McDonald, Joanne, Tom and Zan McGreevy-Yeck, Jim McNamara, Cindy and Doug Moreau, Rosemarie Plunkett, Eric Rosenthal, Anne Savarese, Rosemary Schafer, Jane Schoener, Art Scott, Penny Scott, John and Kim Sitra, Marie Solomou, Michael Steinhorn, Patricia Sinnott-Stott, Scott Thompsen, Jeanne Thompson, Andrea Vaughan, Clare Wharton, and all of the people who shared "Time Capsule Memories".

There was one particular Art Consultant who merits special mention; a person who prefers to remain anonymous, but who helped me by extending unconditional support, and unlimited time and energy. You're one in a million and the world is a better place because you are here.

And of course, a loving hug for Jason, just for being you.

Nickel Parakeets and Grilled Cheese: Welcome to the World's Most Famous Five-and-Dime

F. W. Woolworth store, 34th Street, NYC c. 1954

Rita was 16 years, hazel eyes and chestnut hair.

She made the Woolworth counter shine.

Eddie was a sweet romancer, and a darn good dancer.

They'd waltz the aisles of the five and dime . . .

—Song: "Love at the Five and Dime" by Nanci Griffith

The Woolworth Tradition

Two straws—one dream—all for a dime on Mainstreet, U.S.A.!

For 118 years, the local Woolworth's "Red-Front" was known as *everybody's store,* the place one could find just about anything—including romance. Indeed, Cupid was a steady customer of F. W. Woolworth. During the glory days of the five-and-dime, his golden bow bewitched thousands of young couples at Woolworth lunch counters. It was a common bring-a-smile-to-your-lips sight to see those red vinyl stools brimming over with starry-eyed lovers sharing an ice cream soda after a weekend movie matinee.

Those same lovers were most likely introduced to F. W. Woolworth stores as children. For millions of customers, the Woolworth's tradition started early, and continued to play a part in each stage of their lives. The first stage was usually experienced from the vantage point of a baby stroller, with its pint-sized occupant gazing wide-eyed at this new wonderland which mama called "the five-and-ten." After their strollers were stored away, growing children armed with hard-earned pocket change would walk through the aisles, gazing at the profusion of colorful merchandise, and spend perhaps an hour choosing just the right handkerchief for Uncle Henry, or an Easter corsage for grandmother. There were always a few coins left over for lemon drops at the candy carousel, a "fortune" in the penny weight machine, or a coveted tin soldier.

Teenagers, too, found Woolworth's a province of endless fascination. It was "the" place to buy their first tube of lipstick or hair tonic, a stack of 45 RPM records, or posters of their favorite movie stars.

As the years flew by, and an adult's salary replaced a childhood allowance, one would pass

TIME CAPSULE MEMORY

"Teen-age fun at Woolworth's"

I really believe that Woolworth's had just about everything a person needed! As a teenager, I rarely got past the makeup section, unless it was to buy records. Records at that time were thirty-five cents, and I remember my mother would have a fit over the price.

—Lynda Phebus, Clarks Hill, Indiana

over crayons and whistles in favor of Stardust pettislips, MacGregor cologne and "Fifth Avenue" boxed stationery. A Saturday morning shopping excursion offered a seemingly endless supply of yarn, bobby pins, cotton towels, garden tools and curtain rods. Flashy overhead displays advertised favors and decorations for every occasion, from baby showers to bridge parties. A box of green wax candles and a sugary cake topper guaranteed a rich birthday celebration for even the poorest child.

Not surprisingly, in December, Woolworth's became a holiday mecca for the budget-conscious family, a fantasy of tree angels and fragile glass ornaments, foil garlands, and glitter-sparked pine cones; Nativity figures and wooden Hanukkah dreidels. The original F. W. Woolworth Christmas catalogs featured beautifully illustrated watercolor covers, offering everything from Gene Autry holster sets to Woolco cotton threads—with the promise that the financially strained family could pay with Woolworth's convenient layaway plan. Best of all, this promise, along with the endless supply of bargains, lasted all year, from one holiday to the next.

The twilight years of a dimestore patron often brought the shopping experience full circle. Seniors would bring their great grandchildren to Woolworth's, often as a special treat. On a whim (or at the urging of a tenacious toddler) little Bobby or Missy might leave the store cradling a clear bag full of water, tied securely by a smiling, uniformed counter girl. Inside the bag, a pair of confused goldfish would swim around in circles, awaiting transport to their new home. Grandchildren who had been especially well-behaved were rewarded with a blue parakeet or a green turtle.

When Grandma or Grandpa visited by themselves, the local five-and-dime became a place to browse the aisles and greet old friends. And after the shopping was done, one could always saunter back to the lunch counter for a grilled cheese sandwich or hot turkey dinner. Most people do not realize the Woolworth Company pioneered the concept of offering a turkey dinner *all year round*—not just at Thanksgiving.

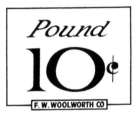

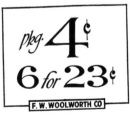

During the 1930s and '40s, placards like these heralded the many bargains of Woolworth's. In the early days, Christmas tree ornaments cost 6 for 23¢!

TIME CAPSULE MEMORY

"The toy farm animals of my youth"

My best friend and I used to visit our local Woolworth's in California in the late 1950s and early '60s. Our mothers bowled for fun, and the five-and-dime was conveniently located right next to the bowling alley. We would sneak away from the bowling alley and head straight for Woolworth's great toy department. In those days, just about every kid had a metal or plastic toy barn, and Woolworth's had many, many rubber farm animals. If we were lucky, we would have money to buy an animal or two. We played with these things until we were old enough to be embarrassed if any of our other friends caught us!

—Cat Campbell, North Fork, Ca.

Back in the 1930s, a complete turkey dinner, including beverage and dessert, cost only a quarter.

For some of us, it is the experience of *working* at the local five-and-dime that triggers the most vivid memories. Through the decades, the F. W. Woolworth Company's "Red-Fronts" employed hundreds of thousands of sales clerks, counter girls, cashiers,

Grand Reopening of Red Bank, N.J. store, c. 1945. Note the penny weight machine far right.

During World Wars I and II, Woolworth's counter girls held down the stores, often taking on the role of managers, while the boys went off to battle.

and stockboys; the latter often started out as minimum-wage "Learners," and then ascended to the upper ranks of the company.

During the war years, the vision of a Woolworth's candy girl, looking snappy in her starched blue uniform and cap, was as familiar a sight as the young soldier marching off to battle.

So loyal were those early employees, that during the women's labor strikes of 1939, when the strikers barricaded themselves in the Woolworth's stores, they continued their cleanup duties. They made certain that every floor they marched upon was swept, and that every single parakeet was fed. And you can bet the company acknowledged their courtesy, even as they haggled over the minimum wage. It was all part of a team spirit instilled many years before, by F. W. Woolworth, the man known as the "Merchant Prince."

The Rise of "Everybody's Store"

From the day of its humble beginning in Utica, New York, in 1879, Frank Winfield Woolworth's "Great Five-Cent Store" filled an unmet need among the masses. While the more privileged could afford to shop at Tiffanys, or have their clothes made by French seam-

In the United Kingdom, the famed Red-Fronts were known colloquially as "Woolies."

stresses, millions of people foundered in the "rest of us" category. Frank Winfield Woolworth recognized this reality and expanded greatly the concept of the general store. He created a retail chain that offered a wide selection of merchandise at prices so reasonable that, half a century later, even the hardest-hit Depression family could benefit. It didn't seem to matter that the products weren't always top quality, or that famous brand names were elusive. The fact was, that if you needed one of the thousands of utilitarian items that kept a household running, you could find it (and afford to buy it) at your local Woolworth's. At F. W. Woolworth's, everyone felt rich, and this was one of the secrets of its unprecedented success.

For over a century, the company's familiar red-and-gold mastheads dotted Main Streets across the United States and Canada, but the wonderful bargains of "Wooleys" were not exclusive to North America. Being a man of great foresight, Frank Winfield expanded overseas as early as 1909, when the first F. W. Woolworth & Co. Ltd. (a "three-penny-and-six" shop) opened in Liverpool, England.

In 1927, eight years after Frank Woolworth's death, his administrative successor, Hubert Parson, adopted Bremen into the family, spawning the German Division's first "25-

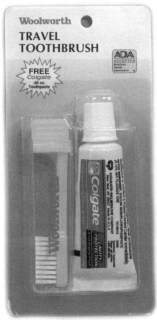

and-50 pfennig" stores. By 1929, eight bustling Woolworth's stores were even operating in the Republic of Cuba. Before Fidel Castro's military coup in 1959, tourists and Cuban natives alike would routinely head for the Havana-based "Tencent" for American yo-yos, Milky Way bars, and Hula Hoops.

After World War II, the company formed alliances with even more manufacturers, allowing it to create extensive lines of "Woolworth-brand" merchandise.

Under the leadership of F. W. Woolworth's president James Leftwich and, later, Robert C. Kirkwood, older stores were remodeled, food service departments expanded, stock was consistently replenished, and managerial training programs were enhanced. Slowly but surely, Woolworth variety stores moved into shopping malls, and long rows of "self-service" aisles replaced the old merchandising format of having a uniformed cashier stationed at individual counters. All of these factors combined to insure that the popular Red-Fronts, with their striped awnings, kept up with the changing American dream. Meanwhile, over in Europe, F. W. Woolworth & Co. Ltd. started to push on, determined to repair the damage rendered by Hitler's aerial assaults.

On New Year's Day of 1961, F. W. Woolworth's executives boasted a milestone: the company had reached a record one billion dollars in annual sales. During this prosperous postwar period, F. W. Woolworth Co. acquired G. R. Kinney Corporation, and started to open colossal Woolco discount department stores in the United States and Canada. In 1969, the company also procured Richman Brothers, a manufacturer and retailer of men and boy's clothing.

The F. W. Woolworth Company had much to celebrate during its centennial in 1979. The corporate giant owned or held majority interest in more than 4000 General Merchandise and specialty stores worldwide, and employed over 200,000 employees. From coast to coast, unprecedented sales and spectacular publicity events heralded the company's achievements.

It certainly seemed as though the boom would never end. The profits were pouring in, the customers were happy, hourly wage employees felt as if they were an integral part of the Woolworth's team, and administrators were feeling secure about their pensions. But behind the scenes, the picture was beginning to cloud.

Nineteen years later, every F. W. Woolworth Red Front in America and Canada was gone.

Bargains Abounded at "Everybody's Store"

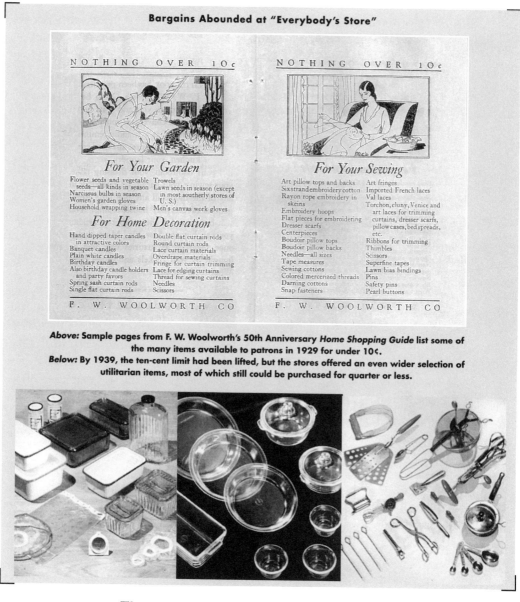

Above: Sample pages from F. W. Woolworth's 50th Anniversary *Home Shopping Guide* list some of the many items available to patrons in 1929 for under 10¢.
Below: By 1939, the ten-cent limit had been lifted, but the stores offered an even wider selection of utilitarian items, most of which still could be purchased for quarter or less.

The Demise of an American Icon

One of the first questions that people ask, when reading about the demise of F. W. Woolworth's, is: *Why? How did this happen?*

The answer is extremely complex. Countless factors and decisions, both good and bad, contributed to the death of these popular Red-Fronts. The exact details are known only to corporate insiders, and to those who have meticulously analyzed the five-and-dime's rich history. Generally speaking, though, it is safe to say that the Woolworth's variety stores perished under the strike of that double-edged sword known as Progress.

Beginning in 1962, with the opening of the first Woolco store in Columbus, Ohio, the company made its first giant leap out of its traditional five-and-dime image. It was now a player in the field of mega-discount stores, competing with other fledgling discount chains such as Grant City and K-Mart. When Woolworth's joined forces with Kinney in 1963, it also ventured into the shoe business. Suddenly, Woolworth's didn't just mean "five-and-ten," Woolworth's meant "diversified retail." The tides were changing, and continued to change with each passing trend. For example, in the mid-1970s, a new health-conscious generation showed an interest in designer sneakers. In response, the company introduced Footlocker stores. When enthusiasm for specialty sportswear climbed steadily throughout the 1980s, Woolworth's was ready with its latest offspring: Champs. There were even experimental forays into small, mall-based shops. Some of these niche establishments like "Afterthoughts" endured, but others, including "Best of Times" did not, causing an additional financial drain on the company's General Merchandise division.

As F. W. Woolworth's focus changed, so did the faces of the powerful inner circle inside the great Woolworth Building on Broadway in New York. A study of annual reports shows that, with each passing term, fewer members of the board of directors were of the "home-grown" variety. The once strictly held traditions of working your way up from stock boy to chairman, or even of requiring that high-level executives have substantial experience in the variety store field, was fast fading. Equally significant, not one direct Woolworth heir was actively involved in the business. All of Frank and Charles Woolworths' children and grandchildren had passed on.

It was a brand-new ball club at the F. W. Woolworth Company. A new guard had replaced the old.

Meanwhile, what was happening to the established Woolworth Red-Fronts? Well, hundreds of the dimestores were holding steady, especially those located in the prime geographical areas. As late as 1992, for example, the 34th Street store in Manhattan (one of the chain's oldest sites) was bringing in over 20 million dollars per year, and the Ala Moana store in Honolulu was generating a sales volume of $24,300,000.

Yet, in some regions of America, customers began to notice a decided change in their once-sparkling Woolworth's stores. Merchandise was not always replenished in a timely manner, pricing code systems seemed outdated, managers that had been in one location for decades mysteriously vanished, and the once-familiar faces of cashiers started to change from month to month. Part of the reason for this drastic shift in ambiance was that, the once-strong feeling of being part of a close-knit "Woolworth family" of employees was diminishing as the company expanded and diversified. Young adults, who once formed the core (and potential management pool) of the Red-Fronts, started job-hopping from retail chain to retail chain in search of better wages. Veteran managers of large Red-Fronts were retiring, or being transferred to other divisions of the company. In some cases, less-experienced employees filled the void. At the same time, the shopping habits of Americans were changing fast. Supermarket chains and discount pharmacies began to carry products that had once been staples of the old dimestore varieties. In the old days, one would automatically stop in Woolworth's for a packet of needle and thread; now one could just as easily pick up sewing notions at the local Shop-Rite, while en route to the produce department. Real estate costs in major cities were also skyrocketing. Consequently, a fair number of Red-Fronts were ousted when their old leases expired and the stores' volume could not support the increased rents.

Further, the North American Woolcos, which were then considered the shining stars of the Woolworth Company, were feeding on the "five-and-dimes." Company executives had decided to funnel large percentages of the established Red-Front's profits into Woolco, and in some cases, to completely replace F. W. Woolworth sites with new Woolco stores. Money that had once been recycled back into the dimestores was now being used elsewhere. These are all common business strategies, but they left the old variety store division with a tighter budget—most noticeably in the renovation and remodeling departments. Prior to the company's 1979 centennial, some of the older F. W. Woolworth stores did undergo extensive remodeling, but these were primarily high-visibility, historically-significant banner stores, such as the one in Lancaster, Pennsylvania. Sadly, a plethora of additional difficulties ensued, and in 1982, all of the American Woolco's were closed. This resulted in a devastating loss of over 30,000 jobs. With Woolco out of the picture, the Woolworth Corporation's athletic and shoe holdings became the new "cash cow" of the Red-Fronts. One former Woolworth executive explained it this way: "The (F. W. Woolworth) division was now the stepchild at the board's table, forced to survive on the proverbial scraps remaining after the favored formats were satisfied." Across America, new and growing chain stores gained momentum. Customers started to migrate to huge shopping malls instead of their home-town main streets.

When the dust settled in the mid-1980s, both Woolco *and* F. W. Woolworth stores, had suffered irreparable damage. The lion's share of company profits were pouring in from its highly-successful chains such as Champs and Lady Foot Locker, and from its growing Northern Exposure and San Francisco Music Box Company mall stores. By 1990, the original focus of Frank Winfield Woolworth's company had completely altered. Where there had once been over 3,000 Red-Fronts in North America, there were now under 1,000. Along with the General Merchandise division (which encompassed the F. W. Woolworth Red-Fronts) there were also four more company divisions: The Athletic Group, Specialty Footwear, The Northern Group, and Other Specialty. At one point, The Specialty Division alone ran over 7,200 stores in thirteen countries. In the overall financial picture of the mammoth Woolworth Corporation, its variety stores had inadvertently become a disconcerting smudge on its projection sheets.

F. W. Woolworth:
More Than Just a Five-and-Dime

In the 1960s, the traditional image of the F. W. Woolworth
Company was forever altered when it developed a line of
large Woolco discount chain stores and catalogue outlets, and
then acquired Kinney Shoes.

By 1993, enough Woolworth Red-Fronts were losing money to arouse serious concern. In response, the newly installed CFO, William Lavin, launched a bold restructuring plan. He and his team cut the company's General Merchandise division in half, by closing 400 of its least-profitable Red-Fronts. The company then sold its 122 Canadian Woolcos to Wal-Mart, and invested much of the resulting capital into more athletic and footwear interests. Meanwhile, as thousands of former F. W. Woolworth employees struggled with sudden unemployment, an accounting scandal broke loose. In the end, no wrongdoing was proven, but Lavin was replaced by Roger Farah.

On the surface, this strategy of "streamline-sell-acquire" seemed to improve the situation. Overall sales in 1996 totaled $8.1 billion with a net income of $169 million, as compared to a loss of $164 million in 1995. The numbers looked good, but the five-and-dime division had experienced an operating loss of $37 million in 1996.

TIME CAPSULE MEMORY

"Paper Doll Fun"

On Saturdays, mother took me to Woolworth's in Tarentum. Excited, I beelined for the movie star paper dolls, or "cut-outs". I spent hours cutting and fitting the fabulous costumes, then designed my own. I still collect paper dolls, but I can't buy them at a five-and-ten. Woolworth's is a lost piece of Americana no modern equivalent can match.

—Rosemary Schafer, Natrona Heights, Pa.

Forecasters speculated that the variety store era had passed. Shoppers were being lured by big name competitors, glitzy malls, mail order, and cyberspace—and even by the corporation's other retail holdings. In 1996, a modernized F. W. Woolworth format was tested in a few cities, including Wilmington, Delaware. Initially, the reaction was good, but for various reasons, the project was abandoned. More than ever, the new wave of corporate VIPs wanted to forge ahead, leaving tradition in the dust. Not everyone was ready to bury this popular mercantile icon, however. F. W. Woolworth stores in prime areas continued to show excellent profits, and consequently, many employees felt that the Red-Fronts could still be turned around. They believed that so many five-and-dimes were in the red because of corporate neglect, rather than a lack of consumer interest. Several people even suggested that, to capitalize on the growing American nostalgia craze, the dimestores revert back to their old-fashioned design of individual wooden counters and vintage decor. By this point, however, the writing was on the wall. The very Red-Fronts which had spawned Frank Woolworth's empire, no longer fit into the company's profit projections.

Good-Bye Woolworth's!

On July 17, 1997, chairman of the board and CEO, Roger Farah, along with the company president, Dale W. Hilpert, announced that the F. W. Woolworth Corporation would be closing the 400-plus remaining F. W. Woolworth variety stores in the United States, and hundreds more abroad. Over 9,200 employees would be terminated; a small percentage would be reemployed in other company stores, such as Lady Footlocker.

Virtually every daily newspaper and every major television network carried the story, proclaiming that another piece of American popular culture would soon be gone.

The unemployment lines swelled and Americans were shocked. From California to New York, and everywhere in between, people dashed to their nearest Woolworth's store to take one final nostalgic waltz around the aisles. Staffer Robert Sietsema of the *Village Voice* was among them. He wrote: "A soothing voice croons over the public address system like a grief counselor, punctuating offers of sale merchandise with, *'It's our way of thanking you for 118 wonderful years together.'* If that isn't enough to swamp the tear ducts, there's the sight of the snacking lunch counter whose streaky gray Formica and twirling stools rocket you back to childhood. The five-and-dime lunch counter will soon go the way of the dodo and Automat."

One New York radio announcer was so upset by the news that she gave out the number of Woolworth's CEO over the air. Within hours, Farah's phone lines were deluged. The announcer, like so many other people, was wondering what would happen to all those goldfish.

Farewell Woolworth's!

In the summer of 1997, when the last of the Red-Fronts were being shuttered, customers from coast to coast flocked to their local stores for one last waltz around the aisles. They were greeted with signs reading "Closed Forever" and "After 118 Years."

In Sante Fe, New Mexico, one multigenerational family posed for a souvenir photo.

TIME CAPSULE MEMORY

"Woolworth's Was More Than Just a Dimestore"

It might seem odd that the demise of a variety store, has caused so much sadness in America . . . but you see, Woolworth's was more than just a store. It was a part of our daily lives. Some people called it the five-and-ten, others the five-and-dime. I always called it plain Woolworth's. For oldsters like myself, it was the place where we took our best girls for an egg cream at the lunch counter. And it was the place we got our first jobs, usually as stock boys, and bought our first tube of shaving cream. Woolworth's was the place to go as a kid and gape at all the penny candy and stroll around the aisles, and later on my wife and I brought *our* kids there to do the same thing. It was a holiday tradition, when I was a kid during the Depression, to try to get as many gifts, for as many people as you could, for fifty cents! F. W. Woolworth's was always there, comfortable, like an old shoe. When the stores folded for good, there were employees caught in the shuffle that had devoted their entire life to the company. They thought they had a job forever and that was sad. I tell you, there's a lot of history in that old Woolworth's chain.

—Art Marshall, Scranton, Pa.

Nearly a year later, on the morning of April 27, 1998, Wall Street buzzed with more news. The great Woolworth Building, which had housed the corporate headquarters for three-quarters of a century, was up for sale. Considering its prime location across from city hall, this "Cathedral of Commerce" could easily sell for $150 million. Such a great influx of cash would certainly make the 1999 balance sheets of the F. W. Woolworth Corporation look greener, but the sands of time were running out for the Woolworth's five-and-dimes that started it all. On June 12, 1998, one day after the company's annual stockholder's meeting, the F. W. Woolworth Corporation became known as the Venator Group. Reportedly, the name *Venator* was inspired by a classical Latin word for "sportsman," which the chief executives felt was a moniker more in keeping with their heavy concentration of athletic holdings.

For those familiar with the rags-to-riches story of Frank Winfield Woolworth and his untiring efforts to establish a posthumous reputation for himself, the company name change struck a particularly discordant chord. It was even speculated that Frank W. Woolworth turned over in his grave at Woodlawn Cemetery, just as he had probably done the day in 1935, when the board of directors voted to lift the twenty-five-cent maximum price restriction on goods sold in the store.

Twelve days after the name change took effect, the final die was cast. On Monday, June 22, 1998, it was announced that the Venator Group had sold the Woolworth Building to a major real estate developer. Within months, workers were dispatched to destroy portions of the seventy-six-year-old building's beautiful Italian Carrera marble highlights, as part of a massive renovation. The Grand Arcade Lobby of Frank Woolworth's Cathedral of

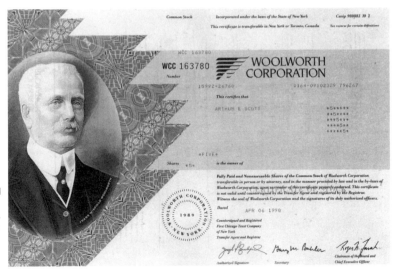

One of the last stock certificates issued that showed a picture of the company's founder, Frank W. Woolworth. When the corporation's name was changed to the Venator Group, the certificates were redesigned.

Commerce would presumably be spared, as it had been denoted an historic landmark. However, the fate of thousands of pieces of the Red-Front's rich history still stored throughout the skyscraper (from early cash registers to glass photo negatives to Frank W. Woolworth's hand-carved desk) remained uncertain. The Venator Group announced that, for the time being, it would maintain its corporate offices in what was once the tallest building in the world, but as of January 1999, they would be tenants of the Witcoff Group.

The decision to obliterate the 118-year-old general merchandise division, to change the company name, and to cast a new corporate facelift, was of course, made after much deliberation. The day after Roger Farah made the announcement about the final store closings, the Woolworth Company's "Z" ticker on the stock exchange was active; the stock rose (briefly) $2.50 per share and trading was four times the normal volume. For the time being, Wall Street was pleased, yet millions of former patrons and thousands of newly unemployed workers uttered a massive, melancholy sigh. Contrary to the fact that Frank Winfield Woolworth's great five-and-dimes had such an impact on America's mercantile history, neither his stores, his name, or his photograph on the company's stock certificates would survive past the twentieth century.

One could almost picture an employee seated before a state-of-the-art computer, pressing the command buttons: Change file name: W-O-O-L-W-O-R-T-H. Refile under keyword: "dinosaur."

From coast to coast, people bid farewell to Woolworth's.

Preserving the Legacy

It is important to note that the familiar red letters of "Woolworth" have not completely vanished from the face of the earth. Overseas, for example, the United Kingdom has hundreds of Woolworth general merchandise stores operating at full-speed, offering the same wonderful values they have since 1909. These days, the UK's Kingfisher Corporation operates its "Wooleys" as a totally independent entity; American Woolworth sold off its last remaining interest in F. W. Woolworth Ltd. of England back in 1982. On this side of the Atlantic, though, the glory days of "Everybody's Store" have receded into mercantile history.

In reflecting upon the five-and-dime phenomena, one journalist summarized it well: "If Woolworth's isn't what made America great, it certainly made you feel great to be an American." In the hearts and minds of millions, the memory of their hometown F. W. Woolworth Red-Front will live on. It will endure through fond memories of dime parakeets, toasted cheese sandwiches, and Lovelee hairnets. It will be remembered as the place to buy "Evening in Paris" perfume for Mom, an all-purpose "4K vegetable peeler" for the kitchen drawer, and a plastic whirlybird for Grandpa's garden. It will certainly be remembered as the store that saved the day, when, en route to your best friend's wedding, you realized you had no film in the camera!

Most of all, Woolworth's stores, in the United States and Canada, will be remembered for the red-and-gold storefront sign designed by its founder, Frank Winfield Woolworth, the Father of the five-and-dime.

To understand just how this uniquely single-minded man managed to turn pocket change into millions, we must travel back 147 years, to a small farm in northern New York—and a special drygoods shop—where it all began.

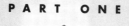

PART ONE

Remembering

Frank Winfield Woolworth:

The Merchant Prince

Frank and Charles Woolworth as boys, c. 1866.

Chapter One

Early Years of the Merchant Prince

> *"Then, by one of those vagaries of Providence found now*
> *and then in all families, a boy appeared who seemed to be*
> *intended for something else besides farming.*
> *This boy, Frank, wanted to be a merchant."*
>
> —*New York Times,* 1 Jan., 1911

Struggling Upward

The true wonder of the Woolworth success story is that it happened at all. One can only imagine the scenario in 1875, when . . .

A wiry young man dressed in raggedy homespun and a pair of coarse cowhide boots, walks into a flourishing dry good store in upstate New York. Smiling politely, he requests a job as a salesman. The elegantly clad shop owner, sitting like a toplofty rooster at his high wooden desk, eyes the boy and frowns deeply. The boy is not surprised by the man's reaction. He has no business skills, has never mastered anything but the drudge work of farming, and cannot even afford most of the luxuries for sale in this fine establishment. In the far corner, the store's employees are listening to the exchange, hiding their smirks. The female clerks dressed in neat skirts and blouses, and the salesmen in high collars and swinging timepieces, are wondering: "Who is this rube, this inexperienced hayseed, with the nerve to ask for a position here?" Undeterred, the young man patiently waits as the shop owner ponders his fate. After all, he has big dreams to fulfill. He knows from all he has read about his hero, Napoleon Bonaparte, that the only way to succeed is to devise a strategy and stick to his guns. His determination is stronger than the sharpest of barbs. In a clear steady tone, the young man quickly lists his assets: He does not drink or smoke and he is a devout Methodist. He knows a bit about bookkeeping, and he wants, more than anything in the world, to own his own store one day.

The shop owner fingers his waxed mustachio thoughtfully. The boy before him is clearly green, but he does seem sincere. Still, times were tough and at least twenty experienced candidates would soon be clamoring for this same job.

And all in all, the boy is a sorry excuse for a potential salesman.

But the owner sees something there.

"Okay," he barks. "The job is yours. You start Monday!"

Trying to control his elation, the young man asks: "What are you going to pay me, sir."

"Pay you!?" The owner exclaims. "You don't expect me do pay you, do you? Why, you should pay me for teaching you the business. Not a half penny until you prove yourself worthy. But I'll tell you what. We won't charge you a tuition fee."

"How long will I work without pay, sir?"

The man smoothes his morning coat, then stares closely at the boy, a spark of challenge in his brown eyes. "Six months," he states firmly.

The young man ponders this meager offer, and the alternative. He thinks about the way he and his brother rise, before sunrise, and work the fields until dusk. He thinks about his back, and how it aches from picking potatoes in the snow-encrusted fields. He feels sad when he realizes that he has never seen his mother in a beautiful new dress with silk ribbons in her hair, the type of which she enjoyed as a child. Or the fact his father doesn't own a proper Prince Albert waist-coat, and works day and night. The boy knows he cannot bear a similar fate for the rest of his life, so his mind, always good with figures, quickly calculates his scanty finances, and makes a counteroffer.

"I have only enough to live for three months without pay, sir."

"Fine," the owner agrees, silently noting the boy's bartering skills. "Three months it is. But there'll be no selling involved—not at first! That's for experienced men. You'll have to do all the mean labor: cleaning, packing, and making deliver-ies. Hard, hard work!"

The deal is made.

And so is history.

This illustration by Gray Morrow depicts a young Frank Woolworth interviewing for his first job at Augsbury & Moore Drygoods in Watertown, New York.

The young man in the previous scenario was Frank Winfield Woolworth, and the place was Augsbury & Moore's Corner Store in Watertown, New York. The shop owner was William Harvey Moore, who, along with his senior partner, Alexander Augsbury, gave Frank W. Woolworth his first real chance at a better life. It was a gesture that Frank would never forget.

Jobs were scarce in post-Civil War America, and chances were high that Frank wouldn't get that post. A less ambitious young man would have given into his father's wishes and toiled on the family farm until he was old and gray.

Given his meager resources, Frank could have easily been discouraged by William Moore's challenge to work three months without wages. The Woolworth story is full of such "ifs"—times when one rash decision, one dollar, one fleeting moment of uncertainty, could have shifted the course of history in a very different direction.

In March 1873, a few weeks shy of his twenty-first birthday, "Wooley" started his business career. In another twenty-two years, this erstwhile farmboy would be a multimillionaire. In 1913, amidst the twilight of his life, he would erect a breathtaking "Cathedral of Commerce," to be hailed as the tallest building in the world.

Most important of all, the Napoleanic inspired empire that F. W. Woolworth dreamed about, would be his—lock, stock, and nickel. He would rule, not as an Emperor of France, but as King of the Five-and-Dime.

Ancestral Trivia:
The Woolworths Meet the McBriers

Like most rags-to-riches' stories, the F. W. Woolworth saga began thousands of miles away from his native upstate New York. The Woolworths were of old English stock, and as far back as the eleventh century, there were Worley, Wolley, and Wooley villages in England. There are varying accounts of Woolworth's ancestry, but several sources trace the genealogical line directly back to William Worley (b. 1482).

The Woolworth Family Through the Ages

Frank Woolworth's paternal genealogical line dates back to eleventh-century Britain. The colonial progenitors of the line were Richard Wolley (or Wooley) b. 1648, and his wife, Hannah Huggins. Some time after arriving in Massachusetts in 1678, Richard changed his name to Woolworth. The photos below show Frank and Charles Woolworth's paternal grandparents, Jasper and Elizabeth, and the boys' parents, John and Fanny. These photos, source unknown, probably date back to the mid-1860s.

LEFT:
Jasper Woolworth, 1789–1873
BELOW:
Elizabeth Buell Woolworth

ABOVE:
Fanny McBrier
Woolworth, c. 1831–1878
RIGHT:
John Hubbell
Woolworth, 1821–1907

Kezia and Henry
Sloan McBrier

Frank Woolworth's Maternal Ancestry: The McBriers

Frank Woolworth's maternal grandparents were Henry and Kezia Sloan McBrier. Henry was of Scotch-Irish descent and immigrated from County Down, Ireland, in 1827 and settled in Pillars Point, NY. Several McBrier cousins joined the five-and-ten bandwagon, including Seymour Knox, Edwin Merton McBrier, Mason B. McBrier, and Gardner T. White. The photo right is of the "Woolworth and McBrier" store in Lockport, N.Y., which Frank shared interest in with his maternal cousins Seymour Knox and Edwin Merton McBrier.

"Woolworth & McBrier" storefront, c. 1887

The progenitor of the American line was Richard Wolley, who was a "Weaver for the King's Bench." Born in 1648, adventurous Richard left England and traveled to Newbury, Massachusetts, in 1679, after which time the name Wolley became "Woolworth." During the 1680s, King Phillip granted Richard's request for land in Connecticut, and the family prospered. The Woolworths gradually spread throughout New England and into parts of upper New York State, primarily settling as farmers. By 1840, descendant Jasper Woolworth and his wife, Elizabeth Buell, had acquired the Old Moody place in Rodman, which lay in Jefferson County, New York.

TIME CAPSULE MEMORY

5&10

"The Hard-working Woolworths"

My father, John, would think nothing of getting up at four in the morning and work until eight at night in the summertime at hard manual labor. Everything that came into farm labor I had experience in, and my mother would break me in into housework, too, I got both ends of the stick. —Frank W. Woolworth

---

John Hubbell Woolworth, the father of Frank W., was born to Jasper and Elizabeth on August 16, 1821. When he came of age, John started to manage the family farm. As John closed in on the age of thirty, the pressure was on to settle down and start his own family. Fortunately, true love was at hand. On nearby Pillar-Point, a New York peninsula extending into Lake Ontario, Canada, lived Henry and Kezia Sloan McBrier and their eight children. One of these siblings, named Fanny, caught the eye of John Woolworth. John was charmed by the blue-eyed, raven-haired beauty and quickly set to courting. Reportedly, well-to-do Henry McBrier was not pleased with the match. He had raised his daughter in fine style, as a lady. It irritated Henry that John Woolworth could not even afford to hire a servant girl to help his daughter with the housework. Overruling her family's protests, twenty-year-old Fanny married John Woolworth on January 14, 1851. The couple moved into a modest cottage located on the Old Moody Farm, which was still owned by John's father, Jasper.

On Tuesday, April 13, 1852, Frank Winfield Woolworth was born in this humble clapboard abode on the hill in Rodman, New York. Four years later, on August 1, 1856, Fanny bore a second son, Charles Sumner.

The sires of the future F. W. Woolworth empire had arrived.

The Farmboy with Napoleonic Dreams

From the beginning, Frank and Charles Sumner ("Sum") were very close, and in the future, Charles would play a prominent role in his brother's five-and-ten empire. In the meantime, the brothers were being raised as frugal, industrious, God-fearing Methodists. In fact, religion was such an integral part of Woolworths' family life, that Frank in 1915, donated a new church and a $20,000 endowment, in the town of Great Bend, in memory of his beloved parents.

Politically, the Woolworths did their part for the Yankee Cause. Fanny was an outspoken abolitionist and had christened her son, Charles Sumner, after a renowned abolitionist senator of the same name. During the Civil War, John Woolworth helped establish the Republican party in northern New York state, and when news of General Lee's surrender reached Great Bend, young Frank joined his parents in a rousing cheer.

The Woolworth family lived contentedly for seven years. The work days were long, and even Frank was helping in the fields by the age of four, but the family had plenty to eat, and Frank's father was spared the burden of paying a mortgage. Then, Grandfather Jasper made an announcement that turned their life upside down.

Jasper Woolworth, at the age of seventy, was weary and ready to retire. John did not have enough money to buy his father out, and he refused to borrow from his McBrier in-laws, who were constantly belittling him. Thus, when Jasper sold his holdings in Rodman, John and his growing family were forced to regroup. In February 1859, John mortgaged a 108-acre farm in Champion. This small hamlet was just a stone's toss from Great Bend, a scenic village situated on a sweeping curve on the Black River. Although Champion was where Frank worked the farm, it was Great Bend where the family shopped, attended church, posted mail, and learned their ABCs. Its population was a comfortable 125, and to John Woolworth, it seemed the perfect area to raise his family, in a place they could call their own.

Unfortunately much of the family's property was rocky and dry, suitable for raising only a smattering of potato crops and enough pasture grass to keep their eight milk cows from starving. The forested areas provided a bit of lumber to sell on Market Day in Watertown, the bustling county seat eleven miles north. But in essence, they were left with a mortgage at seven percent interest and a bleak financial future. It was during this period, from 1859 to 1865, that young Frank became acutely aware of just how much he disliked farm life. He never adjusted to rising at dawn to shovel manure or pitch hay in below-freezing temperatures. In fact, he dreaded it.

Of course, not every moment of every day was spent in the fields; Frank savored those wonderful hours when he was *learning*. One high point of his boyhood, Frank once recalled, was the day he and Charles started lessons with Miss Emma Penniman at Great Bend's one-room schoolhouse. Miss Penniman was a mere sixteen years old herself and had only finished eighth grade, but she encouraged Frank's interest in history and reading.

Both Miss Penniman and Frank's mother, Fanny, also supported his natural love of music. Frank's most prized possession was a mail-order flute, which he practiced on steadily. He also tried learning the piano, on the old family Upright with its yellowed keys and attached pair of candleholders. There, in the tiny living room, Fanny Woolworth would lovingly teach her son the basics of music, along with her favorite Irish ditties. Consequently, the adult Frank W. Woolworth placed a grand piano or organ of exquisite tone in every mansion he owned. He even designed an elaborate system whereby the walls and stair posts of his Long Island mansion, "Winfield Hall" resounded with classical symphonies. The largest Woolworth's stores also had top-of-the-line Uprights, with full-time piano players to help sell popular sheet music. Frank never could carry a tune, but music remained his solace throughout his lifetime. There are several accounts of an elderly, ailing Frank locking himself in his music room at Winfield House and weeping.

Early Adventures in the North Country

Come spring, when the last snowflake had finally melted, the North Country became a beautiful and exhilarating place for young Frank and Charles Sumner Woolworth. The hills were rolling and the lakes crystal clear, providing an idyllic setting for the brothers to play during rare moments of leisure. Best of all, for Frank, this part of Jefferson County was the site of great intrigue revolving around the historic Bonaparte family.

Frank Woolworth was mesmerized by tales about Joseph Bonaparte, who was once the king of Spain, and his famous brother, General Napoleon, who ruled as emperor of France. Miss Penniman had taught Frank all about the Battle of Waterloo in 1812, explaining how Napoleon was overthrown and captured. Frank had read, over and over, about the way Joseph fled to the United States, along with the Spanish crown jewels, and how he dreamed of rescuing his brother, Napoleon, from his captors and bringing him to refuge in northern New York. Joseph even built a special hideaway in nearby Cape Vincent for his brother. Being so close to his own brother, Frank thought this gesture made Joseph Bona-parte a fine fellow indeed.

As adults, both Frank Winfield and Charles Sumner often reminisced about

The Woolworth Farm in Northern New York

This simple farmhouse in Champion, three-quarters of a mile from Great Bend, N.Y., was where Frank and Charles spent most of their boyhood. Their parents, John and Fanny, purchased the farm in 1859, having moved out of the Old Moody Place in Rodman where Frank was born. After Frank's mother died in 1878, a housekeeper named Elvira Austin Moulton was hired to help John Woolworth. In August, 1879, she married John Woolworth and became Frank's stepmother. Frank used to boast about how proud he felt for having built the white picket fence around the old homestead.
From left to right: John Woolworth, his second wife, Elvira, and their adopted daughter, Flora. In the foreground, an unidentified neighbor's child holds a doll.

their explorations of the then-vacant Bonaparte hideaway. "Old Nap's" place, as Frank called it, was only a short ride from the Woolworth farm. It was nicknamed the "cup-and-saucer house" because of its eight-sided octagonal shape, rounded roof, and unusual look-out tower. Young Frank would stare at the great Corsican crest emblazoned on the massive front door, his mind full of adventure. He would peek through the windows, trying to capture the home's former splendor in his imagination. Frank coveted the wealth and esteem the Bonapartes once enjoyed, and to achieve this for himself became a life-long fixation. A half-century later, Frank Winfield would decorate his executive suite in the Woolworth Building in French-European style, adorned with exotic treasures, including an exact replica of Napoleon's own desk.

Throughout his life, the influence of the Bonapartes on Frank W. Woolworth's own aspirations was far-reaching, even obsessive. Unfortunately, back in the 1860s, Frank's time at the "cup-and-saucer house" and his ability to fantasize about royal fame and fortune was highly limited. It was the farm that ordered him back, time and time again.

Frank Prepares to Trade in His Hoe for a Tie

"To the farm boy, the coldest thing in the world was the handle of a pitchfork in the morning," wrote Henry Winkler, author of the 1940 Woolworth biography, *Five and Ten.* Frank W. Woolworth's early lifestyle was not only cold, but emotionally and physically intolerable. It is no secret to historians that Frank Woolworth scorned farm work. To make matters worse, Frank was never a robust boy. Colds and fevers plagued him as a child, and long-term illnesses cropped up rather frequently when he reached adulthood. The harsh winters of northern New York complicated matters, aggravating his health and dampening his spirit.

So, perhaps as much he longed for the riches of Napoleon, the maturing Frank Woolworth longed to flee the farm. He yearned for a dry, warm place to earn his daily bread—preferably in a grand shop, dressed like a gentleman, with a fine tie and a starched collar. His interest in mercantiling started early, when, as a toddler, he met his first traveling salesman. He was fascinated by the peddler's fast-talking ways and saddlebags full of wares. Four-year-old Frank bragged to his parents about the day when he, too, would be "fast-talking" peddler. In the meantime, he and little Charles Sumner played "store" in the dining room. Gathering together miscellaneous doodads from the kitchen and canning room, Frank would carefully set up the "merchandise," make up prices, and invite his brother to be the customer.

Real-life trips to county stores left a great impression on him as well, although not always a happy one. It is true that Frank enjoyed the sleigh ride to Watertown, where the great town square was humming with activity and everyone seemed so purposeful, but he

TIME CAPSULE MEMORY

"Those Harsh New York Winters."

Frank and I went after the cows at half past five in the morning in late September when there was a white frost and we were barefoot. We would stand on the ground upon which the cows had been lying to get a little warmth into our nearly frozen feet. No wonder we yearned to break away from the endless drudgery.
—Charles Sumner Woolworth, c. 1930, recalling
younger days in Great Bend, N.Y.

rarely had more than a handful of pennies to spend. On the few occasions Frank and Charles dared enter the finer dry goods emporiums, the clerks would blatantly shun them, suggesting (rather strongly) that the Woolworth brothers should shop at a more fitting store. They belonged in a shop that sold penny goods, one that didn't mind poorly dressed farm youngsters tracking in mud and wasting the clerk's time.

Nonetheless, Frank was mesmerized by his limited exposure to the business world. The stores were always toasty warm and well lit by elaborate gas lamps. The air was filled with pleasant aromas of candle wax, starch, and perfumed soap. Stretches of long wooden counters with highly polished tops held every imaginable whatsit to make a body's life easier. And overhead, rolls and rolls of colorful fabric were stacked high on shelves, ready to be fashioned into fine garments.

One thing is for certain: these varied experiences instilled a burning desire in Frank to have his own business. He admitted later that he envied the shop owners and clerks in Watertown. They were, he thought, the most fortunate of mortals. Still, he never forgot the shabby treatment bestowed on him by his "betters," or the frustration he felt at not being able to purchase even modest luxuries, such as colorful hair combs for his mother. The maturing Frank W. Woolworth vowed to own a store that would offer quality goods that *all* people could afford. His employees would respect even the humblest customers, making them feel that their nickels and dimes were as valuable as any five-dollar gold piece.

But Frank faced a major dilemma. Just about the time his dreams for the future were crystallizing, he was approaching the milestone age of sixteen. The year was 1868, and he knew he had to make a serious decision about his life, a decision that would cause much consternation at the Woolworth homestead. Like his ancestors before him, both Woolworth and McBrier, he would be soon be expected to live out his days devoted to the land. Until he married, he gloomily forecast, the only time he would don fine clothes would be for Sunday services at the Methodist Church; the only luxury he could ever afford would be a handful of lemon drops.

Nina Brown Baker, author of the children's book, *Nickels and Dimes,* explained Frank's plight perfectly: "In those days, most farmers considered a boy had learned quite enough when he knew how to read and write and do his 'figures.' Everyone left school at sixteen, if he had lasted *that* long. It was felt that at sixteen he had either learned all there was to learn, or else he was too stupid to learn and might as well be put to work."

Of course, Frank Winfield Woolworth was far from stupid, and he had only just touched

Watertown, New York, Through the "Woolworth" Decades

As early as 1855, Frank would join his family for trips to Watertown on market days, where they would sell potatoes and pine. Although the above photo is dated much later (c. 1900) the busy scene on the public square is typical of what young Frank experienced. In 1916, when Frank's dear friend William Moore died, Woolworth erected a new six-story building on this same site, where it served as the company's statutory principal office until 1966. In 1969, the Woolworth Company donated the entire building and all of its leasehold to the Henry Keep Home of the municipality.

the surface of all there was to learn. He hungered for more knowledge, more experience, and the accumulation of more finery than had his hero, Napoleon Bonaparte. He was certain that his dreams would be shattered if he remained at home. His father was a very good farmer, but impractical in business. Unlike his McBrier in-laws, John Hubbell Woolworth had not realized any substantial profit from his long, unrelenting years of labor.

Two things were clear to Frank Winfield Woolworth as he exited Miss Penniman's schoolhouse in Great Bend for the last time. First, that it was in the world of business, not agriculture, where he would attempt to make his mark on the world. And second, he needed a high-falutin' plan.

TIME CAPSULE MEMORY

"A Rags-to-Riches Tale"

When I was in my teens, I remember reading a biography of Frank W. Woolworth, and immediately I thought, "what a fine tale this would make for a children's book. Woolworth's story had all the trapping of a Horatio Alger rags-to-riches story! He started, dirt poor as the son of a potato farmer, suffering through the unrelenting winters of the North Country. He was unhappy with his lot in life and had big dreams for the future. As a boy, he was scorned by most of the wealthy merchants in town, yet he found, among them, a benefactor, who gave Frank the wherewithal to start his own business. He struggled upward and he succeeded, and just like an Alger hero, he never forgot those people who believed in him along the way. If Alger wrote it, the book might have been called: *Frank the Dime-Store Boy: The Tale of the Merchant Prince.* I found his life inspiring, and never forgot it, during my own long, struggle upward.

—James Wilkins, Jefferson County, N.Y.

Chapter Two

The Birth of Woolworth's
"Great Five-Cent Store"

"Surely they thought I was about the greenest fellow who ever came off a farm."

—Frank W. Woolworth

In 1868, sixteen-year-old Frank W. Woolworth, son of a humble potato farmer, set forth to make his fortune in the world of business.

Unfortunately, only a limited number of fortunes could be made in that part of Jefferson County, New York. The Civil War troops had returned home, jobs were scarce, the cost of living high, and young Frank didn't have a lick of mercantile experience. Earnest inquiries brought the same response from each shop owner: "No." So, for several years, Frank was forced back behind the plow, sweltering beneath the summer sun, and freezing amidst the North Country's merciless ice storms. Since his schooldays were over, he didn't even have the lively discussions of Miss Penniman, his former teacher, to divert his active mind.

With every heft of the hoe, Frank's determination to escape intensified. The problem was that on the ladder of mercantile, Frank's muddy boots occupied the bottom rung. Undaunted, he concocted a plan. He'd heard about a small commerce college in Watertown where he could learn the rudimentaries of business. Perhaps, Frank told his mother, if he had a genuine certificate, a potential employer would take him more seriously. Fanny McBrier Woolworth wholeheartedly agreed with her son, but they both knew that the tuition was dear: twelve whole dollars. Brushing aside this roadblock, Fanny championed her son's cause, presenting her arguments to her husband, John. Their son was clearly unsuited for harsh physical labor; he was always taking ill. He'd toiled in the

TIME CAPSULE MEMORY

The education I got in two terms in a business college in Watertown did me more good than any classical education I might have got.
—Frank W. Woolworth

fields since he was a toddler and deserved a chance at something more. He was quick at math and smarter than any other boy in the village—he had potential. She was even willing to give Frank the tiny nest egg she'd been tucking away, penny by penny, since her wedding day. John Woolworth finally relented. Frank could attend school, but he still had to perform his daily chores. Arrangements were made with a professor to tutor Frank at night, and in 1872, Frank enrolled in the two-month commercial course.

Frank studied hard, and by the time he turned twenty, he'd earned a certificate declaring him proficient in double-entry bookkeeping. He had yet to wait on a customer in a real store, but he sensed he was on the road to success. Dressed in his finest wool scarf, Frank headed to nearby Carthage. One by one, he visited every merchant in town: the tiny furniture maker's shop, the meat market, even the undertaker's parlor. The owners were not impressed with the tall, wiry boy and his paper certificate, and promptly sent him packing.

A touch desperate, Frank traveled solemnly back to Great Bend and approached the station master, who ran a tiny grocery at the rear of the train depot shed. The agent was willing to teach young Woolworth the trade, but he couldn't spare any wages. Hungry for practical experience, Frank started working part-time. He performed odd jobs and bagged groceries, and then, a half-hour before train time, he sold rail tickets. His official title was "Assistant Station Master," and since he'd always been fascinated with locomotives, this suited Frank just fine— at least for a while. But Frank's job at the depot was short-lived. It was just not sensible for a young man to work without pay, so he was pressured back into full-time farm life.

"But I still had higher ambitions," wrote Woolworth in 1919, "and I got acquainted with a gentleman [Daniel McNeil] who ran the Country Store at Great Bend. I tried to get a clerkship there, but without success, and I envied the young men behind the counter who dealt out the dry goods and groceries."

Dan McNeil knew of Frank's ambitions and respected his enterprise. The kindly, spirited proprietor told Frank that he knew several merchants in Watertown, and he would keep his eyes and ears open for opportunities.

Meanwhile, back at home, the situation reached another turning point.

Early in March 1873, Frank's uncle, Albon McBrier, offered his nephew a job at his prosperous farm, Pierpont Manor. Frank would receive room, board, and $18.00 per month. If he lived frugally, he could even send some money home to his parents. Frank's brother, Charles, was out of school, and could take over Frank's chores at home. It was a logical plan, in the best interests of everyone—except for Frank.

When it came to tilling the soil, Frank had always felt emotionally torn, and now his trepidation heightened. He knew that the success of a farmer was inextricably bound to the whims of Mother Nature. One drought, one rainy season, could wipe out a family's income for a year. He longed to have more control, to own his own business. He wanted to build a great building, piece by piece, much the same way he'd built boyhood palaces out of spare lumber and rocks. If Frank went to work on Uncle Albon's farm, he would never achieve his Napoleonic dreams. Yet he was being presented with an offer he couldn't honorably refuse.

Just as he had countless times before, Frank trudged to McNeil's Country Store, hoping for good news. One late winter evening in 1873, Frank's efforts were rewarded. While McNeil was conducting business in Watertown, he'd heard of an opening at Augsbury and Moore's Drygoods. McNeil gave Frank an encouraging pat on the back and a letter of introduction to Mr. Alexander Augsbury.

The door of opportunity had materialized. It was up to Frank Woolworth, a few weeks shy of his twenty-first birthday, to step through that door and make his mark.

Watertown, New York—City of Opportunity

Watertown, New York, Jefferson County's seat, was an exciting place for an ambitious young man in the 1870s. The town featured a central square encircled by wooden sidewalks and flanked by shops. Hand-lettered signs advertised everything from silver tea sets to the services of legal solicitors. Well-dressed children nibbled fine chocolates, and tantalizing aromas seeped from the bakery. On special holidays, such as Christmas, bands played merrily in the wooden gazebo, and gentlemen in black coats tipped their hats to ladies in swirling hoop skirts. Frank reveled in this scene. His own hometown harbored only 125 people, but Watertown boasted a population well over 7,000.

Frank had traveled the eleven-mile stretch to Watertown many times before, of course, on open-air market days. Ever since he could remember, his family had journeyed in a wooden sleigh led by pack horses to peddle their wares. On those cold mornings, their mission was to sell wood to the sawmills and papermills that stretched for miles alongside the Black River. This time, however, he'd arrived to secure a respectable position with Augsbury & Moore, the finest of drygood merchants. Located on the corner of the public square and Arsenal Street, the shop's well-lit interior beckoned to Frank, a beacon of freedom. As Frank wound his way toward his mark, he was praying, with typical Methodist fervor, that all would go well.

The first news Frank received was far from encouraging. Elderly Mr. Alexander Augsbury had taken ill and was abed. Clutching his letter of introduction, Frank headed straight for Augsbury's home. Years later, Frank would chuckle, recalling his daunting experience with Mr. Augsbury. Frank Woolworth told financier B. C. Forbes that he was shaking in his boots as he was led by a proper maid to Mr. Augsbury's sick room. After Frank stated his business, Augsbury shot out a series of rapid-fire questions about Frank's character, his experience, and his attire.

William Moore, Frank's first employer in Watertown in 1873. Thirty years later, Frank would thank Moore by making him one of the partners of the great F. W. Woolworth Co.

"Bub, don't they wear any collars in your neighborhood?" asked Augsbury. Frank shook his head. "No neckties, either?" pressed the austere merchant. Frank politely explained that he did not yet own a collar or necktie. There wasn't much call for a starched collar while shoveling manure or milking cows.

Somehow, Frank muddled through this nerve-racking interview and Augsbury sent Frank back to town to see his partner. If William Moore liked him, barked Augsbury, then Woolworth had the job.

Fortunately, as described earlier, Frank made it through this second interview with Moore, who, vast experience aside, was only twelve years Frank's senior. From that day on, Frank credited Moore with giving him his first real start in business.

Back on that milestone day in post-Civil War America, Frank headed home, heady with euphoria. Mr. Moore said Frank had three months to prove himself a worthy employee, working for free during his trial. After that, well . . . most anything could happen.

Frank is Crowned the Worst Salesman in the World

Frank W. Woolworth started his mercantile career at Augsbury & Moore's corner store on March 24, 1873. He reported for duty, as scheduled, on Monday morning, and was promptly instructed to leave and secure a proper white shirt, collar, and tie. By the time Frank returned, duly rigged up, the boss was busy, and Frank was left in the care of the head clerks, Mr. Edward Barrett and Mrs. Adelia Coons. Both of these people would eventually become trusted colleagues in the Woolworth empire, but that first day, they spent most of their free time tittering at Frank's ineptitude. "Surely," Frank remarked later, "they thought I was about the greenest fellow who ever came off a farm." No one spoke to Frank. No one told him what to do. He stood around, awkward and nervous, hoping for guidance.

A farmer walked in, made a beeline for Frank, and gruffly requested a spool of number 40 thread. *Thread?* wondered Frank. Why, he hadn't a clue where the thread was, nor did he realize they had special numbers!

Frank was justifiably befuddled. Back in the mid-1880s, many finer shops, including Augsbury & Moore's, kept smaller merchandise hidden in drawers, with valuable items locked up like Fort Knox. Complicated price codes were listed on special sheets, or most likely, in the memories of the clerk. Few items were marked with price tickets. (This was one of the first problems Frank would remedy when he had his own store.) To complicate matters, there were often two prices. The savvy salesman was to quote the highest amount first. If the customer balked, then he quoted a second, rock-bottom price. In a nutshell, a novice employee like Frank had much to learn. He was particularly unprepared because Mr. Moore had made it quite clear that Frank would not be conducting any sales transactions, at least for a few months.

Meanwhile, the farmer impatiently awaited his thread.

Frank fumbled through the drawer but could not find thread number 40. "The thread is right in front of your nose, young man," Mr. Moore snapped, pointing to the item. Frank quickly lifted out the thread and handed it over to his first customer, beaming with pride.

"How much is it?" asked the farmer, riffling through his wallet.

Once again, Frank didn't have a clue. Back to Mr. Moore he went, seeking the answer. The thread was 8¢. The farmer handed over a ten-cent paper shinplaster. Now Frank had a new dilemma. *How does one get change?* Blushing furiously, Frank watched as his boss illustrated the procedure: Go to Mr. Moore's desk, fill out a sales ticket, hand over ticket and money to the store cashier, and then get the change. Hand the change to the customer, wrap the item, and smile and say "Thank you." Frank eventually mastered the mechanics of pricing and change, but he made a veritable mess of the sales transactions. In one instance, a customer walked in and asked for ten yards of material. As the customer (and Mr. Moore) watched aghast, Frank zealously pulled out a bolt of fabric, and promptly sent calico cascading across the floor. The owners decided that Frank Woolworth was the worst salesman they'd ever hired. Still, he was eager and polite, worthy of another chance. They again limited Frank's duties to starting the stoves, washing windows, and delivering packages. He assumed the role of salesman only during emergencies.

Frank persevered and made it through the three-month grace period. By June, he was making $3.50 per week. Six months later he was awarded a fifty-cent raise. By that time, Mr. Moore was spending less of his time sighing at Frank's antics, and the other clerks had become more amiable. Frank worked from seven in the morning until nine at night, waiting for the day he was allowed to do more than sweep the floors.

A New Talent, A New Hat and a New Love

Frank toiled for over a year at Augsbury & Moore's before the next door of opportunity unexpectedly swung open. One scorching summer afternoon, William Moore ordered Frank to "gussy up" the front display. Frank viewed this as a personal challenge, and worked long into the night. He removed the musty goods, washed every inch of the wood and glass, then gathered together some bright red fabric from the stock shelves. He arranged, and rearranged, a plethora of everyday items, adding in a few strings of inexpensive "golden" paste jewelry for color. The next morning, when Mr. Moore arrived, he spotted a group of customers peering excitedly into his front window. Mr. Moore remained silent, but Frank knew that his boss was pleased. From that day on Frank was responsible for window and merchandise displays. He remained a sorry salesman, but he'd found his creative niche.

By summer 1875, Frank was working twelve hours a day and earning six dollars a week at Moore & Smith's, the successors of Augsbury & Moore. (Sickly Alexander Augsbury had by then sold his interest to Perry Smith.) Feeling quite the gentleman of means, he acquired his first high plug hat for Sunday church and repaid his mother every cent of the twelve dollars that she'd loaned him for business school. He even procured a new violin, which he practiced with gusto, much to the dismay of his fellow boarders. One of these young men, Edgar Emerson, eventually became a Supreme Court Judge. Emerson recalls wanting to take Frank *and* his noisy fiddle, and toss them both out the door. Nonetheless, Frank played on, as always, to his own tune.

> **TIME CAPSULE MEMORY**
> ### ⑤&⑩
> ### "Frank and His Fiddle"
> On Sundays, we clerks would frequently visit friends on Pillar Point, and Frank Woolworth would do his [futile] best to make music with that fiddle of his. Maybe because of that, some people who knew him in his early Watertown days never thought he'd amount to anything!
> —Former Supreme Court Justice
> Edgar C. Emerson, c. 1920.

Mentally, he was just entering his prime, but physically, Frank was fatigued. With the carelessness of youth, he ignored the warnings of his body and concentrated on his heart: Frank W. Woolworth had met his true love.

Young Jennie Creighton of Picton, Ontario had ventured to Watertown in search of work, where her skill with a needle allowed her to make a modest living. Jennie would often leave her rooming house on Franklin Street and visit Moore & Smith's Drygoods for sewing supplies. The moment he met her, Frank was charmed. He thought she was lovely, with her soft blond hair and sparkling blue eyes. He was touched by the tale of her father and six motherless siblings, who pined during her absence from their Canadian home, but wished their loved one well. Jennie was sympathetic and soothing, and listened attentively to Frank's dreams of grandeur. In return, he boosted her self-confidence and made her laugh. Over the ensuing months, love blossomed.

Perhaps inspired by the prospect of making Jennie his wife, Frank made a bold career move in September of 1875. He applied for a position at Moore & Smith's business competitor, A. Bushnell & Co. Mr. Moore told Frank that if he could get more money from Bushnell, he should take the job. (Frank admitted later that he believed Moore was relieved to see him go, considering his poor sales abilities.)

With a burst of bravado, Frank requested ten dollars per week and was stunned when Bushnell agreed. The only catch was that Frank had to leave his comfortable boardinghouse and sleep on a hard cot in the store's basement at night. Frank and fellow clerk, seventeen-year-old Harry Moody, were handed guns and ordered to keep the burglars away. His pay raise gave Frank the confidence to propose marriage to Jennie Creighton, something he had been thinking about for months. Between his own ample income and Jennie's sewing work, surely they could start a fine life for themselves. Jennie agreed, her heart full of hope for the future. Unfortunately, their plans were delayed.

Long work hours combined with restless nights spent in the damp basement took their toll. Frank became weaker, developing several respiratory ailments. His new position wasn't all it had been cracked up to be, either. Mr. Bushnell soon told Frank straight out that he hadn't proven himself worthy of ten dollars per week, and promptly cut his pay. He also suggested that Frank stop tinkering with the displays and concentrate on earning his money like a real sales clerk. This was the last straw. Frank collapsed in February 1876.

Frank was carried by sleigh to his parent's farmhouse. His mother provided twenty-four-hour-care, and Jennie would visit often, assisting as able nursemaid. At one point, Frank feared he'd made such a mess of things that he would surely lose Jennie, but she remained true. The couple married in the living room of the Woolworth farm on June 11, 1876. It would be another year before Frank's recovery was complete, but he was certainly in better spirits. The couple lived with Frank's parents until the following spring. By then, Frank was almost twenty-five, eager to be up and about, and anxious to settle down and start a family.

Somehow, Frank secured a down payment of $300 and mortgaged a $600, four-acre farm near Great Bend. Growing potatoes and raising chickens provided a tolerable income, but it was a dreary life. Frank was in exactly the same rut he'd been in four years before. Now that he'd experienced the business world, his plight was a bitter pill to swallow. Just as Frank was about to accept his grim lot in life, he received a surprising offer.

His old bosses, William Moore and Perry Smith, wanted Frank back. They'd always appreciated the value of Frank's display skills and were willing to pay him ten dollars a week again. The problem was, this would require Frank to be in Watertown six days a week, while Jennie remained home, maintaining the farm. Jennie was courageous, healthy, and prepared to make this sacrifice, so on June 11, 1877, Frank returned to Moore & Smith's. Jennie rarely complained, but Frank knew it was a hard, lonely life for his bride. Thus, the couple rejoiced in the fall of 1877, when Jennie was offered a modern sewing machine in exchange for their chicken flock.

The newlyweds sublet the farm near Great Bend, and moved into one small wing of a frame house at 236 Franklin Street in Watertown. The humming of Jennie's hand-powered sewing machine filled the house, and in her free time, she happily helped Frank at the store. As they sat around the woodstove of their tiny home, Frank would entertain Jennie with his dreams of the beautiful mansion he would one day build for her—a mansion fit for a queen. Ironically, years later, sitting alone in the Woolworth mansion, a melancholy Jennie would long for those days in Watertown, when they were struggling but happy, and she had her beloved Frank all to herself.

Canadian-born Jennie Creighton Woolworth (1853–1924) during her later years, living in luxury in New York. Her fondest memories were of the couple's struggling days in Watertown.

The Five-Cent Counter Causes a Stir

Back on the work front, a financial dilemma for William Moore turned out to be a dream come true for Frank Woolworth. It seemed that Moore and Smith suddenly found themselves with a large stock surplus and a handful of bills due within six months. William Moore decided he might be able to get rid of the extra stock (which he called "stickers") by opening up an additional store in nearby Great Bend. He asked a startled Frank to manage the new shop.

Eager to prove himself in his new role as "manager," Frank painstakingly organized the small twenty by sixty floor space in Great Bend, displaying the excess merchandise as attractively as possible. Grand opening sales on February 10, 1878, totaled a disappointing $42. Then, just five days after his less than impressive managerial debut, disaster struck the Woolworth household: Fanny McBrier Woolworth died on February 15, 1878 at age forty-seven. Frank was devastated. His mother had been his staunchest ally, the embodiment of unconditional love, and he would miss her terribly.

Frank returned to his managerial job in Great Bend and threw himself into work. Ridden with grief, he pushed on, trying his hardest to sell off the excess "stickers" and "Yankee notions," but for various reasons, including a less-than-ideal location, the Great Bend store failed. It was closed in May, and Frank was soon back in the Watertown store. This was a terrible blow for Frank, who still had so many dreams of grandeur in his mind. To console himself, Frank kept Fanny's words of encouragement in his mind: "Don't worry, son," she'd often said. "I just know that one day you'll become a rich man."

Another consolation was the fact that Frank would now be working with his brother, Charles. Shortly after their mother's death, Charles had admitted that he, too, was tired of farm life and wanted a shot in the business world. Frank had used his influence at Moore & Smith to get Charles a job. (Back at the farm, a housekeeper named Elvira Austin Moulton was hired to help Frank's father, John, get along.) Since then, Charles had shown great promise. The Woolworth boys toiled side by side, and on busy Saturday afternoons, even Jennie would pitch in, forming a happy trio.

The only fly in the ointment was the fact that business at Moore & Smith's was slackening. The failure of the Great Bend enterprise had not helped matters. By early summer, twenty-six-year-old Frank had to accept a salary cut to $8.00 per week. The timing was horrible, because Jennie was due to give birth to their first child in mid-July. Frank was at another impasse, unsure of which way to turn. Then, he overheard a conversation which would alter his life, and that of retailing, forever.

A young man name Golding entered the store to say hello to William Moore. Golding, along with E. W. Barrett, had left Watertown several years before to start their own "99¢ Store," an idea which had taken hold in the larger western cities.

Moore told Golding that sales were dropping.

Golding mulled this over a bit, and then asked Moore if he'd ever considered selling cut-rate goods to bring in more business. Moore shook his head. His was known as a choice establishment—why, his high-brow customers would be appalled!

As Frank Woolworth listened carefully, Golding explained to the dubious Moore that a small business in Michigan had recently boosted sales by advertising a counter of select items for the fixed price of 5¢ each. Once customers were lured in by the cheap stock, they moved toward the expensive merchandise. This "lure 'em in" device would eventually become commonplace, but back in the nineteenth century it was very much a revolutionary idea. The cut-rate notion made perfect sense to Frank, but he was not in a position to push the issue and reluctantly let the matter drop. That August, William Moore traveled to New York for his routine buying expedition and purchased one hundred dollars' worth of inexpensive goods from Spellman Brothers Co. He was willing to give this five-cent sale a try. Being the sovereign of displays, Frank was assigned the task of making the cut-rate counter a reality.

Frank took great pains to make the counter look interesting and attractive. He lugged two wooden sewing tables out of the back room and placed them side by side in the middle of the store. Together he and his coworker, Mrs. Adelia Coons, enthusiastically festooned the table with Frank's favorite color cloth: bright red. The goods themselves were nothing to ogle at; they included simple baby bibs, thimbles, and tin wash basins. But

From Rags to Riches: Wide angle view of Woolworth's palatial Long Island Mansion, Winfield House, which he purchased in 1915.

Frank did his best to exhibit them in such a way to encourage browsing, placing the most attractive items in the front. For a grand finale, Frank made up a sign:

"ANYTHING ON THIS COUNTER 5¢"

Then he headed home for a few hours of well-deserved sleep.

The next morning was the opening of Watertown's County Fair. The streets outside were crowded, and from his position near the five-cent counter, Frank could hear the merry notes of the steam calliope playing at the main fairgrounds. Folklore has it that a society woman came in for a pin to repair her torn dress and upon her arrival Frank urged her over to the cut-rate table. She purchased her pin, along with several other items, and then went outside and told all her

TIME CAPSULE MEMORY

In those days, Frank Woolworth was a tall, slim young man of twenty-six, rather looked up to by some of his companions, because he was making as much a ten dollars a week—and perhaps, because, as his brother says today, he could tell without hesitation the difference between dress linings and ginghams.

—From *50 Years of Woolworth*, 1919

This illustration from the F. W. Woolworth 1929 souvenir booklet, depicts Frank's famous 5¢ table in Watertown.

friends about the unprecedented sale at Moore & Smith's Drygoods.

That seminal day in September 1878, the five-cent counter caused a sensation. By closing time, Frank was exhausted, but all the nickel items had vanished! William Moore sent Frank running three flights up to the Western Union telegraph office to put in an emergency rush order to Spellman Brothers. They needed a duplicate order and they needed it fast. Years later, Mrs. Coons (who would be one of F. W. Woolworth's first female store managers) said she could still hear the thumping of Frank's shoes pounding up the stairs to send the wire. It was worth the running, though, because on every single day of the fair, the nickel counter completely sold out. The customers spent a tidy amount on more expensive items as well, which thoroughly pleased the proprietors.

When the fair closed down and the crowds dispersed, Moore & Smith continued the five-cent counter, and for a time they even operated as a wholesale outlet for cut-rate goods, but not as their primary business. The profits on nickel goods were so minuscule that they couldn't rely on them to pay the entire staff's wages and operating expenses. Pragmatic William Moore was also a man of insight, however. He told Frank he believed that someone with pluck could probably make a success with a store devoted entirely to nickel goods. During that post-Civil War era, when prices were so high that a fixed-price "99¢ store" was considered a compelling bargain, surely people would respond favorably to a 5¢ shop!

Frank Woolworth wholeheartedly agreed. He'd witnessed first-hand just how much patrons enjoyed choosing their own stock from the table, an early form of self-service. He'd noticed how pleased they were that every item was the same low price, eliminating the need for haggling. They liked both the convenience and the variety. Just imagine, reasoned Frank, how even the poorest of patrons could feel rich, if they were shopping at a five-cent store.

In the ensuing months, the nickel table caught on among upstate merchants, and it soon became a full-blown craze. One enterprising farmer purchased fifty dollars worth of nickel goods, carried his stock to Adams Center, New York, and placed it on sale outside his barn. It appeared that Frank Woolworth's five-cent sales counter spawned one of the first garage sales in America.

The success of the cut-rate sale gave Frank a new dream. He would establish his own five-cent store, perhaps an entire chain of such establishments. He would simply make a steady profit through bulk sales. He'd certainly experienced moments when one penny made the difference in what he couldn't buy. In turn, a penny or two of profits from items anyone could buy would surely add up to dimes and quarters and dollars, perhaps even hundreds of dollars.

Frank rushed home to discuss his idea with Jennie, who was completely supportive. The problem, as usual, was money. Mr. Moore had said a man in the nickel business would need at least a few hundred dollars of capital. Frank approached his uncle Albon McBrier, but Albon turned him down. He said it was all "stuff and nonsense" and that Frank should stick with his steady job.

Frank was too far along in his scheme to let this rebuke stop him, and he promptly sought out other backers. In the end, it was William Moore who came through for Woolworth. Moore told Frank that if he could find a good location, he would give him a note to finance his own store. To add credence to the deal, Frank's father, John, agreed to endorse the note.

Frank and Jennie were grateful and promised to do all they could to make a go of the new business. Back at Moore & Smith's Drygoods, and throughout the town of Watertown, Frank's coworkers wished him well. Several of his old Watertown friends, including Mrs. Coons and Harry Moody, would one day form the foundation of his five-and-dime empire. Frank W. Woolworth never forgot those who were kind and supportive to him as he reached for the stars.

It was a good time for Frank to branch out on his own. Lifestyles were changing rapidly. The last World Exhibition, held in Philadelphia, had showcased marvels unheard of twenty years before, and there were rumors that New York City had started to install some newfangled communication device called a telephone. As New Year's Day 1879, approached, great fortunes were being made across America. P. T. Barnum had his circus, Rockefeller had Standard Oil, Hartford had A&P, and Frank Woolworth would have his five-cent store.

Frank was ready to pounce on the entrepreneurial bandwagon, not only for his own fulfillment, but for the sake of Jennie and their seven-month-old daughter, Helena. In February, Frank bid his loved ones good-bye, then trudged through the snow to the train depot. A few five-cent stores had already sprouted up in large cities such as Syracuse, and he planned to check them out, first-hand, to assess the lay of the retail land. Then, he vowed, he would find the perfect site for "Woolworth's Great Five-Cent Store."

Frank's First Store Opens in Utica

The next few weeks were bittersweet for Frank. He scouted out several different cities between Watertown and Rome, New York, looking for the ideal site for his first store. The results there were disappointing, so, on a hunch, he took the train into Utica. He was not in the best frame of mind when he stepped off the depot, having just spent a bleak Sunday

TIME CAPSULE MEMORY

"Frank's First Landlords in Utica, New York"

The store was owned by a couple of bankers. One of them had a little faith in me, the other had none; and I had great difficulty in renting the store for $30 a month . . . I showed them the bill for how much merchandise I had coming, and everything was all right to start in the 5¢ business; yet I lacked courage . . . I would have given up all the old boots I ever had in life to be back in my old position, as I never had much experience in the cold, cruel world before. All I had to do was send a telegram . . .

—Frank W. Woolworth, 22 Feb., 1919, recalling the establishment of his first store in Utica, N.Y.

visiting one of his aunts, who, he recalled sadly, "did not try to encourage me."

Fortunately, Utica was hopping when he arrived, which energized his spirits. He watched the flow of traffic, both pedestrian and carriage, his mind reeling with possibilities. Utica was full of hard-working factory workers, all potential customers. The five-cent craze had somehow missed Utica, so he would be operating on virgin sales ground. After using up a fair amount of shoe leather, Frank spotted a "To Let" sign on the corner of Bleeker and Genesee. The storefront measured thirteen feet wide and twenty feet deep; it was not a large space, but it would be ample for his needs.

The landlords were bankers who drove a hard bargain. They wanted thirty dollars per month for rent, a year's lease, and the first month paid in advance—with cash. Combining his charm and tenacity, Frank talked the landlords into deleting the "year lease" clause, and into waiting until the end of the month for the first rent installment. When asked to explain the nature of his business, Frank hedged. "Oh, notions and general merchandise," he replied lightly. He feared that, being bankers, they might smell a cheap-goods fad with no hope of making a long-term profit.

Twenty-seven-year-old Frank Woolworth had achieved his preliminary goals. He had the place. He had the means. He had the energy. All he had to do was wire William Moore back in Watertown and tell him which stock to set aside for transfer to Utica. Still he hesitated, realizing the ramifications of such an action. This would mean leaving a steady job, uprooting his family, and risking everything. If he didn't play his cards right, he would soon be back to hoeing potatoes. Years later, Frank recalled this moment of truth in one of his general letters to his staff. He wrote: "That telegram seemed to mean a definite casting of the die. I kept it in my pocket and walked past the telegraph office many times before summoning courage to send it. I didn't wire my wife because I wanted to tell her myself."

Faith in himself finally superseded his doubts, and he did send that wire. Consequently, the first merchandise bill from William Moore turned out to be much more than Frank had expected: $315.41. That left only $34.59 to purchase wood for counters, a cash box for the money, board in a rooming house, and money for cleaning supplies. The leased space was rather dilapidated, full of dust and grime, and needed to be thoroughly revamped.

At this point in the story, the Woolworth chronicles grow cloudy. There are two different versions of how the milestone emporium actually came to be. John Winkler's biography, *Five and Ten,* relied on an unpublished autobiography that Woolworth imparted (shortly before his death in 1919) to confidante Edwin Mott Woolley. Frank reportedly told Woolley that after he sent the wire to Moore and Smith, he caught a train back to Watertown. Upon arrival, he stopped home to share the latest news with an excited Jennie. Then he walked to Moore & Smith's to oversee the shipment of stock to Utica. Once that was accomplished, he quickly returned to Utica to get the store prepared for opening day.

Frank worked like a Trojan, and scrubbed and cleaned the place all by himself. He shrewdly arranged for two thousand flyers to be distributed by a young boy. The handbills read, in part: "Grand Opening—Eight O'Clock on the evening of Saturday, February 22, 1879." Even though the boy dumped piles of a hundred at a time on local doorsteps, enough were scattered about to spread the word. All was going well, but Frank had underestimated the amount of work required to get his business organized. Years later, he reportedly told Edwin Woolley:

> *"On Friday evening I had the goods all in the store, but everything was in a great litter, with loose paper scattered about on the floor and the goods in a general mix up on the counters and shelves. To keep people from satisfying their curiosity and thus anticipating the grand opening, I had fastened paper at the doors and windows. While I was working in this muss, about nine o'clock, somebody knocked at the door . . ."*

An older woman, who'd seen his flyer, wanted to purchase a five-cent fire shovel. Hence, Frank made his first official sale on Friday night, and then locked the door behind her. The store opened, as scheduled, the next evening at eight o'clock. He did not have a rush of customers, but business was steady. At midnight, when he counted his receipts, he'd found he had made an even nine dollars.

There is, however, another version of the story, which was taken directly from a General Letter that Frank sent to all his stores on February 22, 1919. It was entitled: "Fortieth Anniversary of the Five and Ten Cent Business. Ancient History." In this memo, Frank explained that after he had secured the Utica lease and wired Moore & Smith, he felt suddenly invigorated, on the brink of a new life. The goods quickly arrived, and he was on his way. Contrary to the prior account, Frank didn't stop back at Watertown to visit his family, nor did he say he shouldered the store preparations alone. Instead, he headed back to his Utica store and hired his first employees: two young people (probably teenagers) known to historians as Miss Stebbins and Mr. Edwins.

> *"We worked all day Friday and all day Saturday," wrote Frank, "but we did not open for business, as the store was not ready. In the meantime, we sent out some circulars, giving the list of all the goods we would sell for 5¢. For fear the cus-*

tomers would get there before the store was ready for business, we sent the first circulars out to New Hartford, a place about two or three miles outside the City. Along about six o'clock on Saturday evening a woman came into the store. . . . "

Frank told the woman that they weren't quite ready for customers, but she was insistent. She'd seen the circular and she *wanted* a five-cent fire shovel! Frank quickly dealt with his very first customer, forever regretful that he didn't learn her name. He then locked the door, finished his preparations, and reopened, as scheduled, at eight o'clock P.M. "By then," he enthused, "there was a great crowd outside the front door, demanding to get in . . . !"

After reviewing these two accounts, we may presume that somewhere along the line, Frank's original version was altered, edited, or enhanced by his various biographers or secretaries. The most accurate story of his first opening day is probably a combination of the two, but the truth died with him.

One thing is certain. In setting up his first store, he used his capital mindfully, limiting his personal spending money to a mere five dollars per week. His records show only two notable business indulgences. The first was ten dollars' worth of a proven best-seller—painted red jewelry (composed of sour milk)—which added color to his displays and lured in the town's ladies. The second was a large, three-dollar sign which read:

"THE GREAT FIVE CENT STORE."

A Glory Short-Lived

During Frank Woolworth's opening day in Utica he netted just under ten dollars in toy dustpans, biscuit cutters, apple corers, ribbons, and cheap necklaces. Monday's sales totaled $50.20. By week's end he'd made $244.44. Within three weeks he was able to pay back William Moore, satisfy his landlord, pay his staff, and purchase his wife's first luxury item: a $45 fur Dolman.

Frank always referred to his Utica enterprise as his "five-cent" store, but in reality, he could have called it "Frank's Great Five Shinplaster Store." Most of the money he received came in the form of shinplasters (Civil War-era paper currency), which were issued in cent denominations of 2, 3, 5, 10 and 25. Regardless of whether cents or shinplasters passed hands that spring, by April 1879, his business was booming. Back in Watertown, Jennie was happily packing. She was ready to move to Utica, to fulfill her own dream of renting out an entire house, with a small play area for daughter Helena.

Then, unexpectedly, the bottom dropped out of the market.

Ladies' hair ribbons and accessories were best-sellers at Frank's Utica store, and remained so for the company's 118-year-old history.

There were only so many items Frank could sell for a nickel, and after the patrons had seen them all, the store's novelty waned. He tried to boost business by distributing more handbills, but by mid-May, Woolworth knew he had to close down voluntarily, or his debtors would do it for him.

Frank was dismayed, but not yet ready to toss in the shinplasters. He absolutely disagreed with the critics who insisted the cut-rate trade was just a fad. Frank suspected the primary problem was a lack of variety. Until then, he'd been content to stock his store from the rather limited supply of "stickers" and cheap excess merchandise that Moore & Smith had left over from their wholesale lot. The next time, Frank would carry what was left of those items (he hated to waste anything) along with new commodities, including a wider selection of the brightly colored hair ribbons that had proven so popular with his female customers. Frank admitted that most of the other five-centers had failed, but *he* was just "regrouping."

Frank swallowed his pride and sent the unsold merchandise back to Moore & Smith's for storage. William Moore promised to give Frank another note, if he found a better location. Woolworth closed his doors in Utica in May 1879, but it was not the last the Mohawk Valley would see of him.

The successor to the Genesee Street store would open in 1888 (under the banner "Woolworth & Peck"). In the meantime, Frank stopped at the neighborhood bank on May 28, 1879, and made a modest withdrawal. On a hunch, he was off to northeastern Pennsylvania; a land lush and green, populated by a simple Amish people with a nose for thrift. His long, exhausting trip to Lancaster would prove to be a road well traveled. Frank Woolworth left Utica with only thirty dollars in his pocket, but forty years later, he could boast that his store chain was making one hundred and seven million dollars!

The first permanent five-and-ten-cent store was about to be born.

Chapter Three

Frank Sires a Million-Dollar Baby in Pennsylvania

Dear Father: I opened my store here (in Lancaster) for trade yesterday.
We managed to sell $127.65, which is the most I ever sold in one day.
I had 7 clerks and they had to work—you bet!"

—Excerpt from a letter from Frank W. Woolworth
to his father, John. Dated 22 June 1879.

Watertown, New York, will always be remembered as the city where Frank Woolworth began his legendary career, testing out the five-cent counter at Moore & Smith's emporium. Genesee Street in Utica will always be known as the site of Store Number One, a failure financially, but worth its weight in gold in terms of grit experience.

Yet, it is Lancaster, Pennsylvania, that reigns as Woolworth's inaugural commercial success. There, in 1879, smack in the middle of Pennsylvania Dutch country, young Frank opened his first successful store, one that would prevail as the home of America's first permanent five-and-dime.

In many ways, Lancaster still remains "Woolworth country." A marble plaque in North

Woolworth "skyscraper" and roof garden c. 1903

Queen Street Park commemorates the site of the inaugural store. Just down the road, one can see the remains of the remodeled store, dedicated in 1950, which still has the "Woolworth" name imbedded into the sidewalk. From that central part of town, one can stroll into any eatery, enter any bookstore, pause at any bus stop—and meet up with someone with a unique

Plaque commemorating Frank's first permanent 5&10 on North Queen Street in Lancaster, Pa.

Woolworth tale to share. Equally important, Lancaster's fine Historical Society, libraries, and newspaper archives all work to preserve the Woolworth legacy.

Indeed, the archives house hundreds of newspaper articles recounting Frank's adventures. In 1900, in particular, columnists waxed prolific about the unprecedented splendor of the magnificent new six-story "skyscraper" on the corner of Queen and Grant, erected just in time for Christmas. Reportedly, during the grand opening, thousands of people streamed through the glass doors of this architectural wonder, oohing and ahhing at the marbled stairways and gold-tiered roof garden. The 100th anniversary in 1979 was no less exalted. Frank himself had long ago passed away, but his corporate descendants threw a week-long extravaganza, featuring live entertainment and special sales, with VIPs from coast to coast gathering for the annual stockholder's meeting. In the window, a colorful array of items from 1879 was displayed for one and all to see, and the governor of Pennsylvania declared June 11 the official "Woolworth Day."

One hundred and twenty years ago, Lancaster took Frank Woolworth into its heart, and he, in turn, added to its already rich history, by highlighting it prominently in the archives of his mercantile empire. The Lancaster chapter in F. W. Woolworth's life involved a series of financial ups and downs and emotional round-robins that would have broken a lesser man. But Frank Woolworth persevered . . . and won.

Lancaster City: Birthplace of an Empire

Shortly before the demise of his Utica store, Woolworth received a tip from a traveling man, encouraging him to consider Lancaster City for his next enterprise. He was told that the thrifty German immigrants and the established Pennsylvania Dutch would appreciate good wares at inexpensive prices. There was even a depot in town, which brought hundreds of people into the city for market days. Frank was intrigued enough to take a shot at it. He was certainly far from ready to give up his dream of opening a chain of successful stores.

The train ride from Utica to Lancaster took an entire day. Given the fact that he'd only

ITEM	COST PER GROSS
Toy dustpans	$4.75
Tin pepper boxes	3.75
Purses	5.25
Biscuit cutters	3.00
Flour dredges	5.25
School straps	4.50
Skimmers	2.50
Apple corers	5.75
Sad-iron stands	5.00
Fire shovels	5.50
Animal soap	5.85
Stamped-in cup	5.50
ABC Plates	2.50
Lather Brushes	5.50
Pencil charms	5.75
Police whistles	5.00
Red jewelry	5.00
Turkey red napkins	.50 dozen

A list of merchandise that Frank carried in 1879. These prices are by the gross, or approximately 144 pieces. On every gross of "red jewelry" sold at a nickel a piece, he only made $2.20. No wonder he watched every penny he spent!

allowed himself thirty dollars, and that the round trip fare cost twenty, Frank ate sparingly on the trip. He arrived in Lancaster at dusk on May 30, tired, hungry and somewhat subdued. His mood quickly changed to elation when he noticed that the sidewalks were still thronged with people. Gaslights were blazing and horse-drawn wagons jammed the thoroughfares. "Everywhere," wrote twenty-seven-year-old Frank with awe, "there was an amazing air of business and prosperity! Right away, I felt that Lancaster was the place for me." After hours of strolling the streets, he checked into what he termed "a vile old hotel." Bright and early the next morning, he set out in search of a site. In his customary manner, Frank didn't waste any time. By that very evening, he'd made preliminary arrangements to lease a fourteen-foot storefront at 170 North Queen Street for thirty dollars per month.

The next seven days were a frenzy of activity. He returned to Watertown and told Jennie the good news. Then, he arranged for the leftover stock from his Utica store to be delivered to Lancaster. He also secured an additional loan from Moore & Smith in the amount of $300 to pay the rent and order more merchandise.

Once these details were taken care of, he dashed back to Lancaster, and hired some local citizens to help him sweep the floors and organize the stock. His original Utica sign, "Woolworth's Great Five Cent Store," was displayed prominently a few days ahead, in order to garner curiosity. He did not invest a farthing in paid newspaper ads, believing that this was a waste of his hard-earned cash. For Woolworth, "word of mouth" and the occasional handbill were the preferred form of advertising. Naturally, this type of thinking did not ingratiate him with the local press in Lancaster, or in any other city in which he did business. Be that as it may, both Frank and Jennie were excited by the new venture. The couple found rooms on 237 West Lemon Street, and while Frank busily prepared his store, Jennie settled in with their daughter, Helena.

One of the clerks Frank had hired was fifteen-year-old Charles Hoffmeier. Seventy-one years later, in 1950, when a newly remodeled F. W. Woolworth's opened at 21–27 North Queen Street, Charles recalled that the little pioneer crew had worked around the clock for days, racing to prepare the store. Finally, Saturday morning found a large crowd anxiously peering into the windows. Excited, Frank headed for the door, but young Charlie dashed ahead and let in the patrons. Charlie always prided himself on being the one who "officially" opened this milestone store.

TIME CAPSULE MEMORY

"A Hammer For a Nickel"

My father, the late William J. Fraser, II, bought a hammer from F. W. Woolworth personally, on the day he opened the store. A card in the window, "Nothing over 5 cents" had caught his eye. He said, "Woolworth is a nice young man, but this *can't* pay." Dad had quite a big eye opener coming! —S. H. Fraser, c. 1950, Lancaster, Pa.

That first day, Frank sold thirty percent of his stock, a total of $127.65. Reportedly, his new establishment caused a great stir in town; his only media competition being the ruckus caused over on nearby Prince Street when two infuriated horses got loose and almost killed several pedestrians. Frank was so pleased with the initial response of the Pennsylvanians to his little shop, that he dashed off a letter to his father, John, bragging about his success.

As the weeks passed, and word of mouth spread throughout the city and surrounding countryside, Frank's business boomed. The customers were both intrigued and excited by the nickel prices and the array of goods. Unlike at other, larger stores in the area, they didn't have to ask an often stone-faced clerk to open up a drawer and show them merchandise. At "Woolworth's Great Five Cent Store," they could browse to their heart's content, randomly pick up items off the counter, and carefully scrutinize the quality. Since everything was the same low price, they didn't have to haggle and they didn't need to ask for credit. Frank Woolworth's useful offerings blended in perfectly with the simple lifestyles of the native Amish and Mennonites who made up the bulk of his steady patrons. To lure them in, Frank displayed as much as he could fit into the relatively small window space. Inside the store, he arranged the jumble of goods on simple shelves and in plain woven baskets.

Animal cake-cutters, jelly-cake tins, thread, and candlesticks; sugar scoops, biscuit cutters, ABC plates, and flea soap—such was the stock of the first Queen Street store. To spruce up these rather bland utilitarian items, he festooned red bandannas on the rough-hewn shelves. This red fabric was a luxury for Frank, who counted every penny as if were a dollar. He was so thrifty that he made his clerks wrap the customer's parcels in used, local newspapers. The standard brown wrap paper of the time cost 8¢ a pound, while the newspapers could be procured for 2¢ a pound. Each week, Frank would personally trek down to the supplier and carry back the heavy load of newspapers to his store.

Within a few weeks after opening, it was already time to replenish his stock, which, of course, meant that Frank required more capital. His dilemma was that his $300 loan

Days in the Amish Country

Original Lancaster store, 170 North Queen St., Lancaster, Pa.
The young boy in the photo is probably Charles Hoffmeier,
who started working there at age fifteen. A mustachioed
Frank stands far left.

Informal gathering of the Five-and-Ten pioneers, Brooklyn, New York, c. 1889.

from Moore & Smith had been used to stock the store for the grand opening; the lion's share of his profits had been used to pay his employees, apartment rent, food expenses, and daily necessities. He was an absolute stickler about paying back his notes, and he'd repaid William Moore's note as soon as possible. This certainly left Frank a bit short in the billfold. Historians have sometimes questioned how Frank managed to acquire the funds to keep his store full during that lean initial year.

A 1959 piece in the *Lancaster Daily Intelligencer Journal* sheds some light on this mystery. In that article, Dr. William A. Wolf said his father had been a personal friend of Woolworth. His father told Dr. Wolf that the landlady on Lemon Street, Mrs. Kendig, had advanced young Woolworth $200 when he was sorely in need of cash. Woolworth never forgot that kindly gesture, and repaid her as soon as he could. He also went one step further. Every year thereafter, until his benefactress died, she received a check for $200 on the anniversary date of the original loan.

Meanwhile, Jennie Woolworth started to help out at the store, working side by side with her husband. On most mornings, she would bring little Helena with her to Queen Street and gently set the child down behind the cash counter, nestled in a packing crate covered with soft blankets, or surrounded by simple toys. Helena would always have a stream of clerks and customers fussing over her; her every wail or coo was met with immediate gratification.

Jennie enjoyed her work at the shop; it made her feel useful and productive. Years later, when he was basking in his riches, Frank would forbid his wife to labor at any of his five and dimes, feeling this was not at all suitable for a lady of means. He also discouraged her from cooking and sewing, insisting she had servants to perform such tasks. Frank had her best interests at heart, but Jennie was left with too much time on her hands and a feeling of uselessness that no doubt contributed to the mental depression she suffered in her maturing years. She was never comfortable with a high-brow set, and felt awkward spending her time at fancy charity functions with other female members of her financial class. Once her daughters grew up, Jennie became increasingly wary of the outside world. Consequently, she was often left alone in their vast Long Island estate, save for the company of the expert nurses Frank hired to care for her.

In Lancaster, however, Jennie was in her prime. She often served up hearty Sunday dinners to Frank's employees and friends, contentedly socialized with friends, and crafted lovely dresses for her daughter.

Everything seemed hopeful for the little Woolworth family, and Frank started dreaming bigger and better dreams.

The Woolworth Brothers Band Together

By early July 1879, Frank was doing so well on Queen Street that he decided it was time to expand. He found a site in Harrisburg, Pennsylvania, and wrote to his brother, Charles, asking him to manage this new five-cent store. Charles was delighted to comply, for more than one reason. Since March, he'd been running the Morristown, New York, branch of Moore & Smith's, which was located on the banks of the St. Lawrence River, close to the Canadian border. Like his brother, he longed to flee the limited opportunities of the North Country. He'd also had a most unsettling bout with the law; although he'd proven himself a winner in the general merchandise trade, not everyone appreciated his gifts. Charles had recently made a few enemies when he tried to drum up some Canadian business for Moore & Smith's. He hired a boat man to row across the St. Lawrence to Brockville, and started distributing advertising flyers to everyone in town. The Brockvillian merchants did not appreciate Charles's pushy Yankee methods, or the fact that a foreigner was trying to snare their trade. Charles and the boat man were hauled off to jail, handcuffed, and detained. "He had visions," recalled Edwin M. McBrier, "of being branded as a lawbreaker and languishing in a Canadian jail, with the dire consequences of losing his job at Moore & Smith's!" In the end, the magistrate let them go within a few hours, with a firm warning and an earful of fire and brimstone. But Charles's plan ultimately worked; for as long as the store lasted, a considerable part of the business was due to the trade it had from Canada.

In the summer of 1879, Charles bid a genial farewell to William Moore and Perry Smith, and hopped on the first "iron-horse" bound for Pennsylvania. He quickly moved into a rooming house in Harrisburg, and together he and Frank prepared the store for its grand opening on July 19. They took time to send updates to their father back in Watertown, who in August 1879 married his housekeeper Elvira Moulton. No doubt the brothers were relieved that their father was being cared for, even though the memory of their beloved mother, Fanny, still caused so much pain in their minds and hearts.

The Harrisburg store brought in a respectable $84.41 the first day, with sales increasing as the weeks flew by. The Christmas season was moderately busy, but afterward, sales dropped substantially. On top of that, the landlord demanded a rent increase. The brothers decided this was too much to pay and were forced to close the little twelve by sixteen emporium in March 1880.

TIME CAPSULE MEMORY

"One of Woolworth's First Employees Remembers . . ."

Candy, cosmetics, stationery? Oh dear, no, there were none of these on the counters of Frank Winfield Woolworth's first five-and-ten-cent store. At the back of the store, on the platform of a winding staircase, Mr. Woolworth would sit at his desk, watching the clerks at their work, and guarding the sales box. After a sale was made, each clerk (and there were only three) had to walk back to Mr. Woolworth to get change. *Every* amount was recorded on a tablet, and in the evening after the store had closed, the accounts were determined. The store never closed when a customer remained, and many a time it was after 11:00 until the store was locked to trade.

—Mrs. Susan Kane, in October 1938, recalling her early years working at the first Lancaster store almost 60 years before

---

Undaunted, Frank rented yet another spot in York, Pennsylvania. Once again, Charles was installed as manager, with a one-dollar raise, bringing him to $8 per week. Opening week sales were $222.52. After that, it was all downhill. Sales for the sixth week totaled $62.99, and for the final week of operation only $3.05. Three months later the store was locked up, and the cardboard sign that had hung above the door was shipped back (along with the remaining stock) to Lancaster for safekeeping.

At that point, Frank Woolworth could have tossed in the towel, sent Charles back to his old job at Moore & Smith's and simply reaped the profits in Lancaster for the rest of his life. But he wanted more than that: he wanted an entire chain of stores, all featuring the "Woolworth" name. He decided that to achieve this goal he had to do two things. First, he had to find a larger retail space, and second, he had to add ten-cent items to his inventory. As a test, in the summer of 1880, he introduced a dime section in the Lancaster mother store, thus establishing the first five-and-ten in the world.

The patrons were delighted when they saw the latest bargains, including dainty china cups and solid brass cookie cutters. Feeling that his luck had started to improve,

The Woolworth's of 237 Lemon Street

The house in Lancaster where Frank, Jennie, and Helena lived while Woolworth was establishing himself in Pennsylvania. Reportedly, Frank's landlady, kindly Mrs. Anna Kendig, advanced him a loan in time of need, something Frank never forgot. Frank and Jennie Woolworth remained at Lemon Street for four years until they relocated to Queen Street. The family remained in Lancaster until July, 1886, when they moved to 365A Quincy Street, Brooklyn, New York.

Frank spent several weeks touring the Pennsylvania countryside in search of a town with a busy main street and a large space for let. He soon found it in Scranton, Pennsylvania, on 125 Penn Avenue. Charles was installed as manager.

Scranton was the biggest store to date, offering a roomy twenty by seventy-two feet of space, enough to hold an initial $625 worth of merchandise, this time with stock priced at both a nickel and a dime. Opening sales were modest—a mere $43—but the Woolworth brothers persevered. This perseverance paid off, and by year's end they had made $9,000.

That fall, Frank Woolworth left his Lancaster store in the capable hands of his senior clerk (and his wife, Jennie) and set out in search of cut-rate bargains for the holiday season. He visited a Philadelphia import firm named Meyer & Shoenaman, which offered Frank a great deal on glass Christmas tree ornaments. Frank laughed out loud, calling the idea foolish. "Most of them would be smashed before there was even a chance to sell them!" he told the partners. The partners were persuasive, though, and Frank agreed to order a small shipment. The ornaments quickly became the hit of the season, selling out in two days. In later years, Woolworth stores all over the world featured similar ornaments (along with imported German ornaments), which are now highly collectible.

Come New Year's Day 1881, both the stores in Lancaster and Scranton were showing great profits. Because of his personal "no credit" rule, Frank didn't owe a dime to anyone. He had a sizable bank account, and he was proud of the fine parasol his wife carried during their Sunday strolls about town. Soon, he made his first official expansion in Lancaster, adding the corner property at 172 North Queen Street to his original space.

Brother Charles was doing just as well, his warm manner and good humor making him popular with Scranton's customers and his boardinghouse mates. Charles liked Scranton so much that he was seriously considering making the town his permanent home. This possibility became even more likely when his brother walked in one day and made him a surprising offer: Would Charles like to be a partner, rather than just a manager? Frank would allow him to "pay" for his share through store earnings.

Twenty-five-year-old Charles was delighted with the arrangement. Like Frank, he had harsh memories of shoveling manure and milking cows during the North Country's unrelenting ice storms. To be a "real partner" in a profitable store meant he would never have to return to such hardship.

While this was a generous gesture on Frank's part, it is worth mentioning that Frank also had more selfish motives for extending the offer. He'd learned that his uncle, Henry Wesley McBrier, had offered Charles the chance to manage, and hold interest in, a general merchandise store in Michigan. In the past, Albon McBrier had rebuked Frank's business ideas, and now it appeared that *another* McBrier uncle was trying steal away his brother. Frank was determined that this would not happen.

The three Woolworth girls. *Left to right:* Edna, b. 1883, Lancaster, Pa. the eldest Helena, b. 1878, Watertown, N.Y., and little Jessy May, b. 1886, Lancaster.

Consequently, a new sign reading "Woolworth Bro's 5 & 10¢ Store" was posted outside the Scranton site in January 1881. Charles stood by his brother's side that day and for every day until Frank died in 1919. Charles survived his brother by twenty-eight years, and to the end, he was a pivotal force in the great F. W. Woolworth Company.

By now, Frank was feeling financially and emotionally flush, but he was exhausted from the long work hours. During the spring of 1881, he informed Jennie that they were going to return to Watertown for a short vacation. It was time to revel in his success, especially for the benefit of those naysayers who'd believed he would be a failure. Frank, Jennie and three-year-old Helena arrived in Watertown dressed finely in tailored clothes, surrounded by wafts of Jennie's new expensive perfume. The prodigal Woolworth family received a grand welcome, especially from William Moore, who was proud of his protégé. While Jennie was engaged in homecoming social calls, Frank hustled about the town square of Watertown, handing out expensive cigars and sharing his dreams for the future. His success so far, he told anyone who would listen, was just the beginning. He would soon begin expanding throughout Pennsylvania and into the outlying states. This was optimistic thinking for a man who'd recently experienced dismal failures in Utica, Harrisburg, and York, but that was typical Frank Woolworth, a man who refused to accept failure.

At one point, Frank held court in the center of Moore & Smith's store, regaling his old

cronies with tales of the five-and-ten business, and vividly describing the lush, beautiful countryside of Pennsylvania. His circle of admirers included Mrs. Adelia Coons, who'd enthusiastically helped him decorate his first 5¢ counter, and Harry Moody, who had helped Frank keep the burglars away at Bushnell's store. Fred Kirby was also on hand, working as Moore's bookkeeper, but he was ripe for adventure. Indeed, Kirby was so fervent about leaving Jefferson County and seeking his own fortune, he was ready to hop a train to Lancaster on the spot. Since he was underage, his parents forbade it, but Woolworth took note of

Charles Woolworth was instrumental in the success of the F. W. Woolworth Co., serving as president when Frank died in 1919, and on the board of directors until he died at age 90 in 1947. He made Scranton his home and became a prominent citizen and philanthropist. Charles was vice president of the U.S. Lumber Company and the Mississippi Central Railroad. He was a director of the First National Bank (Scranton Lackawanna) and the International Education Publishing Company.

Charles Sumner Woolworth (1856–1947).

"Woolworth Bro's" five-and-ten at 125 Penn Avenue in Scranton, Pennsylvania, c. 1881.

the boy's ambition. Another clerk, Carson Peck, stood to the side, his intelligent eyes watching Woolworth with keen interest. Frank was not yet in the position to offer a business commitment to any of these people, but his enthusiasm for the five-and-dime business was contagious. By the turn of the century, everyone in that room would become deeply involved in the great Woolworth syndicate—and become wealthy in the process.

Before the Woolworths left New York, they stopped off at Uncle Albon's to visit the McBriers and let skeptical Albon see just how well his nephew had done. While there, Frank continued to plant the seeds for his empire. He encouraged his aunt Jane to have her son, Seymour Knox (who was working in the retail trade in Michigan), to keep Frank abreast of his cousin's progress.

Later that week, over a cozy family dinner at the old homestead in Champion, John Woolworth filled Frank in on the lives of his Woolworth cousins, including Fred and Herbert Woolworth. Both of these boys were still in their teens at the time, but they were already showing an interest in business over farming. Frank filed away this information for future reference.

The trip, though all too brief, was both restful and invigorating for F. W. Woolworth. Whether consciously or unconsciously, Frank had laid the groundwork for the next Woolworth milestone—the expansion of dimestores across the United States and into Canada.

1881–1886: Let the March of Dimes Begin!

Over the next five years, life changed drastically for Frank. He'd arrived in Lancaster in 1879 with thirty dollars in his pocket and a vague pipe dream. Yet, his gross sales for 1881 showed an impressive $18,000, and by 1882, they topped out at a mind boggling $24,000. On the homefront, Jennie announced she was going to have another baby, and asked her sister, Sidney Creighton, to leave her native Canada and join the family in Pennsylvania. The Woolworths did not have a servant, per se (although they could have easily afforded one) because Jennie much preferred to rule the growing roost. Still, Sidney Creighton's help was heartily appreciated and, within a short time, sorely needed.

Charles Woolworth was also moving along. Amazingly, the 1882 years' receipts in Scranton had topped those of Lancaster, and in January 1883, he bought out Frank's partnership interest. This was an entirely amicable arrangement; Charles simply wanted to branch out on his own. The brothers continued to share resources, retail tips and enjoyable social occasions together. The upshot of this buyout, however, was that Frank was now back to being a one-man, one-store show. Given his ambition, he didn't like this very much, and wanted to remedy it as soon as possible. The more stores he had, the more he could buy in bulk, leading to greater profits. There was also the matter of his ego.

Frank W. Woolworth had established a presence in parts of Pennsylvania and upstate

WOOLWORTH'S FIRST DECADE

Opening Date	Location	Size of Store (ft.)	Opening Day Data			Manager January 1, 1890
			Stock	Sales	Ownership	
1879						
February 22	Utica, N. Y.	14 x 25	$ 315	$ 50	F. W. Woolworth	*Failed, June, 1879*
June 21	Lancaster, Pa.	14 x 35	410	128	F. W. Woolworth	W. D. Rock
July 19	Harrisburg, Pa.	12 x 20	397	85	F. W. Woolworth	*Closed, March, 1880*
1880						
April 3	York, Pa.	16 x 30	596	26	F. W. Woolworth	*Failed, June, 1880*
November 6	Scranton, Pa.	20 x 72	625	43	F. W. Woolworth	*See note*(1)
1883						
March 10	Philadelphia, Pa. 25¢ Store	15 x 70	1,385	46	F. W. Woolworth	*Failed, June, 1883*
October 27	Lancaster, Pa.	14 x 35	948	63	F. W. Woolworth	*Failed, March, 1884*
1884						
September 20	Reading, Pa.	16 x 45	1,531	209	F. W. Woolworth and S. H. Knox	A. H. Satterthwait
October 18	25¢ Store Reading, Pa.	14 x 125	1,900	127	F. W. Woolworth	*Failed, Dec., 1884*
1885						
August 8	Harrisburg, Pa.	15 x 40	1,615	197	F. W. Woolworth and H. H. Hesslet	H. H. Hesslet
September 5	Trenton, N. J.	15 x 90	2,192	354	F. W. Woolworth and O. Woodworth	O. Woodworth (3)
1886						
May 15	Newark, N. J.	18 x 70	3,675	161	F. W. Woolworth and S. H. Knox	*Failed, Dec., 1886*
August 28	Erie, Pa.	22 x 150	2,493	213	F. W. Woolworth and S. H. Knox	*See note*(2)
October 16	Elmira, N. Y.	15 x 45	2,245	29	F. W. Woolworth and E. Northrup	E. Northrup
October 23	Easton, Pa.	16 x 45	2,293	170	F. W. Woolworth and A. Getman	M. J. Getman
1887						
September 17	Lockport, N. Y.	17 x 60	2,000	166	F. W. Woolworth and Knox, McBrier	*See note*(2)
1888						
July 21	Utica, N. Y.	16 x 65	3,450	212	F. W. Woolworth and Carson C. Peck	C. C. Peck (4)
August 11	Poughkeepsie, N. Y.	15 x 55	2,600	213	F. W. Woolworth	M. A. Creighton (5)
September 8	Wilmington, Del.	17 x 110	2,900	216	F. W. Woolworth and B. W. Gage	B. W. Gage
September 15	Allentown, Pa.	20 x 75	2,800	225	F. W. Woolworth and C. P. Case	C. P. Case
October 13	Buffalo, N. Y.	18 x 85	4,200	261	F. W. Woolworth and S. H. Knox	*See note*(2)
1889						
August 10	Syracuse, N. Y.	20 x 120	4,500	301	F. W. Woolworth	Mrs. A. C. Coons (5)
October 19	New Haven, Conn.	17 x 80	4,800	315	F. W. Woolworth	A. Creighton (6)

NOTES:

1. C. S. Woolworth bought a half-interest (out of earnings) in this store in January, 1881, and the other half in January, 1883.

2. F. W. Woolworth sold his interest in these stores to S. H. Knox as of December 31, 1889.

3. F. W. Woolworth sold his interest in this store to Mr. Woodworth in 1897, and when Mr. Woodworth retired, in 1906, F. W. Woolworth & Co. (a corporation) acquired the store.

4. C. C. Peck sold his interest in this store to F. W. Woolworth as of December 31, 1889, and began his Executive Office career in New York on January 4, 1890, on a profit-sharing basis.

5. Mary Ann Creighton, F. W. Woolworth's sister-in-law, and Mrs. A. C. Coons, Woolworth's co-worker at Moore & Smith, were the first women managers of Woolworth stores.

6. Allen Creighton was F. W. Woolworth's brother-in-law.

This chart illustrates the ups and downs Frank and his partners experienced during the fledgling years of the business.

New York, but he was still an unknown in other regions of America. The fact was, there just weren't enough mastheads bearing his name. In March 1883, Frank opened up a store on North Second Street in Philadelphia. He was certain it would fly, considering the large population there. He was honestly shocked when the store failed within three months. He added Philadelphia to the growing list of places he would return to one day, when "Frank Woolworth" became a name that inspired awe.

Trying a different strategy, he tested out a 25¢ store in Lancaster, which opened in October, in time to capitalize on the Christmas season. That venture also failed miserably. Although he was downcast about his business, Frank took delight in the birth of his second child, whom he and Jennie named Edna. He was amused by the antics of five-year-old Helena (now nicknamed Lena) and enjoyed the way she doted on her new baby sister. The family, including Sidney Creighton, moved out of their rented rooms on Lemon Street and into a larger space on Queen Street, which conveniently adjoined the Lancaster store.

Around this time, Frank decided to initiate a plan that he'd been mulling over for some time. In order to expand more quickly and be able to purchase goods in discount bulk, he would form a series of partnerships. The partner would invest half the money in each new store, and act

Frank W. Woolworth, Seymour Knox, and Charles Sumner Woolworth pioneered the first dimestores in Pennsylvania, New York, and New Jersey in the 1880s. This photo was taken during Seymour Knox's wedding, June 1890.

as manager. Profits and mastheads were to be shared equally, but Woolworth would be in charge of all buying and general bookkeeping. He estimated they would each need to invest $600 to $1,000.

Frank wanted a partner he could trust, someone responsible but daring enough to take a chance in this still fledgling business. Opting for the nepotistic approach, he thought of his cousin, Seymour Knox, who was then in Michigan managing a general store and had expressed great interest in Frank's five-and-ten trade. Woolworth invited Knox to meet him in New York City, where Frank was scheduled for a wholesale buying expedition. After that, he told Knox they would tour Lancaster. Knox and Woolworth had a grand time in the big city. Knox was equally impressed with the Woolworth store in Lancaster. Frank and Seymour struck up a deal and decided to open a new five-and-dime in Reading, Pennsylvania, which was about forty miles away from Lancaster.

Knox was still officially employed by the Michigan firm and had to leave Pennsylvania for a short time, to settle up his former commitments. Meanwhile, Frank started ordering for the Reading site and hiring new employees. In this particular instance, though, his brother Charles beat Frank to the partnership crunch.

Humble Beginnings

According to Edwin M. McBrier, a five-and-dime pioneer (and cousin of Woolworth), the first dimestore proprietors of the late 1870s, had, "goods displayed in tin bread pans, and later these were replaced, in part, with square willow baskets. It was a far cry from the small, narrow and poorly-lighted stores of the 1885–1895 period to the large elegant modern stores of the present day."

Edwin M. McBrier as a young entrepreneur, c. 1888.

While Frank was with Knox, Charles had been meeting with Fred Kirby, whom the Woolworth Brothers knew from Moore & Smith's in Watertown. "Woolworth & Kirby" (as in *Charles* Woolworth) opened in Wilkes Barre, Pennsylvania, on September 20, 1884. "Woolworth & Knox" (as in *Frank* Woolworth) opened ten days later in Reading. It was a fortuitous season, and both stores fared well. Over the next few years, Frank continued to take on "partner-managers". But as the chart on page 56 illustrates, his track record was rather tumultuous. By June 1886, he had opened twelve different stores. Of these twelve, six had failed miserably (including two forays into "25¢ Stores.") and the one in Scranton was now totally owned by his brother. Frank and his new partner, Oscar Woolworth, were indeed seeing profits at their first New Jersey (Trenton) site, but his other New Jersey five-and-dime in Newark, was barely hanging on. This left Frank owning, or holding a partnership interest, in only three truly profitable banner stores: Lancaster, Reading and Harrisburg.

Ambitious cousin Seymour had already expressed a desire to branch out and start his own chain of "Knox" five-and-dimes. Charles Woolworth and Fred Kirby had similar ambitions. Frank had told them he would support their aspirations, as long as they remained friendly competitors; sharing resources yet not interceding on each other's territory. These evolving partnership dynamics, combined with his burning desire to greatly expand his holdings, prompted Woolworth to investigate a new geographical venue. Frank decided it was time to move to New York City, where the already large wholesaling business was growing in leaps and bounds. He needed to be closer to a center of commerce, to be able to take advantage of bargain opportunities and make the Woolworth Syndicate a respectable, Manhattan-based enterprise.

His handful of five-and-dimes were generating yearly revenues of over $100,000; his personal net profits totaled about $10,000. He was totally free of debt, and he had a supportive wife and healthy children. His Queen Street "mother" store was in the capable hands of W. D. Rock, who Frank had personally trained.

And so, in July 1886, one month after his brother Charles married Anne E. Ryals, and two months after the birth of Frank and Jennie's third daughter Jessy May, the Woolworth family bid a bittersweet farewell to their Lancaster acquaintances. Frank rented a home in suburban Brooklyn, New York, and leased a tiny office at 104 Chambers Street in Manhattan. He was ready to make his mark in "Knickerbocker Town."

There is a touching postscript to this part of the story. Before he left Lancaster, Frank did get the opportunity to repay William Moore for the support and kindness extended since the day Frank entered his employ as the worst salesman in the world. In 1885, the old firm of Moore & Smith had dissolved when the ambitious Perry Smith moved west to start his own chain of five and dime stores. Without a partner, William Moore found himself in a great deal of debt, facing financial ruin. Unable to bear this, Frank headed to Watertown, where he discreetly handed Moore $2,000. He also helped Moore organize the store in the likeness of his own successful Lancaster shop. When the site reopened on town square, it was called "William Moore & Son's 5 & 10¢ store".

> TIME CAPSULE MEMORY
>
>
>
> ## "A Salute to the Dimestore Pioneers"
>
> It took great faith and courage, much perseverance and hard work, as well as considerable experimenting and groping along uncharted roads, to arrive at a definite place where success was felt to be assured. Too much credit cannot be accorded the pioneers who gave to this five and dime retail business a radically different conception of merchandising and established a new enterprise which, in many ways, revolutionized retail business methods.
>
> —Edwin M. McBrier, Frank Woolworth's cousin and one of his earliest partners

This simple story illustrates, perhaps more than any other, Woolworth's enduring allegiance to those who helped nourish his personal vision. In fact, he considered all of the pioneering partners, managers, stock boys and counter girls, a part of his extended family. He rewarded them by offering the sky; in other words, they could rise as high as they wanted in his empire, barring the presidential throne he saved for himself. It was this dual sense of "family" and a "challenge to be the best," that formed the core of the early F. W. Woolworth empire.

In the upcoming decades, thousands more would join, and benefit from, Frank's mercantile bandwagon.

Chapter Four

The March of "Five-and-Dimes"

"You are profiting today from the dreams of a man who was considered

a little bit 'wild' only a few years ago—a man who persisted in carrying out

his ideas to the letter—who profited by following up on his convictions with hard

work—and who was happy in being backed up by those in whom

he had confidence, and whom he had chosen to assist him."

—Carson Peck, c. 1900

Frank Woolworth and his family left their haven of Lancaster, Pennsylvania, in 1886 to start a new life in New York. Once they arrived, Frank worked tirelessly for the next thirty-three years to create the greatest chain store empire in the world.

The first part of that era, from mid-1886 to 1905, was a time of expansion and organization. Frank acquired more stores, more riches, and more mercantile knowledge than he ever dreamed possible. As the Woolworth syndicate grew, so did his workforce, requiring him to develop innovative ways to manage his equally innovative business.

By January 1904, Woolworth would own seventy-six stores in ten states, and several in the District of Columbia. Another great period of expansion would ensue, and before the end of this Silver Anniversary year, he would have 120 Red-Fronts in twenty-one states. Sales for 1904 superseded $10 million. By 1919, the year he died, Woolworth owned over 1,000 stores, scattered across the United States, Canada, and the British Isles.

Eventually, against all odds, the farmboy from the North Country would achieve all his ambitions—but it was a long, hard journey.

The Road To Riches

This road to riches had started out rather humbly from the time Frank ventured into New York City in 1886. Each morning, he would leave his family in their cozy home in Brooklyn, then travel to the end of the Fulton Street "L" line. From this point, he took a cable car over the new Brooklyn Bridge, and other public thoroughfares, until he finally arrived at his offices at 104 Chambers Street in Manhattan. One of the first things Frank did when he settled in was to place a brand-new sign on his office door:

Office of

F. W. Woolworth

Buyer and Manager

for the

Woolworth Syndicate

Strictly 5 and 10 cent stores

He also designed the historic "W" trademark diamond that would eventually appear on every F. W. Woolworth letterhead, store, and brand product. As he gazed out his office window onto the busy but simple Manhattan street scene, Frank could not have suspected twenty-seven years later that he would entirely change the landscape by constructing his own sixty-story "Cathedral of Commerce." In the meantime, he set to work at his rickety wooden desk, anxious to make his mark.

For the next few years, Woolworth continued to acquire "partners-managers." This enabled him to share expenses and expand more rapidly, yet remain free to scour the surrounding countryside for virgin main streets. By late summer, 1886, Frank and his cousin, Seymour Knox, owned stores in Newark, New Jersey, and Erie, Pennsylvania. Woolworth soon called upon other ambitious men as well, including E. Northrup, M. J. Getman, C. C. Peck, and B. W. Cage. Between them, by 1888, they managed stores in Elmira, New York, Easton, Pennsylvania, Utica, New York, and Wilmington, Delaware, respectively.

Frank Woolworth's Poughkeepsie, New York, store held a unique distinction. It was run by his first female manager, Frank's lively sister-in-law, Mary Anne Creighton. Ms. Creighton's employ started in August 1888, followed one year later by the addition of another female manager, his old friend Mrs. Adelia Coons from Watertown. Mrs. Coons had actually ventured out on her own in 1885, opening a short-lived five-and-ten in Lowville, New York. She fared even better when she started working for Woolworth in Syracuse, New York. From then on, Miss Creighton and Mrs. Coons became known as the Grand Ladies of the Woolworth Syndicate, and were accepted as "one of the boys" at all reunions and conventions.

Placing Mrs. Coons in his Syracuse store was a honor carefully bestowed by Frank Woolworth. He'd suspected this would fast become one of his banner stores, and knew that Mrs. Coons would not disappoint him. On opening day, August 10, 1889, Mrs. Coons sent the following telegram to her boss:

> *"When I came in sight of the store this morning, I remembered those stories old Mr. Moore told us of throngs battering down prisoner's doors, and I thought to myself: 'I was there!' I got through the back door and opened the front door. There was no use trying to form a line. It was a riot! I sent for a policeman. No sooner did he gaze upon all those beautiful things than he was overcome and joined the melee. So this gray-haired lady formed herself into a police force and tried to keep the crowd from killing the clerks and smashing plate glass. As I write this, the store is jammed!"*

This amazing description typifies the inaugural scenario at most of Woolworth's stores. Patrons of the day just could not believe that "all this" could be had for a few coins a piece. By then, Woolworth was carrying everything from egg whips to tree ornaments to Horatio Alger books. It was the heyday of retail bargains, and Americans were having a field day taking advantage of them.

Except for Mrs. Coons and Miss Creighton, Woolworth's management and executive force was made up entirely of men. Woolworth had an uncanny knack for choosing loyal, reliable men to run his business, and he was willing to give even the youngest applicant a chance. His very first assistant was sixteen-year-old Alvin Ivie, who, beginning in September 1888, did bookkeeping and all around gophering for Woolworth for $6.00 per week. Woolworth felt that Ivie should learn from the ground up, especially in terms of wages; in time, Ivie became an extremely wealthy man.

Four years later, another young bookkeeper was hired, one destined to become the second president of F. W. Woolworth Co. The teenager's name was Hubert Templeton Parson. Parson was eccentric of personality, but he also possessed a photographic memory and remarkable business sense. He learned every aspect of the retail business from his mentor, Frank Woolworth. Ironically, Hubert Parson would spend his twilight years trying to outdo his employer; automobile for automobile, mansion for mansion and million for million. But during the early 1890s, he was just "one of the boys" who helped Frank W. Woolworth build a colossal empire.

A Master Plan Unfolds

One of the turning points in F. W. Woolworth's career occurred in 1888, when he was struck down with a near-fatal bout of typhoid fever. He was laid up for nine weeks, but the second he was healthy enough to sit up, he insisted on running the business from his bed. Telegraphs and messages flew out of the house in Brooklyn with breakneck speed, as poor Alvin Ivie tried to keep up with the master's ever-urgent orders. Jennie Woolworth had her hands full keeping Frank down, although part of her was probably happy to have him nearby, rather than dashing around the city on business until all hours of the morning. When he was no longer contagious, his three daughters flocked to his bedside whenever possible, to spend time with their interesting, entertaining, but often-absent father.

In his quieter moments, between delirium fits, Frank realized that he had to develop some type of structured organizational system for his burgeoning Woolworth syndicate. The business had to be able to run itself, whether he was ill or away on extended business journeys. He had to learn to delegate. Frank therefore developed a plan that would serve both himself until his death, and his corporate descendants and colleagues, for many decades following.

According to John P. Nichols, author of *Skyline Queen and the Merchant Prince,* one of Woolworth's first bedside tasks was to devise an expansion strategy. On a large map, Woolworth marked thirty-five cities east of the Rockies with

TIME CAPSULE MEMORY

"Frank's Bout with Typhoid"

For two months, I took the mail and the orders to Mr. Woolworth's house each day. On all but two of these occasions, when he was delirious, he gave me directions and instructions as to how to carry on the business. It was quite a responsibility for a boy, but in those two months I learned a lot about the business and a lot about the boss. I certainly admired his courage and grit.

—Alvin Ivie, Frank Woolworth's first assistant, recalling 1888

The Executives and Managers of the Woolworth Syndicate, 1901.

This photo was probably taken on the stage of Frank's "Rooftop Garden & Auditorium" on Queen Street
in Lancaster, Pa. during the annual meeting.

a population of over 50,000, and a smattering of towns in the 30,000-person range. His goal was to open a store on each of these city's main streets, preferably close to a train depot. His only ironclad rule was that he would not open on a street where his friendly competitors were already housed with their own five-and-dimes. This so-called "charmed circle" included his brother, Charles Woolworth, along with Seymour Knox, Fred Kirby, Earle Charlton, and William Moore.

He also decided to train scouts to help find lucrative rental sites and then prepare the stores for their grand openings. Specialists would be trained to lay out the stock, prepare displays, and hire help. Only then would a manager of the finest caliber be installed, and the manager would have to prepare written reports for the executive office every single day. Finally, a central warehouse would be secured for the purpose of storing bulk purchases and seasonal stock.

The "Woolworth" moniker, Frank vowed, would soon be a household name in America.

Over the next decade, Woolworth made all of this happen, and in fact, far-surpassed his goal of a dozen new sites per year, establishing himself as a leading force in the world of commerce. During this period, he also earned the reputation of a "retail mother hen." Frank Woolworth knew virtually everything that was happening in his stores at any given time, and would often visit, in disguise, to see how things were progressing.

One morning he walked into a busy store and blatantly shoplifted, jamming handfuls of merchandise off the counters and stuffing them into his coat. Needless to say, he was appalled when he got away with this, and quickly apprised the negligent manager and counter girls of their folly. He rarely fired employees for such indiscretions, as he believed everyone was entitled to a mistake or two. However, he kept at his managers incessantly, sending them daily communications that he titled, "General Letters." These letters were full of tips, news (personal and professional), and countless gems of wisdom. Fortunately, many of these have been reprinted over the years, providing us further insight into Frank Woolworth's busybody mentality:

> *To push trade in the dull season, keep your goods in attractive shape as possible and trim your windows twice a week with big leaders and prices attached on each article. Another thing you must watch close in dull season is your expense account. Be sure and not have more clerks than you can possibly use and don't turn all the gas burners on every night. Again, put leaders to the front. This is our mode of advertising!*

> TIME CAPSULE MEMORY
>
>
>
> ### "That Nosy Boss of Ours!"
>
> **Mr. Woolworth was the most notional individual I ever knew! He wanted to have a finger in every pie, to know what every man in his organization was doing. He used to go poking around among the buyer's offices and desks, looking in corners and examining packages, especially around the holidays, to make sure none of them violated the rule against presents or 'souvenirs' from manufacturers.**
>
> —Recalled by Beecher Winckler, Woolworth's first confidential secretary, beginning in 1911

As the General Letters kept coming, and the Red-Fronts kept profiting, Frank continued to expand and prosper. Along the way, Frank enjoyed some especially satisfying moments. For example, in July 1888, he and Carson Peck opened a new site in Utica, New York, returning to the city of Frank's fledgling attempt to start a "Great Five Cent Store" back in 1879. This time around, due to its better location and Frank's vast experience, Utica proved to be a great success.

Four months later, soon after he and B. W. Cage opened up a site in Wilmington, Delaware, Frank once again switched business strategies. He decided that Wilmington was to be the last "partner-manager" arrangement of his career. Thereafter he owned his stores outright and installed managers on salary who were eventually offered the incentive of profit-sharing. The better their stores did, the better the managers were paid. In time, this made many of them extremely wealthy.

Frank W. Woolworth's drum of progress continued to beat steadily on, until total sales for 1889 reached $246,732.45. By New Year's Day 1890, Frank had five stores in Pennsylvania, one in New Jersey, three in upstate New York, one in Delaware, and one in Connecticut. On February 19, Woolworth embarked on his first European buying trip, sailing on the luxury liner, *City of Paris.* During that three-month excursion, Woolworth made man-

New York, Jan. 14, 1891

To All Store Managers:

This is the time of year to push soaps, paper, envelopes, tinware, woodenware, music, notions, etc. I hope none of the stores will be foolish enough to place toys in the windows. You can make a handsome 5 cent window of soaps or stationery. A window of 10 cent tinware looks good if properly trimmed.

Glassware and crockery are holiday articles. I am convinced that some of the stores pay too much attention to these goods. Bear in mind, there is not so much profit in these as there is in some other lines. Profit is what we are working for, not sales or glory. I know of a store that does not like to put a line of woodenware in the window as it does not look as nice as crockery. This is not the way to make good profits. Don't be afraid to put goods in the window once in a while that pay a good profit.

When you get in that new soap from Cotton Oil Product Co. I would advise you to make a nice show window of soap, and include all the kinds you have in stock.

We do not care to make a run on box paper that costs over 7 cents each, as it interferes with your line of paper and envelopes that you make a big profit on. Some of the stores have worked up a big trade on paper and envelopes, and some of the stores sell very little of them. This is a fault of yours, and not of the goods. In order to successfully get up a trade on paper and envelopes and hold it, you must make a nice display of them in the window. In the background display a large quantity of envelopes in their boxes neatly arranged with the price "5 cents per pack" marked on.

This is not all. Some time ago I was in one of the stores and their display of envelopes and paper looked awful. The envelopes had the bands broken, and there were some of them tied up with strings and some were loose. It was not necessary to ask if the goods sold well, as it was evident they did not. I asked just the same, and the reply was "No, they don't sell at all, I wish you would not buy any more for us." It was my time to talk then. I ordered all the rotten dirty stuff off the counter, and made a nice display of bright, clean goods. The result was this store has established a big trade on these items. I have done the same thing with the same result in several stores.

Frank W. Woolworth

A sample of one of Frank Woolworth's General Letters. There were a total of 187 thick, bound volumes of these letters, dated 1886 to 1918. Collectively, they form the most important "biographical" source about Woolworth and his empire. Historians hope that the letters will one day be available for public review.

ufacturing contacts that forever changed his buying practices. He was able to introduce American customers to marvelous new items such as tiny Dresden china cups, hand-made German dolls, and Christmas ornaments.

When he returned home from Europe, Frank took some time away from his busy work schedule to enjoy more social pursuits. His brother Charles had sired another baby, named Fred, prompting Frank and his family to travel to Scranton, Pennsylvania, to greet the newest Woolworth heir. That June, cousin Seymour Knox married Grace Millard in a grand celebration.

After this, it was back to work for Woolworth. For the next few years he set out with a vengeance to make sure everything was moving along as efficiently as possible in his

Syndicate. He initiated many new policies, and banned others. For example, one of his pet peeves was the outdated Civil War era practice of bothering customers who simply wanted to roam freely around a store. He constantly reminded his managers, that his counter girls were *not* to be following customers all over the store. "That's the country way of waiting on people, but it won't do for us. Give each girl a counter and stick to it. In one of the stores I saw a cashier reading a novel. This you should put a stop to at once and not allow anyone to read or chew gum during business hours!"

Indeed, it was these very counter girls (who made up the majority of his work force) who worked the longest hours for the least pay and the most grief. Woolworth did not show the same regard for counter girls as he did for his managers and stock boys. From Woolworth's perspective, he was giving these young women the chance of a lifetime, to make their own money and get real business experience. Although this was true to an extent, he never really learned to appreciate them as much as he should have. He was always cordial and respectful, ready with an encouraging word to an overachiever, but remained an old Scrooge about wages. In Lancaster, Pennsylvania, back in 1879, his female clerks had started at only $1.50 a week, which remained the going rate in all his stores for over a decade. It was only through the urging of Carson Peck, who one Woolworth manager called "the personal patron saint of counter girls," that Woolworth relented and eventually made the minimum wage $2.50, and later, a minimum of $3.50.

Early in 1895, Woolworth once again allowed himself a respite from business to help plan the Spring wedding of his protegé, Alvin Ivie to Henrietta (Et) Creighton, who also happened to be Frank's sister-in-law.

Frank and Jennie hosted the celebration at their own home in Brooklyn on April 4. As

"Woolworth's in San Francisco"

There will always be a "Woolworth's" . . . or so I thought eighty years ago, when I was a child of eight years. I don't remember the exact year "our Woolworth's" came into being in the Richmond District of San Francisco, where I was born in 1909. But, as the years went by, Woolworths Red-Fronts appeared all over the city. The original downtown Woolworth's fronted on the south side on Market and Powell streets, next store to the elegant Samuel's Jewelry store. Later, they both moved across the street to larger space in the landmark Flood Building.

I remember Woolworth's being glorified in music during the Jazz Age of the roaring Twenties . . . "I Found A Million Dollar Baby In A Five And Ten Cent Store" and "I Can't Give You Anything But Love, Baby, Diamond Bracelets Woolworth's Doesn't Sell, Baby." (However, there, one could buy beautiful rhinestone-studded jewelry "for a song.")

San Francisco, a seaport town, had the largest Chinatown outside of China itself and Woolworth's patrons could purchase beautiful Asian miniature ivory fans, lacquer boxes, woven sewing baskets, paper parasols, incense, and more, for a nickel or dime. "Dish Night" at the neighborhood theaters during the Depression gave movie-goers free dishes that could also be seen on the shelves of Woolworth's. And, of course, long before fast food came into being, one could visit the Woolworth's lunch counter for a bite to eat. I can recall, both as a single girl and later, a mother of three daughters, much too hurriedly eating that quick bite. I was given impetus by the queues of people standing behind each seat, waiting for the occupant to finish. As the food was good and inexpensive, few complaints were heard, especially during the Great Depression, when most of life's niceties were temporarily set aside.

Graffiti is an unpleasant word, but long before its inception, Woolworth's was among the stores that encouraged school children to decorate its huge front glass windows with colorful

he waited for the blessed event to commence, Frank could not resist writing one of his famous General Letters, which in this case, illustrates his marked sense of humor:

"At 4 p.m. today, at 209 Jefferson Avenue all that remains of Alvin E. Ivie, now manager of the Albany store, and Miss Et Creighton, an ex-employee of the New York office, will be united in the Bans of Matrimony and will start immediately on their wedding trip. I understand there have been several bushels of rice ordered and there have been several men employed for a week collecting old shoes. There has been talk of an invisible wire stretched across the door of the room where they are to be married. A balky horse has been engaged to take them to the station. A card has been labeled 'Bride and Groom' to hang on the rear of the carriage."

With the newlyweds settled in, Frank focused on opening his first big city stores; one in Washington, D.C. and one in Brooklyn, New York. For the landmark event in the nation's

painted drawings at Halloween and Thanksgiving. It should be noted that San Francisco's main Woolworth's was in a prime location. Passengers climbing aboard the famous cable cars did so in front of Woolworth's. Like in London, "free speech" from a curbstone in front of Woolworth's was often heard, protesting everything from the War in Vietnam to doom-sayers asking us to, "Repent, the End of the World is Near!"

In its final years, Woolworth's had changed. Merchandise costing dollars had replaced the once-in-demand paper dance cards and bridge game tallies that cost nickels and dimes. But, many of us still remember saying, "Try Woolworth's—they'll have it, and it won't cost an arm and a leg!"

—Roberta Thomson, San Francisco, CA.

capital, Woolworth purposely stayed away, extending his overseas trip in old Bavaria. Though he'd been present at every store opening until then, he wanted to see how his staff would do without him. Frank's Washington manager, J. H. Strongman, sent Woolworth this message:

> "Once again the banner of Woolworth enterprise has been proudly unfurled to the winds of trade—Thou too, sail on, O emblem great, wave on, and keep thy place of state at the head of the Syndicate!"

Translating the purple prose, Woolworth figured out that the Washington, D.C., store was a grand success. In fact, the harried manager took in almost $2,000 the first day, breaking a new record. That wasn't all that broke, however. The crowds were so anxious and excited that the glass side doors on both sides of the entrance were smashed. "Great guns,

what a mob!" wrote Strongman. "They came like an Iowa cyclone and we had to call the police for help!"

Woolworth was so pleased with this news that he doubled his orders for German
toys and purchased thousands of novelty "jack-knifes" before leaving Europe. Frank
had barely docked in Manhattan when he started scouting a good site for his Brooklyn
store. Brooklyn was still not designated a borough of New York City at this time, but it
was a thriving community ripe for exploitation. His Brooklyn site opened on November
16, on Fulton Street, close to busy Flatbush Avenue. Huge placards hailed hitherto-un-
heard-of bargains. It was here that he first initiated his pre-inspection galas, where he
would invite local dignitaries and select members of the public to view his stores before
the official opening. Woolworth's special guests would be treated to fine foods and
drink, lavish displays of fresh flowers and, in many cases, the music of a full orchestra.
Many of the local dignitaries Woolworth invited to his reception on Fulton Street did indeed attend the party, in spite of the five-and-ten's lingering social stigma as a "Cheap
John" business.

The next day, the general public arrived in droves to see Wooley's latest bargain factory. The Brooklyn opening was such a crowd-pleaser that the *Brooklyn Times* devoted an
entire page to the event, stating that the crush was so large that three big policemen had
to be called in. The reporter noted that Mr. Woolworth had a force of 150 pretty girls on
hand to tend to the thousands of customers. While the claim of "150 pretty girls" being
present might have been an exaggeration, it is a documented fact that the first day's sales
amounted to a mind-boggling $3,139.41.

From this point on, Woolworth premiered similar gala openings in other American
cities, almost all of which earned vast media attention. He also made sure that the new
stores were equipped with the latest types of fixtures, lighting and cable cash systems,
which added to the spectacle of the ongoing march of dimestores.

The name Woolworth was fast becoming a household name, just as Frank had
hoped. But the daily responsibilities of overseeing a growing chain store business
soon became too much for one man to handle alone, even this singularly impressive
man. The financial risks started to equal the financial gains, especially since all of this
responsibility was ultimately, and legally, in Frank's hands. He had 120 profitable
stores operating in December 1904 and millions of dollars at stake. He worried about
his continual bouts of sickness, and his eventual mortality. Frank wanted to preserve
his legacy for his family, and for all his partners and associates who had helped him
reach this lofty place in commerce.

It was time to make a bold move.

Sampling of F. W. Woolworth "Firsts" 1886–1900

July 1886	First office in Manhattan	104 Chambers Street
Summer 1886	First red "W" trademark	
1887	First candy sold	Supplier: D. Arnould
July 21, 1888	First female manager	Mary Anne Creighton
September 1888	First office assistant	Alvin Ivie
November 1888	First hired "typist"	Miss Tallman of New York
1889	First "owned" home	209 Jefferson Ave., Brooklyn, N.Y.
February 1890	First European buying trip	S.S. *City of Paris* luxury liner
April 1892	First summer cottage	1109 Grand Ave., Asbury Park, N.J.
July 1894	First company convention	Hathaway Inn, Darlington, N.J.
August 1894	First blanket fire insurance	Columbia Fire Lloyds ($177,500)
1894	First "horse carriage and pair"	
February 1895	First employee paid vacations	
October 1895	First company phone number	"FRANKLIN 1292"
1897	First "food" line tested in five stores.	"Woolworth's Diamond W Pure Foods." Discontinued 1899.
December 1897	First Christmas bonuses for all employees	$5.00 per person
1896	First move to luxury "home" in New York City	Savoy Hotel, Fifth Avenue, New York N.Y.
January 1899	First store opens in Canada	
1900	First Woolworth skyscraper	Six stories, Lancaster, P.A.
1900	First Woolworth's "soda water" fountain	Newark, N.J.
1900	First cash registers replace cable cash systems	

The Great 65-Million-Dollar Merger

In January 1905, fifty-two-year-old Woolworth took one of the most important steps of his career. He arranged for his Woolworth Syndicate to go public. It was formally incorporated on February 14, 1905, when "F. W. Woolworth & Company" authorized and issued outstanding capital stock in the amount of 10 million dollars. His syndicate became a bona fide New York corporation, and the outstanding stock was represented by 100,000 shares, each of par value $100, of which $5 million was seven percent preferred stock and $5 million common stock.

Every newly formed corporation needs a string of company officers, and so the first men on the F. W. Woolworth & Company team were duly installed: Frank W. Woolworth, president; Carson C. Peck and Clinton Pierce Case, vice presidents; Hubert T. Parson, secretary-treasurer; and Charles Griswald and H. W. Cowan as assistant treasurers. The first board of directors included the name of an old friend and colleague, Harry Moody. One month later, F. W. Woolworth & Co. of Massachusetts was formed, followed by F. W. Woolworth & Co. of Pennsylvania. The executive office remained in the Stewart Building in New York City, but a space in Mineola, Long Island, was secured for the principal office.

The common stock of the new company was only offered to officers, executive buyers, and select personnel. The preferred stock was offered to the same, along with store managers and certain "friends" of the company. The stock went like hot cakes, and between them, there were soon seventy-five shareholders, owning a combined 6,431 shares. Frank was happy when he heard about the quick sale of the shares, as this clearly showed him how much his colleagues believed in him and in the success of his company. However, it was with bittersweet emotions that Frank penned his next General Letter.

"This will be the last letter I shall ever write to you as individual owner and proprietor of all the five and ten cent stores running Jan. 1, 1905. It is a sad occasion and I will tell you later on why I am transferring my business to a corporation. Hereafter I will write to you as a representative of a corporation. I am sorrowful, but modern methods must be pursued. Time is fast flying away and I cannot expect always to be in control of this vast property."

It appears that Frank Woolworth would have preferred to remain an autocratic emperor of his five-and-dime domain, but he accepted the decision to go public as the wisest choice. Never a man to dwell in remorse, he quickly made arrangements for new signs to be placed over the doors of his Red-Fronts: "F. W. Woolworth & Co."

To call the next five years "prosperous" would be a gross understatement. Woolworth's Red-Fronts increased in leaps and bounds, and his stores were soon generating more than $50 million in annual gross sales. The only fly in the ointment was the growing "unfriendly" competition: Frank's original idea had spawned a copy-cat industry of five-and-dimes.

Along with his friendly rivals, such as his brother Charles, and colleague Earle Charlton, Frank was faced with increasing competition from a host of ambitious, sometimes ruthless merchants. One of his greatest rivals was his own cousin, Herbert G. Woolworth (brother of Frank's loyal employee, Fred Woolworth), who had taken off on his own after a brief training period with Frank. This was all acceptable until Herbert started plagiarizing Frank's store setups, right down to the red-and-gold mastheads on the front of the buildings. Herbert copied the design and used his "Woolworth" name to create the illusion that he was one in the same as the real Woolworth five-and-dime founder. Soon after, when hostilities heightened, Herbert set out to open stores in the same towns where Frank's stores were already operating. Frank never forgave Herbert for this indiscretion. He felt it was a dishonorable way to conduct business, especially given their blood relation. Frank considered a libel suit, but never followed through with legal action, partly because every time a rival five-and-dime opened near one of his own, it created more business and a fair amount of publicity.

The rival pressure was also increasing from stores such as McCrory, the Titus Supply Co., H. Germain, Rothchild & Co., Kresge, and Kress. So far, F. W. Woolworth & Co. reigned as the largest chain of five-and-dimes in the entire United States, but if Woolworth wanted to maintain his position, he knew he needed to develop a few new strategies. Individually, these rival merchants did not pose a threat, but collectively they did. This threat escalated late in 1905 when rumors started to circulate that his unfriendly rivals were considering a merger with the purpose of putting Frank out of business. These rumors triggered an unprecedented price battle between F. W Woolworth & Co. and his competitors; if Kress was offering china dishes for eight cents, then Woolworth's managers would promptly display the same items for a nickel.

The rumored merger did not occur and, in fact, a financial twist of fate ultimately rid some of these merchants from Woolworth's "worry list." During the depression of 1907, three merchants—H. Germain, Holmes, and Herbert Woolworth—all went bankrupt. However, that still left the mighty Kress, Kresge, and several other chains to put a damper on Frank's business. Woolworth realized that the only way to assure long-term success was to take drastic action.

On April 11, 1911, Woolworth gathered his inner circle of friendly rivals for a secret meeting at the old Waldorf Astoria in New York. It was time to discuss the possibility of merging their own respective five-and-dimes into one giant corporation.

All of these men had done exceedingly well in their spin-offs of Frank's original idea. Seymour Knox had 112 stores in the United States and Canada, Fred Kirby had ninety-six "green fronts," and was the only one operating in the Deep South. Charles Sumner Woolworth owned fifteen five-and-tens, most of them situated in his favorite states, Pennsylvania and Maine, with a few scattered about New York. Earle Charlton had introduced the five-and-dime concept to the region west of the Rockies, as well as Montreal, Canada, and now had fifty-three stores. Frank himself had over 300, located in the eastern and midwestern United States, and overseas in the British Isles. The men met for many hours, first at the Waldorf, then at the Hotel Plaza. They agreed that the advantages of a merger were

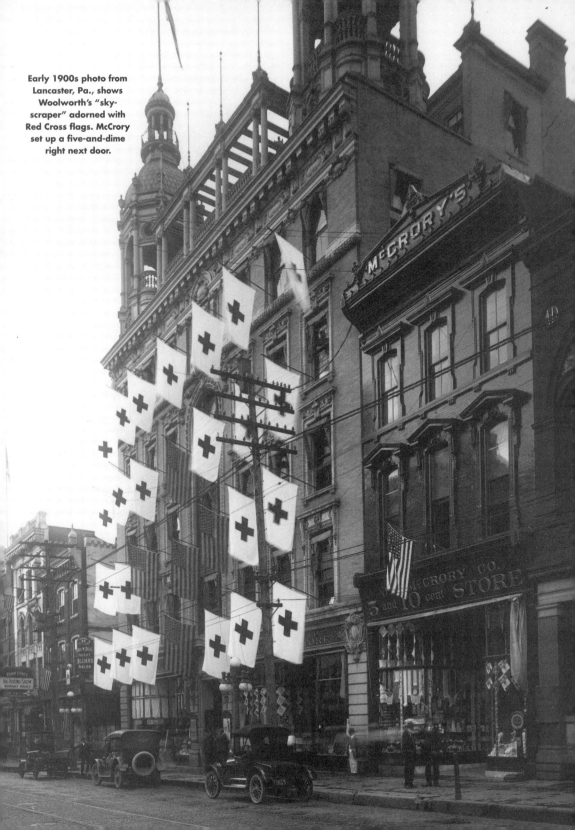

Early 1900s photo from Lancaster, Pa., shows Woolworth's "sky-scraper" adorned with Red Cross flags. McCrory set up a five-and-dime right next door.

More contemporary postcard of Clearwater, Florida, shows that McCrory consistently built his own stores next to rival Red-Front, F. W. Woolworth.

substantial. If they joined forces, they would have almost 600 stores in 37 states, along with a fair number in the District of Columbia, Canada, and Great Britain. They would be able to advertise themselves as a coast-to-coast chain. Their buying power would be unsurpassed, allowing them to purchase goods in bulk, and then reap the profits. Most important of all, they could individually and jointly assure that the business would not fall into the wrong hands. Regardless of the fact there were few male heirs among them, the business could stay in "the family."

The line item that took the longest time to negotiate was Frank's insistence that the merged company bear *his name and his alone*. It was true that he had started the entire craze, and had more stores than the rest of them, but this was still a tough nut to swallow. All of the men in that room had worked extremely hard to build their individual five-and-dime chains.

We can presume that Frank used all of his charm, perseverance, and tenacity to persuade his partners to see things his way. It is not exactly clear how he managed this, but in the end he won.

The new company would be called the "F. W. Woolworth Company."

Frank felt this was a vital step toward preserving the posterity that he had worked his whole life to attain. (It is also one of the reasons why historians, Woolworth descendants, and long-term employees, found it so disconcerting when the Woolworth Corporation changed its name to the Venator Group in 1998.) The details of the merger were ironed

William Moore, the "sixth founder."

The Founding Fathers of the F. W. Woolworth Co., 1912.

Left to right: Sitting: Fred Kirby, Frank Woolworth, Seymour Knox. *Standing:* Earle Charlton and Charles Woolworth.

out in September 1911, and the legal corporation agreement was signed on Thursday, November 2. Along with the Woolworth brothers, Knox, Charlton and Kirby, there was one more name on the agreement—that of William Moore. Frank had asked if Moore could be in on the deal, and his fellow founders had agreed, knowing how much William Moore had done to help Frank Woolworth make his dream into a reality. By then, Moore and his son were trying to make ends meet with his new five-and-tens in upstate New York. Overnight, he became part of one of the most important mergers of the century.

As of January 1, 1912, the combined 611 stores of the circle started operating as a harmonious whole. Frank Woolworth issued a landmark General Letter, announcing that the corporation was about to be formed with a capital stock of $65 million. From then on there would be eight district offices in this country and one in Canada. At the end of this detailed missive, he added: "Please refrain from criticism."

There was much excitement and much speculation about the merger, and only limited criticism. Most of his employees trusted Frank implicitly, and since their jobs were absolutely secure, they decided to roll with the punches. One inspired employee from Milwaukee even wrote a dramatic poem in honor of the occasion. Following the preliminary buzz, there was a virtual stampede for stock shares when the new F. W. Woolworth Co. offered all

$6,000,000

F. W. Woolworth Co.

Incorporated under the laws of the State of New York

Seven Per Cent. Cumulative Preferred Stock

Preferred as to dividends and as to assets in liquidation.

The whole or any part redeemable at the option of the Company on three months' notice, at 125%, and accrued dividends.

Dividends Payable Quarterly April, July, October and January

Par Value of Shares $100

Farmers' Loan & Trust Co., New York, N. Y.   Lawyers' Title Insurance & Trust Co., New York, N. Y.
Transfer Agent   Registrar

CAPITALIZATION

Seven Per Cent. Cumulative Preferred Stock,
Dividends payable quarterly beginning April 1st, 1912:
Authorized and Issued $15,000,000

Common Stock:
Authorized and Issued... $50,000,000

F. W. Woolworth Co. was organized under the laws of the State of New York to take over as going concerns the following businesses:

(1) F. W. Woolworth & Co., a New York Corporation.
(2) S. H. Knox & Co., a New York Corporation.
(3) F. M. Kirby & Co., a Pennsylvania Corporation.
(4) The E. P. Charlton & Co., a Connecticut Corporation.
(5) The five and ten cent store business of C. S. Woolworth.
(6) The five and ten cent store businesses of W. H. Moore and W. H. Moore & Son.
(7) The controlling interest in F. W. Woolworth & Co., Ltd., owned by F. W. Woolworth & Co., and now operating 12 stores in England.

The undersigned are in receipt of a letter from Mr. F. W. Woolworth, President of the Company, which is hereto attached, with respect to the purposes of the merger and the history of the businesses of the above-mentioned Companies. The following is the balance sheet and statement of earnings of the Companies included in the merger, which has been furnished us by Messrs. Touche, Niven & Co., Chartered Accountants.

F. W. Woolworth Co.

(Incorporated 15th December 1911.)

Initial Balance Sheet

Introducing Assets and Liabilities, to be taken over as of the date of January 1st, 1912, of F. W. Woolworth & Co., S. H. Knox & Co., F. M. Kirby & Co., The E. P. Charlton & Co., C. S. Woolworth, W. H. Moore and W. H. Moore & Son, and Assets and Liabilities of the Subsidiary Corporations of the four first named Companies.

ASSETS		LIABILITIES	
Leases, Alterations and Improvements, Furniture and Fixtures and Goodwill	$55,009,387.87	Capital Stock to be Authorized and Issued:	
Real Estate	607,751.15	7% Cumulative Preferred Stock	
Investments:		150,000 Shares of $100.00 each	$15,000,000.00
F. W. Woolworth & Co., Ltd., England $279,928.41		Common	
Real Estate Mortgage 30,000.00		500,000 Shares of $100.00 each	50,000,000.00
	309,928.41		$65,000,000.00
Inventories of Merchandise	8,141,009.75	Purchase Money Mortgages on Real Estate	30,000.00
Supplies and Prepaid Expenses	160,727.30	Sundry Creditors	52,154.68
Sundry Debtors	101,047.43	Reserve for Federal Corporation Tax and Miscellaneous Taxes	75,000.00
Cash in Banks and on Hand	827,302.77		
	$65,157,154.68		$65,157,154.68

New York, February 7th, 1912. We certify that the foregoing is a correct statement of the Assets and Liabilities of F. W. Woolworth Co., as the same will appear upon the completion of the organization of the Company.

We have further examined the Accounts of F. W. Woolworth & Co., S. H. Knox & Co., F. M. Kirby & Co., The E. P. Charlton & Co., C. S. Woolworth, W. H. Moore, and W. H. Moore & Son, the undertakings of which F. W. Woolworth Co. is to acquire, for the six calendar years ending December 31st, 1911, and certify that the combined Sales and Profits of the Merged Businesses have been as follows:

		SALES	PROFITS
Year 1906	- - -	$27,760,664.07	$2,723,354.22
Year 1907	- - -	32,968,144.84	2,971,118.99
Year 1908	- - -	36,206,674.24	3,617,077.15
Year 1909	- - -	44,438,193.39	4,702,802.23
Year 1910	- - -	50,841,546.98	5,065,031.04
Year 1911	- - -	52,616,123.68	4,955,255.57

(Signed) TOUCHE, NIVEN & CO., New York,
GEORGE A. TOUCHE & CO., London,
Chartered Accountants.

The offering circular that introduced F. W. WOOLWORTH CO. to the investor

Stats and Facts about the Great 65-Million-Dollar Merger

of its store managers and executives the chance to buy in at $50 per share for common stock, and $100 for preferred. The sheer number of stores that the F. W. Woolworth Company now owned gave Frank and his partners enormous buying power among distributors. Consequently, the company greatly expanded its selection of merchandise. Lingerie, musical instruments, costume jewelry, men's accessories, and even inexpensive lines of luxury materials (such as velvet, satin, and angora) soon filled the counters of the five-and-tens.

By the time the Great Merger was concluded, Frank Woolworth was a changed man, emotionally, financially, and physically. The legal pressures of the new partnership, combined with the pressures in his personal life, finally took its toll on sixty-year-old Frank W. Woolworth. He began weeping uncontrollably at odd moments. His joints became swollen and his appetite waned. The man already known as the "King of the Five-and-Dime" was diagnosed with a nervous disorder and ordered to Carlsbad, Austria, for a cure among the healing spa waters. It was not easy for Woolworth to agree to this because he was also in the middle of planning for his greatest structural triumph, the erection of the Woolworth Building of New York. However, he promptly sailed off for Austria, with another rest cure following in Spain. He returned many months later, feeling like he could take on the world one more time.

The Woolworths Take Their Place In Society

Following the merger, the momentum in Frank's professional and personal life continued to increase at a dizzying pace. Frank W. Woolworth was now a millionaire many times over, and he altered his habits accordingly. While Woolworth was far from "the manor born," he certainly adapted to a highbrow lifestyle without any visible difficulty. In reality, he had started changing his lifestyle many years before, when the first rush of wealth had begun.

Following the incorporation of F. W. Woolworth & Co. back in 1905, Frank had relocated his executive headquarters into even larger offices in the Stewart Building. This new location offered a view of historic City Hall Park, in the center of Lower Manhattan's original financial district. "There was an imposing entrance hall," wrote John Nichols, " a sample room and private offices for the leading executives. There were overhead lighting and mahogany furniture, upholstered couches and gaily painted wainscoting."

Woolworth's desk was now mahogany and gold, flanked by green Moroccan leather chairs. This setting was a far cry from his original Utica store "desk," which amounted to a tier of package crates covered by cheap muslin. His clothes were now hand-sewn by the best European tailors, his soft leather shoes made by New York's finest craftsman. His belly was growing larger from the elaborate meals he had his servants prepare and the equally sumptuous gourmet treats he enjoyed in France and Vienna. The farmboy who had once survived on boiled potatoes and chicken, now favored prime roast beef and imported caviar. As a matter of fact, he rarely ate chicken at all, so unpleasant were his early memories of tending them on the farm.

By the turn of the twentieth century, Frank's three daughters were no longer children. Helena, the oldest, was twenty-two; Edna was

---

TIME CAPSULE MEMORY

"Angora for a Nickel"

I grew up in Cheviot, Ohio, a suburb of Cincinnati. When I was in high school Woolworth's was *the* headquarters for two items crucial to a teen-age girls' life—nylons and angora. Woolworth's sold nylons for only fifty cents a pair, and it was the only place in town where we could buy angora, in just about every color. The girls who received a ring from a boy just *had* to wrap angora around it so the ring would fit perfectly. Some girls even changed the color daily to match their outfits. Angora was only 5¢ a strand back then!

—Diana Hunter, Chardon, Ohio

---

seventeen; and the youngest, Jessy May, was almost fifteen. They had been spared the difficult hardships suffered by their parents and were instead coddled and spoiled with glee. All were pretty and polite, and enjoyed their frequent vacations and shopping trips. Helena, or Lena as her family called her, shared her father's passion for art and antiques. Unlike Frank, however—who preferred to distribute his money only "within the family"—the adult Helena would set up numerous charitable foundations across the United States, and would become a devoted parent who spent as much time as possible with her husband and children.

Jennie Woolworth found herself married to a corporate magnate, a man greatly changed from the young naïve lad she'd met decades before in Watertown, New York. The new Frank W. Woolworth wanted his wife to take her place in high society—whether she wanted to or not. For several years, he'd been gradually moving his wife, and daughters, from humble abodes to glorious mansions.

It all started when, in 1889, Frank moved his family into their first wholly owned home, a modest but comfortable abode at 209 Jefferson Avenue in Brooklyn. Eight years later, they moved again, this time to the beautiful Savoy Hotel at 582 Fifth Avenue. They lived there, in spacious rented suites, on and off until 1901, when Frank purchased a huge, thirty-room marble mansion on the corner of Fifth Avenue and 80th Street. In time, Frank also bought a townhome for each of his daughters and their families. Helena and Charles E. F. McCann married in 1904, and Edna and Franklyn Laws Hutton in 1907. Jessy would not

Rare photo of the Woolworths in Palm Beach. Frank and Jennie Woolworth along with their daughter, Jessie Woolworth Donahue, c. 1913.

marry for several years, but already had her eye on young dashing James P. Donohue. On Millionaire's Row, the Woolworths cohabited side by side, although, truth be told, Frank didn't have much time for family socializing.

When the breezes turned hot and balmy, the Woolworths often visited the cool country spas in Europe, but they also enjoyed vacationing closer to home. Back in 1893, Woolworth leased his first summer cottage in Asbury Park, New Jersey. For years thereafter, the Woolworths returned to that same cottage, each time with a finer carriage and pair of horses. On the expansive porch of 1109 Grand Avenue, Frank held court in what was then considered the "Monte Carlo of America." Asbury Park, Allenhurst, Deal, and nearby Long Branch were all popular shore resorts frequented by the creme of society. At first, Frank was not privy to this blue-blood world, so he brought along his own population of the F. W. Woolworth & Co. elite. He could never quite understand, though, why he and Jennie were *not* included on all the party lists of the seaside "A" crowd. This fact probably hurt him, but he did his best to keep up a good front. Furthermore, even though some snubbed the Woolworths, there were plenty of other wealthy magnates and politicians who did not.

For one of his General Letters to the boys, Frank asked his old friend William Moore to impart some of their exploits "down the shore" in the early 1900s. In response, Moore wrote:

"The first day the Ocean looked like any Ocean and the thousands of nice looking people did not look any better than our party and surely did not have any more fun. The Razzle-Dazzle ride, imitating a ship at sea was taken in, also Day's ice cream. The bathing is piles of fun, the girls don't look very much . . . when they have their bathing suits on. The suits they rent are awful long and don't fit very good and the straw hats are tough . . .

"Sunday—All went to church, walked, music, singing, talking by the hour on Woolworth's fine piazza. Boardwalk in the evening.

"Tuesday—the 'Tally Ho'—was ready, but it looked like rain; four horses, darky driver—darky 2 with a bugle. What music that darky made with that thing! The top . . . is made with a folding ladder . . . some beautiful photographs of the ladies in graceful attitudes making for the top seats . . . but what a gay party . . . for the 28 mile ride down the beach!"

By 1899, Frank Woolworth's name appeared on the roster of the new, prestigious Deal Golf and Country Club, along with men like President McKinley and William Hearst. His Asbury Park five-and-ten was also flourishing by 1900.

All in all, the summers were joyous for the Woolworths and Frank's select circle of friends. These outings played an important part in Woolworth's life; one of the few times he allowed himself to relax. Frank also had another notable diversion—his motorcars.

For years, Frank's gleaming horses and carriages were the pride of his personal transportation collection, but in October 1903, he discovered the delightful new invention called the automobile. He purchased his first motorcar in Paris; it was a forty-horsepower, 1903 King of Begium model Panhard. He even hired a dashing chauffeur named Julius Billard, an experienced driver who had once won the Grand Prix. Billard would become one of Woolworth's closest confidants, traveling with the Merchant Prince whenever a fancy motorcar was needed to impress. Billard was also Frank's unofficial "social planner," and he routinely traveled ahead of his boss to Europe to make arrangements for special outings. Frank also acquired a lush private Pullman rail car, which he used for dashing across the country on business, or to transport special guests to his headquarters in New York City.

As Frank and his daughters reveled in all this luxury, Jennie Woolworth grew increasingly quiet and withdrawn. She was already slipping into a deep mental depression, her thoughts wavering back to the days of struggle, when she was working close with her darling husband and making herself useful. Now, with her daughters growing older, and her days spent surrounded by an endless stream of pampering nurses, servants, and every manner of seamstress and cook, Jennie was left with an empty nest and a lonely heart. She would never again return to the persona of that shy but happy girl Frank knew in Watertown. Frank was so busy that Jennie rarely saw him, even on holidays. He once told his managers that he had no intention of spending another Christmas Eve at home. He couldn't bear to be away from the excitement and frenzy of the retail holiday season, when the bulk of his yearly profits came ringing through the cash registers. He also kept strict tabs on what his competitors were doing during the holidays and said that he wanted to be ready to "one-up them" if they started offering better bargains than his own five-and-dimes.

It was in this lap of luxury and this arena of ruthless commerce that the F. W. Woolworth Co. family entered its final years with its spirited founder at the helm.

A Tale Of Castles And Despair: Twilight Years, 1912–1919

The final seven years of F. W. Woolworth's life, from 1912 to 1919, were historically significant and productive, but they were also fraught with sadness. Woolworth built homes as big as castles, and purchased every conceivable comfort item he could find—but his bouts of depression struck with more intensity than ever before.

Midway through this period, Woolworth's health also started to decline, and he was feeling increasingly tired. Part of the reason was because his wife, Jennie, with whom he had so generously shared his bounty, was slowly but surely slipping away. With each passing day, the vacant stares of senility inexorably replaced her once shining blue eyes.

On the domestic front, his daughters, Helena and Jessie, were busy with their own families. His lovesick daughter Edna was caught up in the emotional clutches of a philandering husband, broker Franklyn Hutton. Edna and Franklyn's daughter, Barbara, born November, 1914, was being primed for the role she would day assume—that of one of the richest women in the world.

Frank's closest colleagues, Carson Peck and Seymour Knox, died within three weeks of each other in 1915, followed, one year later, by his high-ranking manager C. C. Griswold and then, by old William Moore.

In spite of all this—or perhaps because of it—Woolworth was seized with a renewed desire to physically expand his empire. He'd experienced a similar mania at the turn of the century, when the Red-Fronts became noticeably larger and the first Woolworth skyscraper was erected in Lancaster, Pennsylvania. This time around, he set out to design an entire *series* of elaborate structures, not the least of which was a block-long row of stately townhouses in Manhattan, right on Millionaire's Row; one for each of his daughters, and one for himself. Less looming, but more poignant, was his ornate mausoleum in New York's Woodlawn Cemetery, where for $100,000 Frank commissioned his final resting place.

Clearly, during the twilight of his years, the man the newspapers called the "Dimestore King" did not want to risk being forgotten. He wanted to make sure that his name would continue to reign in mercantile history.

He had already expanded geographically, and had increased the square footage of his thousand or so Red-Fronts; the only place to go now was *up*. And so, Frank proceeded to build his ultimate testimony to commerce and to himself—the Woolworth Building of New York.

Chapter Five

Reaching for the Sky:
The Great Woolworth Building

"The Woolworth Building is a veritable fairy palace, such as we

have all dreamed about in childhood—a dream now happily

come true through the genius of two typical American conquerors

of success in the world of business and the world of art."

—H. Addington Bruce, 1913

On July 10, 1910, the *New York Times* was electric with excitement over news of an extraordinary skyscraper to be erected on the southwest corner of Broadway and Park Place in Manhattan. Frank W. Woolworth, the famed dime store magnate, had purchased the tract with the full intention of creating a building that would surpass any other in New York, perhaps in the world. Normally, the press begrudged its coverage of a man and a company who never used its pages for paid advertisement, but this story was too exciting to ignore. The electrified edifice was to be twenty stories high, with a tower thrusting up ten stories more. It was rumored the cost would be an unheard of five million dollars.

In fact, the completed Woolworth Building far surmounted that original twenty-story projection, topping out at sixty stories from sidewalk to observation tower, with not one ceiling under eleven feet high, and many of them twenty feet. The final cost was almost three times the original estimate, due to the fact that every possible safety feature was awarded equal consideration with architectural beauty.

The skyscraper took thirty-six months to build, leaving ample time for public anticipation to mount as well. As opening day approached, press releases were issued in rapid succession, proclaiming that Frank Woolworth's new command center would be the tallest building in the world. Consequently, on Thursday evening, April 24, 1913, thousands of on-

Woolworth Building
Fact Box

FINANCIER: F. W. Woolworth, $13.5 million

ARCHITECT—Cass Gilbert

OFFICIAL DEDICATION: April 24, 1913

HEIGHT FROM SIDEWALK: 792 feet

STORIES: 60

WEIGHT: 206 million pounds

FLOOR AREA: 15 acres

EXTERIOR WINDOWS: 3,000

HIGH-SPEED ELEVATORS: 30

TONS OF STEEL: 24,000

ELECTRIC WIRING: 87 miles

MARBLE WAINSCOTING: 12 miles

NICKNAMES: Cathedral of Commerce &
Skyline Queen

TALLEST SKYSCRAPER IN THE WORLD: 1913–1930

lookers crowded around 233 Broadway and nearby City Hall Park, waiting for . . . well, they weren't exactly certain what they were waiting for, but the papers had assured them it would be a night to remember. It was rumored that Frank Woolworth had grand plans for the christening of his steel-and-terra-cotta Skyline Queen.

Most of the spectators were staring upward, where even on that dark spring night, they could see a magnificent gothic spire glistening almost 800 feet above the sidewalk. The building's gargoyles had been hand-chiseled by skilled craftsman; the decorative Italian marble quarried in the Isle of Skyros. The looming exterior side walls were painted white, but highlighted with soft shades of ecru, light olive, and mauve, resulting in an ethereal patina. It looked more like a fifteenth-century church than a twentieth-century corporation headquarters. One could understand why, before the night was over, Dr. S. Parkes Cadman would dub it, "The Cathedral of Commerce."

Inside the building, eight hundred eminent men who had assembled in the mezzanine for a cocktail reception were led through Tiffany-bedecked elevators for a high-speed ride upstairs. Under the direction of Frank's public relations chief, Hugh McAtamney, the twenty-seventh floor had been transformed into a gala banquet hall, to honor the building's architect, Cass Gilbert. Within the hour, the guests would be feasting on cotuit oysters, roast squab, and vintage Cordon Rouge; but first, they would partake of Wooley's latest spectacle.

Gradually, the lights were lowered, until the banquet hall, and the entire building, were plunged into darkness. Behind the scenes a Western Union telegraph was simultaneously dispatched to Washington, D.C., signaling that it was time. At precisely 7:30 P.M., President Woodrow Wilson pressed a button in the White House connected by wire with the building in distant New York. Seconds later, 80,000 brilliant electric lights flashed throughout the skyscraper, illuminating the tip of the observation tower to the depths of the sub-basement. The hushed twenty-seventh floor suddenly exploded with activity. A hidden orchestra emerged from behind a curtain to play the National Anthem, followed by "The Woolworth March." Eight hundred dignitaries leaped to their feet, some rushing to the windows, white linen handkerchiefs waving in tribute to architect, builder, and financier.

"Outside the skyscraper," reported the *New York American,* "waiting thousands in New York and its suburbs saw, flashing in outlines of fire, the greatest mountain of steel and stone ever erected by man—the gigantic Woolworth Building." The crowd gasped, and then let loose with a rousing cheer. Many of them were members of the working class, living without benefit of modern electricity, and not one among them had witnessed a marvel as magnificent. Somewhere in the throng, an oft-repeated exchange was overheard by a reporter: "How did he do it?" one charwoman asked another. "'Twas easy," replied the second, "with your dime, and mine." One of Frank's esteemed guests reportedly speculated that Frank's deceased father, John, also looked down from the heavens and echoed one of his oft-repeated comments: "It's nice, Frank, you always did like to lay it on thick."

April 24, 1913, was certainly a glorious night for Frank Winfield Woolworth. Ever since he was a boy in Great Bend, building houses out of colored rocks, he'd longed for his own palace, one stamped with his name to assure his memory would live on forever. It had taken six decades, but the Merchant Prince finally had his own kingdom. Let Wall Street snigger about his "Cheap John" business. Let those snooty Vanderbilts slight his family from party lists. Let his arch-competitor Kresge try to match him store for store. Frank Woolworth had proven, once and for all, that an enterprising American from humble beginnings, could turn pennies into billions. He had the tallest, most beautiful, and safest skyscraper in the world to prove it. And the twenty-eighth president of the United States had helped him celebrate his achievement.

Best of all, this Cathedral of Commerce was all his—lock, stock, and gargoyles. The ever resourceful Frank had paid a hot 13.5 million for his steel kingdom—all in cash.

The Story Of The Skyline Queen

The size and beauty of the building made F. W. Woolworth an internationally known personality. The story of how the Skyline Queen came to be is another example of Frank's penchant for dreaming big, and then working day and night to make his dream a reality.

When Woolworth was first seized with the mania to reach for the sky, his business life was humming along, devoid of any major calamity, save an occasional wage strike by his counter girls. His five-and-ten syndicate had been publicly incorporated four years before and was running as smooth as a top. His inner circle, along with a stream of stenographers and errand boys, were comfortably housed in elaborate offices at 280 Broadway in the Stewart Building. The company even had a new private phone number—"WORTH 3557"—there were to be no shared party lines for the great F. W. Woolworth.

Frank was reaching his zenith professionally, but his personal life was another matter. He was feeling restless and anxious, even amidst the luxurious surroundings of his Fifth Avenue home and his quaint Asbury Park summer cottage. His wife was slipping farther and farther into her own world, offering him little comfort or rational conversation. Frank worried constantly about his beloved Edna, who had wed that pompous upstart, stockbroker Franklyn Hutton (brother of E. F. Hutton), a man Frank was certain would break his daughter's heart. Health-wise, Frank was shaky at best. He was on the wrong side of fifty, overfed, overweight, and underexercised. He sensed that his time was limited and he needed a big project to keep his mind off such somber thoughts.

In 1909, Woolworth had purchased a plot of land in lower Broadway, on the corner of Park Place, a stone's throw from the F. W. Woolworth Company's offices. He'd been tracking the activity on that corner, and felt it had great commercial potential. The question was, what exactly should he do with it? He had already erected four multistoried Woolworth

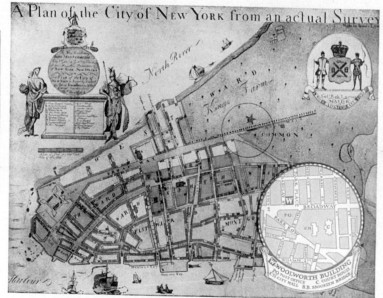

This pre-American Revolution map of New York shows the site of the Woolworth Building was once designated as the "King's Farm." The site of the Woolworth Building is rich with history. In Dutch Colonial days, its fertile ground was owned by the powerful West India Company, who fenced it off for cattle-grazing and private farming. Later on, after the Dutch succumbed to British and the British to the American colonists, the site of the future Woolworth Building hosted the palatial home of Philip Hone, mayor of New York in 1826, who'd "brazenly" entertained the literary likes of Daniel Webster and James Fenimore Cooper. Along surrounding streets, New York's first theater district featured vaudeville, plays, and musical reviews.

Buildings, including one in Lancaster, Pennsylvania, and one in Trenton, New Jersey—but he longed for something more imposing. Perhaps the site on Broadway, across from historic city hall, and a short trolley ride from buzzing Wall Street, was the place to assure his posterity. After some intensive thinking, he decided to erect yet another Woolworth Building, more beautiful than its predecessors. Although his body was weakening, Frank retained his boyish zeal for enterprise. This new brainstorm fueled his energy.

At first, Frank thought a twelve- or fifteen-story building would suffice, but he soon changed his mind. He'd need at least twenty stories to top the gold-domed Pulitzer Building and the Singer Building, also nearby, which clocked in at 612 feet above the sidewalk. If he managed to outdo those two, he'd have the tallest building in lower Manhattan, but would still be faced with formidable competition. The 700-foot high Metropolitan Tower loomed in solitary splendor over the midtown skyline. As of 1909, it had been crowned the tallest skyscraper in the world. Its majestic architecture and four-sided clock had earned international acclaim through photographs, postcards, and magazine articles. This irked Frank. He didn't want to be known as the man who built the *second* highest skyscraper in the world. He wanted to construct a skyscraper unparalleled on earth; a majestic headquarters that would allow him to bask in comfort and accolades before—as his preacher used to say—the Lord called him home. The steel gauntlet was tossed. He decided that his building would be taller than 700 feet and at least 40 stories high.

To achieve this goal, Woolworth needed more land. Under his instructions, realty broker Edward J. Hogan gobbled up a stream of connected downtown properties. Soon, Woolworth owned the entire block front on lower Broadway between Barclay and Park Place, with a frontage of 105 feet on Broadway alone.

The land was rich in history and had been in use steadily since Manhattan Island had been purchased from the Indians. By the time Frank acquired this tract, the stately mansions of prior decades had succumbed to genteel decay, and most of them had been converted into storefronts. Even though the neighborhood was run down, Frank had to pay the Mercantile Bank $750,000 for just one of the small plots on 237 Broadway. He felt it was worth it, though. Projections indicated that New York would soon be the greatest commercial city in the world, with lower and midtown Manhattan connected by great avenues guaranteed to bring in a steady stream of natives and tourists to see his skyscraper. One day, Woolworth vowed, his own steel-and-mortar zenith would be honored in twentieth-century chronicles.

The Architect, The Builder, And The Bankroll

Cass Gilbert, architect.

By New Year's Eve 1910, Frank was legal owner of the land required. Now he needed an architect and a builder to help create his masterpiece. Woolworth's architect of choice was Cass Gilbert, a man known for his astounding designs, including the Minnesota State Capitol and the New York Beaux Arts Customs House. Frank knew that Gilbert had a reputation for doing wondrous things with stone; his powers of design were unequaled in infusing mass with delicate beauty. He was a true gentleman, even of temper and meticulous of task. Cass Gilbert agreed to take on the job, with the understanding that Woolworth's skyscraper would top the Metropolitan Tower.

Over the next six months, Frank concentrated on organizing the rest of his team. One of his biggest concerns was assuming the role of landlord for a sixty-story skyscraper; an edifice that large would require hundreds of commercial tenants. Taking the bull by the horns, Frank invited a young banker friend, Lewis Pierson, to a lunch-hour powwow. Frank had known Pierson for years, well before the latter had risen to the presidency of the National Exchange. Pierson had since engineered the exchange's 1906 merger with the Irving National Bank, of which Frank himself was an influential director. Over a table at the Hardware Club, which was groaning with the weight of rich and sumptuous foods (most of which his doctor had advised him not to eat), Woolworth asked Lewis if he thought the Irving National Exchange would be interested in leasing a floor or two in his new building.

Lewis replied affirmatively. Frank was elated; he had his first tenant, one so prestigious it was guaranteed to lure in more of the same quality. But this was really just the beginning, for with each passing day, Woolworth's dreams became more elaborate.

Woolworth required a builder of unquestionable reliability to pull off the gargantuan task he was planning. After spirited bidding, the construction contract was awarded to Louis Horowitz, president of the Thompson-Starret Company. The pieces were finally in place. He had Cass Gilbert as architect; the Foundation Company as escavators; Gunvald Aus, the steel engineer, to erect the superstructure; Irving National Bank as first tenant; and Frank J. Hogan, the rental agent, to fill up the rest of the floors—barring of course, those reserved for F. W. Woolworth Co.'s executive headquarters.

Escavation officially began during the summer of 1910. The wrecker's ball swung. Timbers buckled and splintered. Down came the history-haunted buildings that had once stood shoulder to shoulder. To prepare the escavated site for the new building (estimated to weigh over 200 million pounds), the Foundation Company sank great metal tubes into the Manhattan bedrock, to make certain that no cave-ins would occur during or after construction. The supporting structures were imbedded 115 feet deep below the curb level, then topped off by a fully finished cellar, subbasement, and boiler room. The underground section of the Woolworth edifice was so high that it was actually a building unto itself. Seeing an opportunity for media attention, Hogan's real estate firm erected a huge billboard outside, proclaiming:

HIGHEST IN THE WORLD!

The magnificent WOOLWORTH BUILDING,–

to be erected on this site.–

Ready for occupancy, 1912.

Woolworth Co. booklets have long boasted that not one life was lost during the project, but a small article in the *New York Times* belies this claim. On the morning of December 13, 1910, a fifty-foot boom, supported by a cable attached to a derrick, was carrying a load of dirt and rocks to the street. The cable snapped and the boom crashed to the ground, killing an unidentified man and fatally injuring a young boy. Amazingly, considering all the heavy machinery on hand, there were no further casualties during construction.

The Eighth Wonder Of The World Takes Form

Even as the steel framework of the Woolworth Building first inched through sidewalk level on November 15, 1911, Frank had still not decided exactly what materials would be used to adorn the outside of his skyscraper, how the interior lobby would be designed, or exactly how tall the building would be. A harried Cass Gilbert had already drawn up numerous architectural sketches, but Mr. Woolworth was not yet not satisfied. Nonetheless, Gilbert persevered. "It was clear to [Gilbert]," wrote James Brough, "that if his patience outlasted his new client's vacillations they might together awe the nation with the breadth of their vision. Still, he could not guess how severely his forbearance was to be tested."

Frank Woolworth was all over the project, asking questions and meddling in decisions that only engineers had the expertise to resolve. For example, Woolworth wanted to cover the entire exterior in marble, but Horowitz and Gilbert dissuaded him in favor of terra-cotta; marble was much too heavy and might, in time, collapse under its own weight. At one point, Woolworth slyly suggested that, because of the prestige of being attached to the world's tallest building, Horowitz and Gilbert ought to forgo their fees. Their refusal was as stony as the building itself—and as firm. Somehow, they all remained friends through the ordeal.

After much ado, the final architectural plans were approved. Frank's building was to be gothic in style, but state-of-the-art in mechanical design. On his frequent trips to London, the lofty spires of the houses of Parliament had taken his breath away, and Frank considered this to be the ideal architectural model. Both aesthetic and interior construction plans also

Laying the Groundwork

Rare photo from 1911 shows workers from the Foundation Company, during excavation for the Woolworth Building. Notice the lack of hard hats and safety glasses.

The Engineering Report of Saturday, April 12, 1912 described the first phase of the project, and how the projected 200 million pounds of weight would be supported. The Foundation Company's muscled workers, known as "sand-hogs," painstakingly scooped out sand and fill with orange peel buckets, which were then hoisted to waiting wagons in the street above, drawn by horses clip-clopping impatiently and snorting steam into the air. Great metal tubes were brought in so that no cave-ins would occur during construction, or after. These tubes were sunk, through soil, mud, silt and water, to bedrock, along the Manhattan schist. The tubes were emptied by means of pneumatic pressure and filled with concrete, forming 69 solid piers, on which the steel columns of the structure would rest. The project was one of the most challenging of its era.

included a host of safety features. The 1890 Chicago fire was still fresh in America's mind; the cinders of 17,000 dwellings and the ashes of countless victims were grim reminders of the folly of careless construction techniques. Woolworth told Gilbert and Horowitz that no expense should be spared in making his corporate castle as safe as possible.

At this point, the matter of additional financing reared its pesky head. Woolworth had already spent considerable sums on preliminary architectural plans, escavation, and other costly projects. Suddenly, he realized there might be a way to foot the remainder of the bill.

During the period he was setting the cogs in motion for his skyscraper, he had also been busy finalizing the $65-million merger that created the F. W. Woolworth Co. Since the merger was finalized on January 1, 1912, Frank thought it perfectly logical that his skyscraper should be bankrolled through profits from the new company's capital stock enterprise.

He consulted with Goldman, Sachs & Co., the investment firm that had handled the stock issue for the grand merger. Without preamble, Frank asked for the money to finish his building. Henry Goldman promptly rebuffed him. The new shareholders might be disturbed, explained Goldman, if Frank pulled millions out of the new corporation's bank account. Naturally, this response did not sit well with Frank, who was accustomed to getting his way.

In the end, Frank called upon his good humor, flexibility, and his bulging pockets to resolve the dilemma. He informed Goldman that he would pay for the entire building himself, in cash. He then set up another business, Broadway Park Place, to manage the details.

Thus, the Woolworth Building became one of the only skyscrapers in the world, past or present, to be erected completely unencumbered by mortgage or other debts.

Woolworth Building "Firsts"

As New Yorkers gaped from the sidewalks, the Skyline Queen slowly stitched upward, like embroidered lace, against the New York sky. On July 12, 1912, a flag was flown in the breeze at the pinnacle of the tower, signifying the completion of the structural steelwork. Ten months later the entire building was finished.

The completed Woolworth Building was full of firsts. It used the largest, most efficient steam and water pipes to date. To contain any unexpected fires, the internal rooms were designed with steel reinforced doors and walls. Its lofty spire was resistant to 200 m.p.h. hurricane-strength winds, and also had an ingenious lightning deflector system. This system was put to the test less than one month later, when a severe thunderstorm, accompanied by huge hailstones, hit Manhattan Island. Heavy winds buffeted lower Broadway and lightning crackled down, until suddenly, the Woolworth Building was struck head-on. Showers of sparks rained down, but there was no fire and only small damage. Not a splinter of wood had been used in its external superstructure, and its deflecting system (a copper roof, connected by copper cables to the steel framework) had saved the day.

The Woolworth Building was equipped with its own mini-hospital.

During lighter moments, executives could relax in the ornate, Olympic-sized pool.

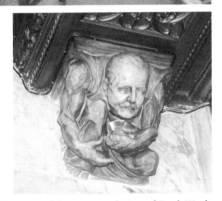

ABOVE: A humorous caricature of Frank Woolworth counting his money was incorporated into the upper section of the Grand Arcade Lobby. BELOW: Caricature of architect Cass Gilbert holding the building.

Another first included the building's elevator system; its thirty-four high-speed cars encompassed a string of safety features, the most important being an air-compression and cushioning system. Theoretically, if a major cable snapped, the pressure in the elevator was designed to compress, allowing very little air to escape. This would limit the speed of the drop, allowing the car to slowly come to rest at the base of the shaft. Woolworth felt it necessary to test this theory, so he had his engineers load the forty-fifth-story elevator car with over 7,000 pounds of material, well exceeding the weight limit. On top of the pile, they placed a glass full of water. As expected, within a short time, all preliminary safety precautions failed and the elevator plunged down in a noisy free-fall. The air cushion system worked, though, and when the car reached the bottom level, the load was unharmed and the glass of water was still full.

Besides being lightning proof, hurricane proof, and fire-resistant, the Woolworth Building was the first to have its own in-house police, fire, and mini-hospital departments. Never before had a commercial landowner placed so much money and effort into safety, or luxury.

Inside and out, the Woolworth Building was hailed as a work of pure, soaring art, an architectural masterpiece, looking like an elongated church viewed in a convex mirror. Due to its U-shaped design, every office, from the base of the building to the twenty-seventh floor, enjoyed an outside view. In the Grand Arcade, a beautiful, stained-glass "Labor and Commerce" fresco was inset into the second-floor balcony. (According to folklore, the faces on the fresco were both modeled after Woolworth's beloved mother, Fanny.) The building featured marble interiors, gold-and-turquoise terrazzo ceilings, gilded tracery, majestic external spires, flying buttresses and gargoyles. On almost every floor, little "W's" were carved into the woodwork; a subtle but distinct reminder of the man who had made it all possible. Frank was taking no chances that his name would be lost to posterity.

Unbeknownst to Frank, a few little extras had been added to his magnum opus. Tom Johnson, one of Cass Gilbert's team of artists, designed a series of gargoylelike caricatures of the building's prime movers and shakers. He then placed them high under the supporting crossbeams in the main entrance lobby. To this day, visitors can look up and see Gunvald Aus measuring a steel girder, and Hogan closing a real estate deal. Pierson, the first bank tenant, and Horowitz, the builder, are also there, along with Cass Gilbert holding up a model of the building.

Tom Johnson did not, of course, forget the King of Commerce. Johnson added a humorous and fitting caricature of Frank Woolworth himself, hunched over, intently counting his nickels and dimes. Reportedly, when Frank first saw the gargoyles, he dissolved with laughter and ordered that they never be removed.

There is another popular story, which brings to mind the Frank Woolworth of younger days; the boy who avidly investigated the old mansions of northern New York. Early in 1913, Frank suggested to his friend, organist Frank Taft, that they explore the nearly completed Woolworth Building. The upper floors were still closed to everyone but workmen and officials, so, like a mischievous child, Woolworth waited until after hours, then snuck Taft inside. Together, they made their way upward. They used the elevators until the elevators ran out, and then proceeded up the winding stairways. At the topmost landing, Frank stopped to rest, out of breath from the unaccustomed exertion. He was about to give up and start back when Taft noticed a ladder leading to a small trapdoor. He let out a little cry of glee and began climbing.

"Wait a minute," wheezed Frank. "I don't propose to let you go higher in this building than I go myself." And up the ladder he went.

Taft later recalled that the two men soon found themselves hunched over at the peak of the tower, just below the roof. Then Frank got a brainstorm.

"Say, let's write our names up here!"

Carving initials on trees was something he and brother Charles had done as boys back in Great Bend. The idea of leaving his mark on an entire building, his own building, pleased him immensely. And so, Woolworth and Taft set to work and left their distinctive signatures in the tower, beneath the rafters. It is probable that those names are up there still.

Not too long after Woolworth and Taft explored the tower, Frank finally had the chance to show off his skyscraper in grand style. The aforementioned grand opening dinner list of April 1913 included engineers, bankers, scientists, attorneys, and men of letters from all over the world. Everyone who was anyone was fascinated by Frank's Skyline Queen, then the tallest inhabited building in the world.

When the first waves of exultation began to wear off, Frank traveled back to Paris, for a bit of rest and inspiration. He revisited several of Napoleon Bonaparte's old haunts, and decided to design his executive office in the Woolworth Building in the style of Napoleon's Empire Room at Compiegne. The ceiling of the room was cream white, embossed in gold. The walls were of marble. He commissioned a large desk (also a replica of one of Napoleon's) made of polished mahogany and gilt. The top was covered in dark green Italian leather. At knee level, on the left side, a small panel, a sort of command center, was inserted to make certain his official whims were met with expediency. One of the buttons was connected to his secretary, one to his senior partners' offices, and one simply said "boy." Frank also purchased a life-sized bust of Napoleon and a clock owned by Napoleon himself. On the west wall, opposite Frank's desk, hung a huge portrait of Napoleon in his coronation robes. Frank Woolworth felt it was important to impress powerful people when they came to call. Frank himself described his own Empire Room as "the handsomest office in the country, and possibly the world."

By erecting his Skyline Queen, with its office fit for a king, Frank had not only created the tallest and most beautiful skyscraper on earth; he had embodied, in wood and stone, his three main passions: commerce, religion, and Napoleon. In 1915, the Woolworth Building was awarded the Medal of Honor for the highest and finest office building in the world.

Frank Woolworth's lavish Empire Room in the Woolworth Building was his base of operations, and his pride and joy. The office featured a life-sized portrait of his hero, Napoleon, and a leather-and-gold desk modeled after Napoleon's own.

The prestigious honor, which Frank hung prominently in his office, was given to him by the Department of Liberal Arts of the Panama Pacific International Exposition of San Francisco, California. He said later, that it was one of his finest moments as man, and merchant.

Frank was sixty-one years old when his Cathedral of Commerce was christened. He would only enjoy it for four more years, until the night he died from pneumonic complications at his Gold Coast mansion in Long Island.

He was lucky to enjoy it for even this short period, though, and in one sense, it was the Woolworth Building that inadvertently gave Frank those four extra years of life. Early in 1912, Frank was so stressed that one of his colleagues suggested he take a pleasure trip. There was a new ship that was all the rage with society, and many of America's biggest magnates had already booked passage. Frank gruffly declined, saying he had too much work to do on his skyscraper to be pottering around on the open sea.

The pleasure ship in question was the *Titanic.*

The Cathedral Of Commerce Through The Decades

The Woolworth Building reigned as the tallest building in the world until 1930, when the New York Chrysler Building topped it by 254 feet. One year later, the Empire State Building took the prize, holding the title until 1971. Today, the Woolworth Building is dwarfed by the many other skyscrapers that dot downtown Manhattan, but it is still considered one of the most beautiful twentieth-century structures on earth.

In the years following its grand opening, more than 300,000 tourists per year strolled through the Woolworth Building's Grand Arcade, taking pictures and purchasing souvenirs. From the Observation Deck Gallery, 58 stories aloft, they viewed up to forty miles of skyline in each direction. By 1920, the Visitor's Register Book listed names from fifty countries, and thousands of American cities and towns. Sadly, the observation deck was closed to the public during World War II, as the U.S. Navy feared that enemy spies could use it to track Allied movements. It was never reopened.

The Woolworth Building has remained a popular address for hundreds of notable corporations who have leased offices there since 1913. One section was even used as Thomas E. Dewey's clandestine headquarters during his racket-busting days in the 1930s.

Unfortunately, not every part of this historic building has fared well. For example, Frank's pride and joy, his corporate Empire Room, was long ago renovated and modernized. For a time, his desk, along with the priceless portraits of Napoleon and the one of himself, were featured in a mini-museum display on the twenty-fourth floor. As of 1998, they were being kept in storage rooms. Many of the priceless antiques that adorned his Empire Room, and other lavishly decorated rooms of the building, were auctioned off or mysteriously vanished. The fate of the remainder of the building, including all those hand-carved "W's" that Woolworth was so proud of, is uncertain.

In June 1998, the name of the Woolworth Corporation was changed to the Venator Group. Soon after, the building was sold to a real estate developer, the Witcoff Group. The street-level Grand Arcade and the splendid mezzanine have been declared historical landmarks, and are, presumably, safe from demolition, but more than that is at stake. The Woolworth Building housed not only antiques, but irreplaceable documents penned by Frank himself, along with vintage glass negatives of the building, massive bound histories of the company compiled in 1949, and countless trophies and plaques commemorating company executives of days gone by. Some of these plaques have already been chopped up for scrap marble and brass. Historians and veteran employees alike are hoping that if the Venator Group ever moves its corporate headquarters out of the Woolworth Building, the remaining artifacts surviving from its rich history will be justly preserved.

Tradition Lost . . . Tradition Remembered

Like every other segment of the Woolworth story, the building, as it stood regally in glory days, lives on in the minds of the millions of people passed through its glass doors. During the centennial celebration of the company, banners flew in the entranceway and a special reproduction display of the original Red-Fronts was constructed for the lobby. Even now, not a working day goes by when groups of school children and tourists do not pause for a moment in the Grand Arcade, wide-eyed with awe at the sheer immensity and beauty of this landmark.

While researching *Remembering Woolworth's,* I interviewed many former employees of the company who actually worked in the Woolworth Building, some of them for more than forty years. The types of memories most widely shared involved the building during the Christmas holidays. Reportedly, straight up until the mid-1990s, each floor occupied by Woolworth departments had beautiful Christmas trees, with several departments vying to have the most beautifully decorated tree of all. Of course, downstairs in the lobby, the "official" Woolworth tree rose a full story high, glittering for the enjoyment of tourists, set against the colorful background of stained glass and marble.

For almost as long as the building existed, there had been a special holiday tradition of organizing a seasonal choir. During December, Woolworth employees who worked in the building would join together joyously for a Christmas sing atop one of the mezzanines in the Grand Arcade. The employees would give up their lunch hours to entertain visitors and other employees, their voices ringing in cheer throughout the hallowed halls. People from all over the city hall area would bring their bag lunches, find a spot in the lobby, and listen. In 1996, this tradition was mysteriously terminated by current company executives.

Another strong wave of memories involves the months following the final demise of the F. W. Woolworth General Merchandise Division in the summer of 1997, the time when

the last of the five-and-dime stores started to close across North America. Seemingly overnight, the busy offices with their hundreds of employees were suddenly empty of equipment and people. With over ninety percent of them left without jobs, a skeleton crew of employees was temporarily retained to tie up loose ends and work a hot-line for customer inquiries. One employee recalled how absolutely still everything was—it was almost like working in a mausoleum. The only noise generated came from the ringing phones. Some of the hot-line calls involved general inquires, but most were from former customers honestly upset about the closing of their favorite five-and-dime. One woman from the Midwest asked if there was any way to get a bottle of Blue Waltz perfume for her elderly mother. Apparently, her mother had been suffering from memory lapses and depression, and all she wanted was to go down to Woolworth's for a bottle of the scent. Of course, Blue Waltz hadn't been sold for decades, and so could not be secured for the ailing woman, but this story's poignance reflects

TIME CAPSULE MEMORY

"Special Moments at the Woolworth Building"

I worked for the F. W. Woolworth Company for almost thirty years, and for a good part of that time I worked in the beautiful Woolworth Building itself. My bosses and co-workers were like a family to me, and I missed them terribly when my department, Region 2, was disbanded. My boss, Mr. Charles Green was a wonderful man; he was demanding but fair and had a great sense of humor. I remember that every year, the various Woolworth departments in the building would try to out-do each other when it came to the office Christmas tree. Mr. Green always wanted our department to have the biggest, best, most beautiful tree. He supported our efforts to make sure that happened, and there were always plenty of presents under the tree. During the holidays, some of the Woolworth Building employees would form a choir, and they would sing during lunch hour in the lobby downstairs. They sang so beautifully it made me cry. That tradition started a long time ago, and I am not really sure why the company made them stop.

After all the Woolworth's five-and-dimes were closed down in 1997, our department was no longer needed. It was very quiet in the office, with everyone gone. I was one of the few employees left, and I was working the hot-line we set up to answer questions. People from all over the country called up to ask why the F. W. Woolworth stores were closing, and most of them were sad and upset. I tried my best to answer their questions; some of which were general questions, and others specific requests for items like the "Silent Secretary" which was one of the company's longest, best-selling items. After work, or during my breaks, I would sometimes stroll down to the lobby, and think about all the different experiences that happened in that building. There was always a group of tourists gazing up at the beautiful artwork and architecture. I would proudly point to the stained-glass windows that were named "Labor & Commerce" and tell the visitors that Frank Woolworth had had the women's face on the glass designed after his beloved mother. (That was the story that I was told.) I will never forget my experiences working in the Woolworth Building. I always thought I would retire with the F. W. Woolworth company, but I, too, had to find another job. —Olga Freeman, New York

Woolworth's place in the collective heart of the nation. Clearly, the memories of the old dimestores ran, and still run, deep and true.

For many people, especially those who patronized Woolworth's during its heyday, it was more than a store, it was part of their lifestyle. And that is exactly what Frank Winfield Woolworth would have wanted.

The rags-to-riches story of the merchant Woolworth is only part of the whole story. Most Americans do not not realize that F. W. Woolworth Co. was an international retail marvel. Just as thousands of United States' main streets were dotted with the familiar red-and-gold Woolworth signs, so too were countless streets in cities and villages across Canada, Europe, and South America.

PART TWO

REMEMBERING WOOLWORTH'S...

AROUND THE WORLD

This *American Weekly* illustration by R. F. Schabelitz, depicts
a disgruntled Frank Woolworth pointing out the high-brow
antics of "titled European fortune-hunters" who were seeking
his daughter Jessy's attentions in 1909.

Chapter Six

Woolworth's *International*

"I think a good penny and six pence store run by a real live Yankee

would create a sensation here."

—F. W. Woolworth, writing from London, 5 March 1890

The Woolworth story is often hailed as a prime example of an American rags-to-riches tale. Frank Winfield Woolworth, along with other self-made men of his time, such as John Jacob Astor, Henry Ford, and Thomas Alva Edison, are the kind of entrepreneurs who Americans proudly point to and boast: "See, look what can happen in this land of unlimited opportunity!"

To a great extent, this is an American tale. Frank was a self-professed, "dirt-poor, home-grown Yankee" with big dreams who used the resources of his native country to help make those dreams-come-true.

But Frank Woolworth's experiences in the United States represent only one part of this success story. His variety stores also enjoyed unprecedented international acclaim. Indeed, a large part of the Woolworth tale unfolded thousands of miles away, far from Frank's sixty-story "Cathedral of Commerce" in New York City. During the 1970s, for example, the F. W. Woolworth Co. operated over five thousand flourishing general and specialty merchandise stores worldwide, more than twenty-five percent of them located throughout the United Kingdom, formerly known as the British Isles. According to Woolworth historian, John P. Nichols, "At year's close 1971, that 62-year-old mercantile Goliath [F. W. Woolworth LTD of England] operated 1,108 British Woolworths and five British Woolcos in England, the West Indies, Ireland, Scotland, Wales and Africa." Further, along with its scores of stores located in the U.S. mainland and into the remotest provinces of Canada, the F. W. Woolworth Co. once operated flourishing Red-Fronts in Cuba, Germany, Hawaii, Mexico, Puerto Rico, Spain, and the Virgin Islands. Amazingly, in 1997, just a few months before the company announced that it would be doing away with its entire Red-Front Division, the total number of establishments it owned or controlled had topped 7,000, a respectable percentage of which were still foreign holdings.

Frank and his partners actually set the seeds for this global expansion by branching out into Canada during the 1880s. For the next thirty years the Woolworth team steadfastly moved beyond North America's borders to create "three-and-sixpence" shops in the British Isles and sprawling warehouses in France and Germany. After Frank passed on in 1919, his successor, Hubert Parson, established the first "25-and-50 phennig" stores in Germany. Several years later, after World War II, Parson orchestrated the massive rebuilding of F. W. Woolworth variety stores in battle-torn Europe. In 1929, the F. W. Woolworth Co. opened stores in Cuba, being one of the first American retailers to infiltrate that highly popular resort country. Another surge of international expansion was initiated during the reign of Woolworth president, Robert C. Kirkwood, who, beginning in 1958, led North America's Woolworth's into the age of shopping malls, self-service, and modern merchandising, while simultaneously devoting his energies into increased presence of the famed Red-Fronts in South American countries.

When Kirkland retired from the presidency, the company's annual sales had surpassed the $3 billion mark, and executives started focusing on newly acquired and newly formed subsidiaries, including Woolco, Kinney Shoes, Richman Brothers, the Norvell Company, and later, Footlocker and the San Francisco Music Box Company. As these and other retail concepts caught on, foreign branches of these were established, enhancing the strong presence their five-and-dimes already enjoyed. (Red-Fronts in island resorts did especially well, and until the bitter end, the Virgin Islands were bringing in over 20 million dollars in annual revenues.)

By the early 1980s, the F. W. Woolworth Co.'s interest in the international retail market began to shift. Political and import complications in Spain and Mexico proved problematic, and the British holdings were not performing as well as before. In a landmark move in 1982, American Woolworth's sold off all of its remaining interest in the United Kingdom's Red-Fronts. Beginning in 1993, the Canadian Red-Fronts started to close, along with the first wave of U.S. dimestores. The last Red-Fronts in the United States were being shuttered in 1997, and finally, in September 1998, F. W. Woolworth LTD, Germany, was sold. After the dust had settled, the company (now the Venator Group) still owned thousands of specialty stores, such as Lady Footlocker and Champs, but by selling off the German five-and-dimes, the company had also severed America's proprietary ties with any Red-Fronts *anywhere* in the world.

However, the historical connection between Frank W. Woolworth and "Woolworth's International" can never be severed. His nineteenth-century buying expeditions in England

and Germany forever altered the scope of international import, export, and shopping habits. Here in America, the sudden availability of previously unseen items, such as hand-painted German holiday ornaments and "angel hair," directly influenced the way millions of Americans decorated their homes and Christmas trees during the Christmas season. Equally important, the presence of so many Red-Fronts overseas helped to make "Woolworth's" the household name it is today.

The aforementioned accomplishments were a direct result of Frank Woolworth's original foresight to bring his concept of "good merchandise at fair prices" to millions of people outside of the United State's borders. In turn, hundreds of thousands of foreign suppliers, managers, and wage earners also benefited greatly.

In spite of all this global fanfare, the actual tale of "Woolworth's International" began in a humble way, across the Canadian border, just a train ride from Frank's home town in northern New York state.

Woolworth's In Canada

Woolworth's of Canada holds special significance in the expansive and rich history of the F. W. Woolworth Company. The Red-Fronts were nearly as popular in Canada as they were in the United States. However, the origin of F. W. Woolworth's Limited of Canada is rather unique.

The first city-based "Woolworth's" was founded in Montreal in 1896, but the name on the original masthead was not Woolworth, it was *Charlton*. One year later, the very first five-and-dime opened in Toronto, the masthead reading neither Woolworth or Charlton, but *Knox*. By 1911, Canada had thirty-one successful five-and-dimes operating in its country, dotting busy thoroughfares in Ontario, Nova Scotia, Quebec, and British Columbia. These stores were still being influenced by men with the names Charlton and Knox, yet by then their mastheads *all* said "F. W. Woolworth".

The reason for the name discrepancy is that the Woolworth stores in Canada were actually "founded" by two of Frank Woolworth's dimestore protégés, Seymour Knox and Earle Charlton. Later, during the famous $60 million merger of 1911, the Canadian holdings of Knox and Charlton were added to those of Frank Woolworth's to help form the mammoth F. W. Woolworth Co. Although the Woolworth name would become the best known in Canada, it is important to recognize the vital importance Knox and Charlton played in the history of that country's favorite five-and-dime.

Charlton & Knox: Canada's Dimestore Pioneers

Back in 1884, Mr. Woolworth was still struggling along in Pennsylvania. His Lancaster store was doing exceedingly well, as was his store in Scranton, which he'd recently sold to his brother Charles. However, Frank wanted to expand to a full-blown chain of five-and-dimes, and knew he could not do it alone; he needed partners. He had a meeting with his cousin, Seymour Knox, who showed great enthusiasm for a partnership agreement. Together, they opened a store in Reading, Pennsylvania, which fared well, and another in Newark, New Jersey, which did not fare as well. During this period, Frank taught his cousin all he knew about the five-and-dime business.

Seymour Knox, a farmer's son from Russell, New York, was an ambitious man, as determined as his cousin Frank to make a name and a grand success for himself. After several partnership ventures with Woolworth, Knox decided to branch out on his own. The two cousins agreed they would share suppliers but not geographical territory. In 1887, Seymour Knox then teamed up with his cousin Edwin Merton McBrier to open a store in Lockport, New York, and later, in 1890, he joined forces with Connecticut-born traveling salesman, Earle P. Charlton. Together, the team of "Knox & Charlton" opened a string of five-and-tens across New England.

Seymour Horace Knox, 1861–1915.

They set up their stores exactly the way Knox had been taught by Frank Woolworth, and soon, both men were prospering. In 1896, Mr. Charlton decided that he, too, wanted to work independently. Over the next year, he expanded into the uncharted territory of America's Pacific coast and into Montreal, Canada. Hence, Earle Charlton introduced Montreal to the five-and-ten concept, probably late in 1896, or early 1897. As far west as Vancouver, British Columbia, Charlton's venturesome nature was rewarded. Seymour Knox quickly followed suit, opening Toronto's first dimestore on April 30, 1897. Knox had a tendency to remain

Earle Perry Charlton, 1863–1930.

in the Ontario region, but Charlton ventured forth into the Province of Quebec, and beyond.

There is some discrepancy in Woolworth Company records as to which of these two men first ventured to Canada. Records dating before 1949 credit Charlton, while those afterward credit Knox. The two men established their stores within such a limited time frame that is safe to say that they were cofounders of the dimestore expansion into Canada. From the beginning, the Canadians readily accepted the idea of a discount variety store. This allowed for speedy and profitable expansion.

When the five-and-dimes first debuted at the close of the nineteenth century, Canada was still primarily an agricultural nation, and the types of items stocked in Knox and Charlton's earliest stores reflected this. As Canada become more industrialized, the same lines

Doll display from one store in Quebec, c. 1960.

of items that were carried in the United States were then being offered in Canada.

By 1954, the year of its 57th Woolworth Anniversary, there were 170 Red-Fronts located in every single province except Newfoundland. By 1960, that number had jumped to 250, including a site in Newfoundland.

For most of its long history, F. W. Woolworth Co., Limited, Canada, was managed and staffed by Canadians. It was, however, wholly-owned by the United States' parent company, which always had one or two representatives on its board of directors to represent Canadian interests. Until 1912, the division's principal office was in Montreal, but they were moved to 357 Bay Street Toronto in 1916. During the 1950s its headquarters were moved to lavish offices at 33 Adelaide Street.

During the 1920s, about sixty-five percent of the goods sold in Canada were manufactured in Canada, with twenty-five percent being imported from the United States, and ten percent from England.

On May 9, 1945, the board of directors approved a resolution to change the Canadian division from a limited public company to a private company. This meant that no further transfer of capital stocks were to be issued except via special approval, and that the shareholders were temporarily limited to only fifty!

Along with the substantial revenues generated by the Canadian subsidiary, F. W. Woolworth Co., Ltd., Canada was also noted for the wealth of talented manpower it generated for the parent company. For example, Charles C. W. Deyo, president of the Woolworth Co. from 1936 to 1946, started out in the five-and-ten business in London, Ontario. R. D. Campbell, who eventually became managing director of the Canadian division, started as a stockboy in the Windsor, Ontario, store back in 1916. I. W. Keffer, a Canadian by birth, started in Hamilton, Ontario, stocking shelves in 1912; he eventually managed both the German and Canadian divisions.

During a Newcommen Society address in 1960, Woolworth President Kirkwood had this to say about F. W. Woolworth, Ltd., Canada: "While all Woolworth family ties are very close, we are particularly proud of our Canadian operation and grateful to our friends in Canada who have made it so outstanding successful. In our opinion, the future of the great country and our business there was never brighter."

As part of a massive restructuring strategy in 1993, 240 Canadian Red-Fronts were closed down, affecting 3,000 employees. One year later, F. W. Woolworth, Ltd., Canada (by then known as Woolworth Canada, Inc.) again made headlines when, after eighteen years, the company closed down all 82 of its Kinney Shoe stores. January 1997 brought another shake-up, when the American discount giant, Wal-Mart purchased the remaining Canadian Woolco stores.

Today, Woolworth Canada, Inc, is a specialty retailer that operates 1,400 stores in Canada and the United States, under names like the Northern Group and Weekend Edition. The company continues to move along profitably, but the once-bustling Red-Fronts are now only a part of their past.

> ┌─────────────────────────────────┐
> TIME CAPSULE MEMORY
>
>
>
> ## "Strawberry Shortcake & Wonder Woman"
>
> The Woolworth stores were very popular in Canada. In fact, for many years in my own city of Guelph, Ontario, Woolworth's was the biggest store downtown. I used to go there as a youngster every week (or weekend) with my grandmother and she would buy me a toy from the downstairs section which held the toy department. Then, as a treat, we would go upstairs to the restaurant and have a strawberry shortcake. Ahh, I have special memories of that strawberry shortcake, as well of buying and reading the latest Wonder Woman comics! —Ryan Lawrence, Canada
> └─────────────────────────────────┘

Frank Woolworth's Maiden Journey To Europe

By the time Seymour Knox and Earle Charlton started to make dimestore history in Canada, Frank Woolworth had already begun making his own form of history in Europe. Officially, Woolworth opened his first "three-and-sixpence" Red-Front in England in 1909, but the seeds for that milestone were planted many years before, in 1890.

Frank Woolworth was thirty-eight-years-old when he embarked upon his maiden trip overseas. His official reason for the journey was to seek out inexpensive manufacturers of pottery, dolls, toys, and glassware, which he'd heard were available in abundance in the British Isles, Germany, Austria, and France. But to travel abroad was also Frank Woolworth's personal dream. At long last, he would roam the same cobblestoned streets and vast battlefields as had his hero, Napoleon Bonaparte. He longed to meet a member of the British royal family, to feast on Vienna pastry, to see the Louvre in Paris, and to enjoy Europe's renowned musical concerts.

Prior to his departure, Frank worked around the clock to put his business and personal affairs in order. His brother, Charles, and his general manager, Carson Peck, tried to assure their leader that all would be well in his absence. Nonetheless, Frank took an extra day to draw up a detailed, handwritten will, and to make arrangements for his family's care in the event of his demise. Meanwhile, his servants meticulously packed several huge trunks filled with enough necessities for ninety days of traveling. Among his belongings were a rubber mackintosh, a steamer cap, a box of medicine, and a state-of-the-art Number 2 Kodak camera. The camera was one of his prized possessions. He was absolutely thrilled to be able to capture his adventure on film.

With a hearty farewell to his wife, Jennie, and a promise to his three daughters to return with the prettiest "dollies" he could find, Frank W. Woolworth set sail on February 19, 1890, on the luxurious steamship *City of Paris.* According to the brochures, he would arrive in the port of Liverpool, England, in less than six days.

Puffed with ambition, Frank boarded the liner's expansive deck, his mind reeling with plans, his heart full of pride. He was now a man of substance. The year before, in 1889, sales from his five-and-tens totaled $247,214.26 in American dollars, with ample profits to do the Grand Tour in style.

From the very start of his trip, Frank began a routine of writing that continued throughout his pilgrimage. He wrote by gaslight, by candlelight, and by moonlight. He was determined to preserve the details of his trip for his managers and for posterity. These voluminous letters were mailed back to New York and multigraphed in the form of "General Letters" for distribution to Woolworth's employees. Reportedly, hundreds of boxes of such precious historical documents are housed in the present Woolworth Building in Manhattan. Public access to these archives is not permitted, but portions of Frank Woolworth's papers have been reprinted in numerous forums, allowing readers a glimpse into the mind of the Dimestore King.

Not surprisingly, given his frugal tendencies, one of Frank's first missives to his boys back home dealt with the topic of money. Woolworth drew a bold line between the shillings he planned to spend seeing British actress Ellen Terry star in *Dead Heart,* and the money frittered away on foreign postage. On February 20, he wrote:

> *"Postage on letters to Bremen will be five cents per half ounce, so you must use thin paper and envelopes to save expense."*

Typically, Frank did not hold back in his general letters. He expressed unabashed feelings about all aspects of his adventure, including his jarring bout with the sea god Neptune:

"On deck part of the day but awful sick from morning till night. I don't see any pleasure in going to sea. I wish I was home. Why was I such a fool to leave home? The sea is black and ugly and the ship rolls and pitches!"

Fortunately, when they passed the Fastnet Light and moved into the calmer Irish Sea, Frank fared easier. The rough seas were soon forgotten, replaced with the excitement and sights of the dry lands of Europe.

A Tour Of London . . . And Beyond

Woolworth didn't waste a moment when the liner docked in Liverpool, England. He hadn't been able to stomach a decent meal in days, so his first priority was to head into town and sample the local cuisine. His simple repast of mutton, Gorgonzola cheese, marmalade, and plum pudding renewed his vigor.

By March 1, Frank W. Woolworth was already bustling about Staffordshire investigating the pottery. He and his small band of associates managed to visit twenty-five potteries in three days. From Staffordshire, he was off to London, a city Frank especially wanted to explore.

Woolworth was temporarily discouraged by the dense coal smoke that pervaded London, which reminded him of the gritty steel city of Pittsburgh, Pennsylvania. But after enjoying an ample dinner at a fashionable restaurant on the Strand, complete with a fine orchestra and gracious personal waiter, Frank stifled his grumbling and carried on with good humor. His traveling companion, international importer, B. F. Hunt, Jr., toured with Frank Woolworth for miles, taking in the shops and penny bazaars, while Frank assessed the mercantile situation. The first thing he learned was that they did not have "stores" in England, they had "shops." They were smaller than American establishments, and often dark. An ace window dresser himself, Frank paid particular attention to the trimmings. He wrote on March 5, "The way they trim the shop windows here is new to me. They trim them close to the glass from the top to the bottom, and it is impossible to look into the store . . . [but] I think a good penny and six pence store run by a live Yankee would create a sensation here!"

Almost twenty years would lapse before the first "Wooleys" did indeed cause a sensation. In the meantime, Frank was free to hunt down wholesale bargains for resale in the United States. Throughout the trip, he left ample time for sightseeing, as well as to indulge his legendary passion for fine food. Once again, his General Letters offer a rare glimpse into Woolworth's somewhat off-handed humor:

"We took lunch in a restaurant in the Old Palace of Richard the Third in the Throne Room. The bill of fare was dated 1466, but fortunately the meats and vegetables are comparatively modern."

"Frank Causes a Stir at Westminster"

We then visited the House of Parliament, or at least looked at it from the outside, and Westminster Abbey, which I consider the greatest sight in London. The guard at the door would not let me pass until I opened my Kodak and proved to him that there was no dynamite in it! —F. W. Woolworth, 6 March 1890

To Frank, the greatest sight of all was Westminster Abbey, where he had to prove to the guards at the door that there was no dynamite in what they considered "that newfangled contraption" called a Kodak camera.

From London, Frank hopped a steamer for Holland. From there he set off for Sonneberg, where he discovered that Germany's toy and tree ornament business was positively booming. Woolworth immediately purchased thousands of items at a fraction of the usual cost. His trek to Vienna was also memorable. He referred to the city as a "regular kaleidoscope," waxing prolific about the mouthwatering pastries, stunning statuaries, and incomparable musical concerts. France was next on the itinerary, the country where his childhood dream was finally realized. He walked the same streets Napoleon once walked, and took a drive out of Paris to tour the emperor's former summer palace.

It was a hectic yet productive three months. Toward the end of his journey, Woolworth returned to London, which he commented now seemed "almost homelike." He then arranged passage on the steamship *Etruria,* which sailed from Liverpool on May 10. Shortly after dawn, the liner docked briefly at Queenstown, enabling Woolworth to take his first step onto Irish soil, in the country of his maternal ancestors. He had a grand old time in Queenstown, touring in a rollicking jaunty cart. As a special bonus, Woolworth learned a bit about his McBrier grandfather, a topic that intrigued him:

> *"We hung on [the cart] with all our might while the driver whipped up his horse and cracked jokes for us, which he seemed to be as full of as a nut of meat. I asked him if he knew my Grandfather [Henry McBrier] when he lived in Ireland. He replied: 'Oh, yes, I knew him well. He was a foine man with strait hair, curley teeth and only half an upper lip.'"*

The week-long excursion back to New York harbor was stormy and rough, and when he ultimately arrived, Woolworth admitted he was relieved to be home. "Such hugging and kissing I never got before!" he enthused. Frank's three daughters, Helena, Jessy, and Edna May, were delighted with their beautiful "dollies" from Sonneberg, although frugal Frank was less pleased that he had to pay $2.10 duty on them!

The Birth of "Woolies" in Liverpool

His experiences in Europe convinced Frank Winfield Woolworth that he should open a retail variety chain in the British Isles. Unfortunately, every time he broached the topic, his trusted associates scoffed. They questioned his decision to risk all in new, even antagonistic territory. Silently, they also wondered if their leader, then fifty-seven, was beginning to experience the daffiness of old age. It was common knowledge that most of the Brits considered him an eccentric American capitalist who would inelegantly invade their mercantile territory. But nothing, and no one, would deter Frank's spirit for foreign expansion.

He traveled overseas many times after 1890. "The more Woolworth visited England," recalled Robert C. Kirkwood, "the more impressed he became with the country, its people, and the business possibilities." One spring morning in 1909, Frank Winfield Woolworth suddenly informed his aghast New York colleagues that he was leaving for an extended trip with the express purpose of finding a suitable location for his first British store. There was to be no more discussion of the matter; he was simply going to do it.

Carson Peck, Hubert Parson, and even Frank's own brother, Charles, were not of a mind to join Frank on this particular escapade, so Frank called for volunteers among the newer members of the Woolworth ranks. Three entrepreneurs stepped forward. Fred Woolworth (Frank's third cousin), Byron Miller, a former errand boy turned company superintendent, and Samuel Balfour. They were all young, ambitious, and game for adventure, particularly after an earful of positive persuasion from Frank.

The small party set off in May 1909. It was Decoration Day (our present Memorial Day), and for this particular trip, Woolworth brought along his wife Jennie and their lovely twenty-three-year-old daughter, Jessy. Once settled in England, Frank added a Brit to the mix, young William Lawrence Stephenson. Little did Stephenson know, that he was destined to become the chairman of the British Woolworth's division, and upon retirement, one of the wealthiest men in all of Europe.

They investigated potential shop sites in Northampton, Croyden, Birmingham, and Reading, but it was Liverpool which earned the honor of hosting the first Woolworth's store. Woolworth and his colleagues scuffled to order stock, secure permits, and scout for employees. In late-night meetings, his head bowed over piles of financial sheets, Woolworth outlined his strategy.

Frank had done his homework. He knew that the working-class British were accustomed to frowning clerks and small, dark shops with limited goods. Only the richest and most fashionable enjoyed the fine shops with attentive proprietors and quality products. *His* store would change all that. It would be bright and airy, packed with so many colorful, inexpensive items that even the poorest of patrons would feel they were on holiday. Most important of all, Frank would allow his customers to browse freely throughout the premises. Frank frowned upon the colloquial Liverpool tradition of "shopping," which amounted to staring in the crowded, poorly lit windows. "The moment you go in," he complained, "you are expected to buy and have made your choice from the window. They give you an icy stare if you follow the American custom of just going in to look around the store."

Frank was determined to change all that; he informed his colleagues that his Yankee-styled "three-and-six pence" would soon have tongues wagging across Europe.

F. W. Woolworth & Co. Limited, was legally incorporated on July 23, 1909, with the startup capital financed by the American parent company. The capital amounted $50,250.00, seven percent of which was represented in the form of 5,000 preferred shares sold at $10 per share and 5,000 ordinary shares at one shilling per share. After much political and financial ado, a lease was signed on August 13, 1909, for his first British Red-Front to be located at 25 Church and 8 William Streets, Liverpool. Armed with information and capital, everything started to move along so smoothly that Woolworth became bored seeing to the last minute details. He was also exhausted, and so he decided to take his family on a short pleasure trip to Switzerland. The beauty of Switzerland impressed him, but he was absolutely horrified by the young fortune seekers who so blatantly wooed his daughter, Jessy. "These cheap titled people are after the American girl and her money," he wrote home. "You must respect their good judgment in hoping to get both money and a fine-looking wife. But the poor American father and mother over here have their troubles if they are not sympathetic with this sort of courtship!"

Meanwhile, back in Liverpool, the Woolworth argonauts were trying desperately to keep the finer details of their mercantile plans a secret until the last possible moment. They did not relish the thought of bad publicity. The atmosphere in England was not as genial as Frank had hoped. The British had already made it clear they were not fond of private enterprise, especially from a brazen upstart from America. Several prominent businessmen before Frank Woolworth had been literally run out of England in disgrace.

Naturally, word did leak out to the press. In blazing headlines, columnists compared Woolworth to the infamous showman Barnum, and warned the public against the cheap perils of his proposed penny shops. A rival competitor circulated rumors that the Americans were opening at a seaport—Liverpool—in order to be able to flee the country quickly!

Awash in bad publicity and growing infamy, the first Woolworth's store opened in Liverpool on Friday afternoon, November 6, 1909. A band concert heralded the occasion, and newly trained British clerks stood sentry behind highly polished counters. Frank had planned to be present for the premier, but was called back to New York for a business emergency. From his desk in the Stewart Building, he nervously reviewed his managers' reports and shot back replies by wire. All in all, he was pleased with the feedback, and smug in the knowledge that he'd been right all along. It seemed that unabashed curiosity had overpowered the skeptical British public: over 60,000 people passed through the first Liverpool store in the first two days.

This new marvel of Liverpool's "three-and-six" brimming over with goods you could actually handle, was a tremendous popular success. Opening day sales totaled

£562.6s.11d. Regional pottery, candy, and enamel-ware sold swiftly, and the American wares caused an outright stir. Byron Miller remembered one customer who gleefully picked up an American bathroom "gadget" (probably an ornate faucet) and cried out: "I says, wots this blasted thing for? Woota you do with it?" As the weeks progressed, the crowds continued to mob the little store.

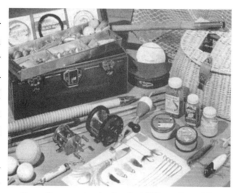

Another site was quickly leased in Preston, Lancashire, followed by a second in Liverpool. The latter heralded an opening day event that would be forever etched in the minds of its original employees and patrons: customers became so exited that a riot ensued. Shop girls swooned and several people were injured.

From the very beginning in 1909, and straight through until World War II, tools, hunting equipment, and fishing gear were among the best-selling items in the "three-and-sixpence" Red-Fronts of the British Isles.

Fortunately, the next series of store openings (in Manchester, Leeds and Hull) were more subdued.

The wonders of Woolworth's variety stores eventually reached London, prompting expansion into that great city in April 1913. That same month, F. W. Woolworth, Ltd. moved into expansive offices in Central House. For a time, the more sophisticated shoppers stayed away from what that they considered a very déclassé operation, but within a year, Frank Woolworth received reports of titled ladies and gentlemen (sometimes in disguise) slipping into "Woolies" for an odd American whatsit. He was thrilled.

The Growth of F. W. Woolworth & Co., Ltd. England

In keeping with Frank's cash-and-carry philosophy, the American F. W. Woolworth Co. never invested another pound in its British holdings. Growth and expansion derived from earnings and profits alone.

When the British division was formally incorporated in July 1909, Fred M. Woolworth became chairman of the board and managing director. Byron D. Miller was appointed director, a position held until he returned to the States in 1932 to serve as president of the American company. When Fred M. Woolworth died in 1923, British-born William Stephenson moved up the ranks to become chairman of the board and managing director.

With few exceptions, F. W. Woolworth & Co., Ltd., England managed, trained and staffed its workforce from its own country's human resources. The British division rapidly became an independently run retail operation. Of course, a majority stock interest of sixty-two percent of the ordinary shares was maintained by the American Woolworth Company—thus assuring a steady stream of earnings into the States. F. W. Woolworth & Co., Ltd. soon expanded to Ireland (April 1914) and Scotland (October 1914), where it was accepted with great warmth and enthusiasm. By 1930, virtually every major town in

This Woolworth building in Blackpool, England, featured a roof-top cafe and a large, street-level "three-and-sixpence" Red-Front.

the British Isles had a "three-and-six-pence" shop of its own.

Fred Woolworth and Byron Miller remained loyal to the chief until the day Frank Woolworth died in 1919, generally heeding his wise counsel and wishes. There was one wish, however, that they did not quite heed. It seemed that Fred Woolworth and Byron Miller were both clean-shaven Americans when they settled in London to run F. W. Woolworth & Co., Ltd. Shortly thereafter, Frank decided his boys needed mustaches to give them a look of distinction among their British colleagues. He ordered them to grow some facial hair posthaste. Fred and Byron dutifully grew mustaches, but they also shaved them off the second Frank Woolworth sailed back to the states. For years afterward Fred and Byron grew back their mustaches only when their leader was due back in England. Supposedly, Frank Woolworth never caught on.

Whether mustachioed or clean-shaven, the Woolworth, Ltd. management team led the chain into a great period of prosperity and expansion. By 1912, Frank Woolworth boasted twenty-eight British holdings—all of them operating at a neat profit, and twenty-six of them managed by Englishmen. In 1914, there was a total of 44 stores in England, Scotland, Wales, Eire, and Ireland. Another marked period of expansion ensued during the 1920s, where William Stevenson pioneered the famous "Wooleys" chainstores into South Africa and the British West Indies.

In 1931, British Woolworth's changed its status to a publicly owned company. This decreased the American Woolworth's stock interest to 52.7 percent. Nonetheless, in 1954 alone, the F. W. Woolworth & Co., Ltd., generated over $7 million (US) for its parent company. Stockholders on both side of the globe were duly pleased. Then war intervened.

Both World War I and II were devastating for the company. Records show that during World War II alone, twenty-six of the company's 766 stores were completely destroyed by enemy bombs, and 326 others were seriously damaged. Over 2,600 British male employees and large numbers of females left their jobs with Wooleys to serve in the National Service. Hundreds of women grasped the reins and carried on as managers and clerks during these harsh times. The British Woolworth's executives voluntarily contributed money to the next-of-kin of employees who were serving, to help augment the lost pay, and they made certain that copies of the company's in-house magazine, *The New Bond,* were sent to the men and women at the front. The *Christian Science Monitor* reported that, "the company's service flag was emblazoned at war's end with 5,848 stars."

After World War II ended, the Brits were tireless in their attempts to rebuild. By 1960, there were over 1,000 stores in operation, one in almost every major city of England. On the golden anniversary of the F. W. Woolworth & Co., Ltd. in 1959, Chairman John Berridge proudly hailed the efforts of post-war British to rebuild:

TIME CAPSULE MEMORY

"The Woolies' Riot in Liverpool"

On the opening day of the second store in Liverpool [1909] there was a near riot! The counters were mobbed by shawl-clad, bare-footed women in such numbers that the very sales counters were pushed about the floor; shop girls fainted; and the customers helped themselves to the goods without the formality of paying for them.

—R. John Berridge, former chairman of Woolworth Ltd., Britain

---

**F. W. Woolworth Ltd.
"Firsts"**

FIRST SHOP IN LIVERPOOL: **1909**

FIRST SHOP IN LONDON: **April 1913**

FIRST CARDIFF (WALES) SHOP: **1913**

FIRST SHOP IN DUBLIN: **April 1914**

FIRST GLASGOW (SCOTLAND) SHOP: **Oct. 1914**

In spite of the interruption of two world wars and the destruction during the second of so many important stores, the British Company bounded back and increased the number of its units at an average rate of one every eighteen days for the whole of the fifty years!

And so, Woolworth's, or "Woolies" as it was nicknamed in Britain, persevered after the war, stronger and more visible than ever before.

Remembering "Woolies": Then and Now

Just like their American counterparts, many patrons of F. W. Woolworth & Co., Ltd., England, can fondly recall their first trip to the local Wooleys for a tin soldier or a pair of warm woolen socks . . . for a composition book or "magic" painting book . . . or a pocketful of delicious penny chocolate. Many a retired early twentieth-century laborer spent leisurely afternoons at the lunch counters, sipping tea and munching on fish-and-chips, or in some shops, tasting their first American hot dog.

The decades rolled by, bringing about changes in the types of merchandise offered, as well as in the prices. In November 1940, the company was finally forced to lift its "nothing over a sixpence" policy. Regardless of this, for many years afterward, much of the merchandise was still available for under five shillings, which was then roughly equivalent to one American dollar.

During the 1950s, F. W. Woolworth & Co., Ltd. introduced its customers to the concept of self-service shopping. Slowly but surely, all the Woolworth stores changed over to self-service, doing away with the tradition of having a uniformed sales girl posted at every counter, waiting to personally help patrons. From the largest stores in London, to the smallest stores in villages, such as Cobham in Surrey, Wooleys entered the modern age. Simultaneously, the actual premises were revitalized. Sometimes this amounted to a simple paint job, while in other cases a entirely new building was created to accommodate the growing numbers of merchandise and customers. Stores, including those on High Street of Guildford and Holborn in London, experienced a major face-lift.

By the 1960s, fresh-frozen foods shared space with hot scones. Foam plastic mats replaced hand-embroidered place napkins. And, with the exception of the smallest, most remote stores, the wonderful wood counters were replaced with multitiered gondolas. The old counters were not practical anymore for displaying bulky goods like plastic washing-up bowls or large imported rugs.

Regardless of all the modernization, F. W. Woolworth & Co., Ltd. remained a colorful, bustling, amiable place to find a great bargain in the leanest of times. Wooleys was still the place to find items one just could not seem to find elsewhere. It also offered the comfort of a familiar red masthead sign for Americans traveling abroad.

In 1982, the Woolworth American parent company sold off its entire U.K. interest in F. W. Woolworth & Co., Ltd. to the Paternoster Group for £300 million. The group was known as "Woolworth Holdings" until 1989, when it changed its name to Kingfisher.

TIME CAPSULE MEMORY

"Boyhood Memories of High Street"

I still remember shopping at the local Woolworth's on High Street in our town (one of the older towns in England) and gaping at all that lovely, cut-rate merchandise. One of my favorite boyhood buys was a wonderful color map of the Front, which was issued soon after World War II. I have it to this day.
—Jonathan Gash, author of the "Lovejoy" mystery series

Today, Kingfisher is one of Europe's largest non-food retail groups. Along with Woolworth's shops, they own several large chains, such as B&Q garden centers and Superdrug health and beauty stores. Kingfisher describes its Woolworth's stores as "the high street chain for consumers' everyday shopping needs." Along with kidswear, toys, and home items, they recently added newspaper and magazines and lottery tickets to the mix. As of 1998, there were 781 Woolworth's stores and over 30,000 employees in the U.K.

Clearly, the retail baby to which Frank Woolworth first gave birth in 1909 is in good hands. Of course, many of the patrons of Kingfisher's Woolworth's are not aware of its Yankee roots. The Woolworth's abroad have developed their own personal history and style—but for Americans traveling to London, Glasgow, or Dublin, the familiar red letters of Woolworth's still offer a pleasant reminder of their own days at the five-and-dime.

In the United Kingdom, the Woolworth legacy lives on.

TIME CAPSULE MEMORY

"The Woolworth's in Stevenage"

I grew up in England in the '50's, when the currency was still pounds, shillings and pence before decimalization in the early 1970s. There was a Woolworth's store in the town of Stevenage, four miles from where I lived. It was a great treat for me when my mother took me to Woolworth's; it seemed such a large store to a 5-year-old. My greatest treat was to spend sixpence on a new pencil and a composition book, or, maybe, a "magic" painting book. Woolworth's had its own peculiar smell, probably a mix of garden products and everything else they sold, from pots and pans to hammers and plimsolls, the cheap, black tennis-type shoes we wore for gym class. The floors were scrubbed wood and the shop assistants wore rust-colored overalls and a hat. —Susan J. Pope, Freehold, Twp., N.J.

Souvenir thimble from modern U.K. Woolworth's, which are now owned by Kingfisher.

Wilkomen, Woolworth's!
The Story Of F. W. Woolworth Co., G.m.b.H.

The history of the Red-Fronts in Germany is inherently linked to Frank Woolworth's first experiences in that country during his maiden journey to Europe in 1890. From the moment he first stepped onto German soil, Frank was enamored with the country. He reveled in the cultural bounty, the musical concerts, the stunning architecture, and the beautiful hand-crafted dolls and Christmas ornaments. He was also dazzled by the shops. There were already quite a few "50-pfennig" stores, which he visited and analyzed with great fervor (50 pfennigs at that time were equal to roughly 3¢ in American money). Of one such visit in Nuremberg, he wrote:

> "We took a walk tonight, through the old city and it was very interesting indeed. Very large show windows were trimmed up in elegant taste . . . and some of the goods were about the same as those sold for 25¢ in America, and some of them could be found in our own 5 & 10 cent stores. Goods in most of the windows were displayed in fine taste with prices marked on each article."

Frank was impressed, especially when he saw just how many German natives and tourists were streaming in to these variety stores. He immediately saw an opportunity to bring his own brand of Yankee discount chain store there, which of course would offer items for even less than the going rate of fifty pfennigs. It is probable that his American colleagues scoffed at this idea, the same way they scoffed at his idea for expanding his Red-Fronts into the British Isles. So, rather than pursue this venture at that time, Frank let the matter drop. He settled for placing large orders for Christmas ornaments, marbles, dolls,

Remodeled Bremen, Germany, store, c. 1979. The first "25-&-50 phenning" Red-Front opened in Bremen in 1927.

and other German-crafted goods, which he planned on selling in his American stores by December.

Before he left Germany, Frank and his party found time to enjoy more of the local sights. His letters home were filled with details about the incomparable food and concerts, the expansive art galleries, and the beautifully dressed women. He did have mixed feelings, though, about his trip to Berlin. On April 19, 1890, he wrote from the Grand Hotel de Rome:

> *"We arrived in this handsome city last night at 9:15. Visited the Royal Palace this forenoon and the National Gallery in the afternoon. One of the great sights in Berlin are the soldiers. Today the soldiers were all called out to salute the Empress as she was passing in her carriage and nearly every person took off their hats except myself. I could see no sense in such nonsense. . . .*
>
> *Today I wandered into a show of waxed figures and while looking at a tattooed girl heard her drop a few words of English! She told me she was an American and had come to London with Barnum's show and will perform in the various cities of Europe."*

Following Frank Woolworth's first sojourn to Europe, he returned many times in the ensuing years. Many of the products he purchased in Germany became instant best-sellers in the States. He eventually opened F. W. Woolworth warehouses at 8 Lange Strausse, Fuerth in Bavaria, and in Sonneburg in Thuringia, so as to house the bounty of items he and his buyers continued to find in available in Deutschland.

The idea of expanding his Red-Fronts into Germany continued to haunt Frank, especially after he saw the tremendous success of his first store in Liverpool in 1909. At one point, he strongly encouraged "his boys" to start training promising American young men in the languages and cultures of other countries, including Germany, as a way to prepare them for future expansion overseas. However, time got away from the innovative chief, business matters in his own country consumed most of his time, and the actual idea of opening a German division was once again shelved. Perhaps one of the most pivotal reasons for Frank Woolworth not expanding into Germany during his lifetime was the onset of World War I.

For the duration of the war years, 1914–1918, both of Woolworth's German-based warehouses were closed down by the German government. This caused a multitude of problems, as the chief had begun to rely on several German imports as big sellers in his established five-and-dimes. But Frank Woolworth was not a man to let anything, even war, interfere with his profits. He quickly commissioned American manufacturers to duplicate the German dolls and tree ornaments that had become so popular, at the same time he arranged for American cottons and threads to replace the now unavailable British-made brands.

Frank Woolworth died in 1919, unable to pursue expansion into Germany. However, Woolworth's successor, Hubert T. Parson, picked up the reins and made his mentor's dream come true.

F. W. Woolworth Co., G.m.b.H. was legally formed in 1926 with a capital of Rm 3,500.000.

F. W. Woolworth of New York owned 97% of the corporation, although they planned on staffing the new division almost entirely with Germans, and stocking the stores primarily through German suppliers. The basic plan was to create hundreds of new jobs overseas, to make a healthy profit for the parent company, and to simultaneously make the "Woolworth's" name more visibly global.

In the fall of 1926, Hubert Parson sent Richard H. Strongman to Germany to organize a new branch of the company. By then, war-torn Europe was recovering from its losses, and regardless of prior differences between the two countries, it was assessed that "Yankee anything" would sell in Germany. Strongman reported back that the Germans hungered for inexpensive necessities. Luxury items were not yet a priority with the still-recovering population, so it was decided that Woolworth's in Germany would, for the time being, stock their store with a heavy dose of the same utilitarian items that had launched Frank Woolworth's empire in America back in 1879. Of course, several novelty items and luxuries such as toys were also on hand.

R. H. Strongman along with Germany's first managing director, Ivan W. Keffer and his assistant, Rudolf Jahn, scouted out sites and made all the preliminary arrangements. The very first "25-and-50-pfg" Red-Front opened in Bremen on Saturday, July 30, 1927.

The opening was as grand as any the F. W. Woolworth Company had ever staged in America, with a preopening reception on Friday complete with an orchestra and refreshments, and an "official" opening for business on Saturday.

The local *Bremen Zeitung* newspaper reported:

"An orchestra played at the pre-opening the night before and early purchasers found, with astonishment, that anything they needed could be bought. On the counters, you can buy razors for only 50 pfennig!

". . . The young mother can find nearly everything for her little darling. If the child is older and wants toys, the Woolworth Company will help again with the cheap and pretty toys. With all these above mentioned articles, the assortment is not exhausted. If you want to know exactly what you can get there, look over the displayed goods and you will be convinced."

And so, with favorable free advertising being provided by the local media through reviews, and scores of Bremen patrons raving about the unprecedented variety and bargains at Mr. Woolworth's "Yankee" shop, F. W. Woolworth Co., G.m.b.H. was on its way. Within five months, there were nine more German stores and an executive office was opened at Friedrich Ebert Strasse 6, Berlin. By December 31, 1927, the stores were bringing in half a million American dollars in sales, or about 2,100,000 German

> **Woolworth Trivia**
>
> The sites of the first nine "25-&-50-phennig" stores in Germany, c. 1927:
>
> Bremen • Berlin • Dusseldorf
> Bochum • Wiesbaden • Barmen
> Dortmund • Hamborn • Duisburg

marks. One year later, Mr. Strongman and his staff were boasting forty-seven stores and over $28,500 (U.S.) in sales. Meanwhile, back in New York City, company president Hubert Parson smiled when he saw the ample proceeds from the German holdings being funneled into the American company's bank account. From his grand desk in the Empire Room in the Woolworth Building, Parson tipped his hat to the memory of Frank, who'd had the idea for entering Deutschland so long ago.

Woolworth's in Germany continued to grow and prosper throughout the late 1920s and into the early 1930s. American F. W. Woolworth Co. was more than pleased with the sales figures; the executives overseas were becoming quite wealthy, and scores of German employees and suppliers were enjoying a steady, generous income. Woolworth's was extremely popular during this period, basking in prosperity along with several German-owned variety store chains, including Epa, Ehape, and Wohlert.

Then the bottom started to drop out of the market. Within a few years, this trouble would explode into another full-scale world war. And just like its English Woolworth's counterparts, German Woolworth's employees and stores would suffer immensely.

A privately printed company document, *Milestones of Woolworth,* prepared by John P. Nichols in 1949, offers great insight on the effects of World War II on F. W. Woolworth's in Europe.

According to Nichols, F. W. Woolworth Co., G.m.b.H. operated seventy-seven successful stores in 1932. That same year, a government policy he refers to as "the Bruening decree," was instituted in Germany. It stated that all of Germany's variety store chains, including F. W. Woolworth, were prohibited from opening any additional fixed-price stores. The ever-resourceful Woolworth's administrators managed to sidestep this policy, arguing that they already had four new sites under construction. They were begrudgingly granted permission to open these four stores, along with several more.

As Adolf Hitler started to gain power in Germany and other parts of Europe, the plight of the "25-&-50-phennigs," along with their German executives, suppliers, and employees, increased in leaps and bounds. Hitler was a rabid opponent of fixed-price chain stores, especially those owned by Americans. He viewed chain stores as a serious threat to the commercial prosperity of his homeland. "Among others courted by the politically ambitious Hitler," wrote Nichols, "were the retailers of the Republic many of whom, at this stage, were nearly beside themselves with worry over the manifest popularity and rapid growth of the one-price chains, Woolworth, Epa, Ehape and Wohlwert".

By January 1, 1933, Woolworth's Germany had moved their headquarters to Belle-vuestrasse II, Berlin W 9. The director, Mr. Richard Strongman, had resigned and passed the leadership over to Ivan W. Keffer. Keffer struggled on, doing his best to continue under the onslaught of increasingly dictatorial government controls, and of course, among the horrific consequences of anti-Semitism caused by the Nazi Party. It is also important to note that Hitler was zealously guarding all outgoing profits by then, and trying to keep all the profits from Woolworths and other retail chains, right there in Germany. In 1938 alone, the United States parent company lost Rm 5,527,217 in unrealized dividends and undis-tributed surplus earnings.

F. W. Woolworth Co. of New York, which owned 97% share in German Woolworth's, quickly voted to set aside a $6 million reserve against potential war losses. In September 1939, as the Third Reich marched on Poland, Woolworth's German manager, Ivan Keffer, was recalled to Canada by the American parent company. A limited power of attorney for the Germany holdings was given to Heinrich F. Albert and Dr. D. F. Albert, legal counsel to German Woolworth's.

After almost six years of war, an unconditional surrender agreement was signed by Germany's Reich on May 7, 1945. By this time, a total of seventy of the eighty-eight prewar Woolworth stores operating in Germany had been either completely destroyed or seri-ously damaged by bombing and fire. It took many years for F. W. Woolworth Co., G.m.b.H. to recover. The remaining employees and managers, along with a new ambitious group of employees, all banded together to put German Woolworth's back together again. They were led in this effort by Rudolf Jahn, a German who had been trained in the Woolworth organization in America and had been with the German division since its inception.

During the war, Jahn had been ordered by the Nazi government to act as custodian of German Woolworth's. According to *Milestones of Woolworth,* Jahn continued this post under the control of the Allied military government. In time, the United States Department of State issued a directive ordering the release from American military government control of all properties in the American-German Zone and in the U.S. Sector in Berlin. Once this was granted, Jahn was totally free to get German Woolworth's on track.

By the end of 1946, forty-four Woolworths were back in business. But this was a very different Germany than the one Frank Woolworth had visited in 1890. The new Germany was restructured and divided, with Woolworth's restricted to only West German localities. By 1954, they had fifty modern-looking stores, and by the time American Woolworth cele-brated its 100th anniversary in 1979, F. W. Woolworth Germany celebrated its 53rd, with 199 stores and sales exceeding $600 million (U.S.).

The German stores continued to prosper as many of the original "25-&-50 phennig" signs from the 1920s and early thirties were replaced with simple white signs, on which the word "Woolworth" was emblazoned in red letters.

Along the way, German Woolworth's Yankee origins became clouded, and for many post-

War patrons of the German Woolworth's, the variety stores were an innately German invention. Several German immigrants who arrived in America after 1960 said they were shocked to see F. W. Woolworth signs when they walked the streets of New York. They honestly believed that Woolworth's belonged exclusively to Germany. This was a similar response shared by United Kingdom patrons, who thought "Wooleys" was purely British in origin.

As with all of Woolworth's divisions, Germany had its own sales and stock preferences. Sports equipment, bicycles, leisure apparel, and home improvement lines were the biggest sellers. The larger stores even sold ladies fur coats, in many styles and price ranges. And, of course, in the Woolworth's equipped with cafeterias, the German patrons enjoyed luncheon repasts of bratwurst and fresh-baked rolls.

On September 22, 1998, Venator (formerly F. W. Woolworth Co.) announced that their seventy-two-year-old German division had been sold for $552 million. Before the end of the year, Deutsche Woolworth G.m.b.H would be in the capable hands of its own German management and Elektra Fleming, a London-based private equity group.

At the time of its sale, the division had 357 stores and 13,000 employees, and was rated one of the largest retailers in all of Germany. Although the division had experienced some losses over a period of years, the *New York Post* reported that it had shown a healthy profit of $16 million on sales of $1.3 million in 1997. Projections indicate that *Deutsche Woolworth G.m.b.H* will continue prospering, under its new management, for many more years.

In terms of the history of Woolworth's itself, the German division holds special and marked significance. By selling off its interest in the German stores, the Venator Group also sold off the last of its Red-Fronts in the world.

TME CAPSULE MEMORY FROM GERMANY

"Bratwurst and Beer at Woolworth's"

Some of the larger Woolworth's stores in Germany had counters where we could enjoy lunch. I always found it amazing, and convenient, that a family could shop for necessities like socks and yarn, and then browse over to the food area for refreshment. In Germany, we did not eat out "franks" on a bun like the Americans did. We had a plate with say, a piece of bratwurst, and beside it a warm roll and a bit of mustard. We would dip the meat into the mustard as we ate. Of course, there was always good German beer to finish off the meal. When I first came to America, I was living in New York, and one of the first things I noticed was a big Woolworth's sign. I was quite shocked, as I had always believed that Woolworth's was a German invention!

—Werner Reschmeier, Rumson, N.J.

Woolworth's In Cuba

"The republic of Cuba has taken Woolworth's to

its warm and friendly Latin heart."

—From company souvenir booklet dated 1954, several years before Castro's hostile takeover of F. W. Woolworth, Cuba

By the early 1920s, the F. W. Woolworth Co. was basking in great financial success. With his passing in 1919, the chief had left behind a multimillion-dollar legacy—the largest retail chain in America. Just across the United States' border, the Canadian division was profiting. Overseas, F. W. Woolworth & Co., Ltd. Of England was growing in leaps and bounds, and the Woolworth product warehouses in Germany and France were providing a steady stream of imports for eager American buyers.

The late Frank Woolworth's massive desk in the Empire Room of the Woolworth Building was currently being occupied by his hand-picked successor, president Hubert Parson. Charles Woolworth was installed as chairman of the board, and a talented team of managers were making sure that all the Red-Fronts were in tip-top shape. While everyone mourned the passing of their leader, Frank Woolworth (and other revered Woolworth men such as Seymour Knox, William Moore, Carson Peck, and Charles Griswold), the company's executives knew they had to carry on. World War I was finally over, and it was a fortuitous period to expand the business. This time around, company leaders looked toward one of the most notorious and prosperous resort islands in the world.

The year was 1923 and the Republic of Cuba was thriving. Thousands of wayfarers were heading to that small isle, ninety miles off the Florida coast, to enjoy the beautiful beaches, resort hotels, and legendary night life. Several American-owned businesses were already making millions on sugar and cigar plantations. Locals were cashing in on souvenir straw hats and voodoo charms. The famous and infamous, rich and poor, Samaritans and mercenaries, all thronged Cuba's hot spots twenty-four hours a day, with only a short respite for afternoon siesta. The island was a *touristos'* paradise.

One of its *touristos* happened to be Frank Woolworth's nephew, Roy Creighton, then supervisor of merchandise for the company. Upon returning from his Latin pleasure trip, Creighton presented a proposal to the board of directors on April 9, 1923. He was convinced that Havana was ripe for a Woolworth's five-and-ten, and suggested they expand into Cuba immediately.

Sensing an ideal business opportunity, Hubert Parson pressed Creighton for details. Creighton explained that he'd already scouted out several sites for the premier store. The ideal spot seemed to be 51–57 San Rafael Street in Havana. A new building was being erected there, on the busy corner of Amistad. The rental price was $24,000 (U.S.) per year plus taxes and insurance, and the landlord was open to a fifteen-year lease. After some deliberation, the board approved the proposal. Parson sent Roy Creighton back to Cuba to set up shop, this time with official power of attorney to enable him to conduct the necessary paperwork.

Hola, Habana!

The first F. W. Woolworth's on San Rafael Street was called "La Casa de 5+10 Centavos." It opened, with great fanfare, on Saturday, December 20, 1924. Its red-and-gold masthead blazed electric in the shadow of Morro Castle.

From day one, the American "centavos" was a huge hit. Expansion was swift, and by the end of 1928, there were eight such Woolworth's units on the Island. Four stores were located in Havana, with the remaining "centavos" dotting Matanzas, Santiago, Camaguey, and Cienfuegos. (Eventually, the original San Rafael store moved to the crossroads of Galiano Street, nicknamed "Sin Corner" because of the brisk prostitution trade.) The locals referred to F. W. Woolworth's as the "Ten Cent" or the "Centavo".

Unlike F. W. Woolworth, Co., Ltd. in the British Isles, which shared ownership with the parent company, the Cuban stores were owned 100% outright by F. W. Woolworth Co. of New York. The profits continued to roll in for decades, holding steady even through the Great Depression. The 1930s brought the American fascination with movie stars, hot dogs, and yo-yos right into Cuba's backyard. During the 1940s, piped-in tunes of the Andrew Sisters and Bing Crosby shared store air time with Latin mambo music. By the late 1950s, total annual sales in its eight Cuban Red-Fronts had topped $10 million (U.S.).

The late forties and fifties represented a zenith period for the small Latin subsidiary. Hula hoops and costume jewelry, radios and sewing notions, frying pans and Tangee lipsticks—were all grabbed up by bargain-hungry patrons. The candy and food service areas were always busy, and for good reason. They offered clean, modern air-conditioned dining facilities and convenient take-out service. Lunch counter ice cream was a favorite treat of local students returning from hot schoolrooms. In fact, when Woolworth's first introduced ice cream into its Havana stores, it caused a sensation among young and old alike. At first, the company had to import this delicacy, not a simple task in the pre-electric freezer days of the 1920s. The problem was resolved when Cuba started its own booming ice cream industry, inspired by the American "Ten Cent." Woolworth's

This large Havana "centavos" store, c. 1955, featured rows of circular lunch counters staffed by uniformed counter girls.

then had its own island supplier to help meet the steady demand for vanilla cones and cherry-topped sundaes.

The company's 1954 promotional booklet, *Woolworth's First 75 Years,* proudly extolled its Latin stores, stating: "The republic of Cuba has taken Woolworth's to its warm and friendly Latin heart."

Unfortunately, by 1958, not every heart in Cuba was friendly.

Woolworth's Under Siege: Castro's Takeover

The spring of 1957 was a time for celebration at the New York headquarters of F. W. Woolworth Company. Its recently remodeled Havana store was showing record sales. Preliminary plans were underway to expand further, perhaps even to branch out to other Cuban resort towns. Unfortunately, just as the Cuban Woolworth's was basking in its greatest success, its eight "centavo" sites suffered a menacing and irreversible fate. In 1958, Fidel Castro began what he called a "total war" against the Batista government. Seemingly overnight, the country changed from a popular resort to a confused center of turbulent uprisings. By 1959, Cuban President Batista had fled, seeking refuge in the Dominican Republic. Fidel Castro was left behind, a loose cannon, to take over as premier. Castro didn't waste any time capitalizing on his quarry. Relying on the strength and loyalty of armed revolutionaries, he started to expropriate all the U.S.-owned sugar mills. By March 1960, he had "nationalized" every large estate in Cuba, native or foreign-owned. One by one, he forcibly procured all nonsympathetic foreign businesses. Of course, the American-owned five-and-tens were directly in the line of fire. The United States government, and businesses like F. W. Woolworth Co., vehemently protested the continued Cuban expropriations, but to no avail. In 1961, America broke off all diplomatic and trade trade relations with Cuba.

Later that same year, Cuban-exiled rebels (covertly organized and funded by the United States) attempted an unsuccessful invasion of Cuba at the Bay of Pigs, a fiasco which was followed by the frightening Cuban Missile Crisis in 1962. Fortunately, nuclear war was averted, but Cuba officially became a Communist regime.

It is not clear what exactly was happening at the American-owned Woolworth's stores in Cuba during this period. During his address to the American Newcomen society in 1960, Woolworth President Robert C. Kirkwood, discussed the company's foreign holdings at length, including the success of its newest Latin operations in Mexico—but not one word was uttered about Cuba.

Several Cuban expatriots and former American Woolworth's employees, however, clearly remember that time in history, providing a partial picture. Apparently, Fidel Castro sent armed revolutionary troops into the eight Woolworth's stores sometime between 1958 and 1960, to "relieve" the managers of their store keys. The American staff was then ordered to leave the island immediately (in some cases, before midnight). Some employees left with only the clothes on their backs. After the nationalization of the stores, the names of the F. W.

Woolworth "Centavos" were changed to read "Variedades." When referring to a particular store, customers would include the name of the street; for example, *Variedades de Galiano.*

Castro's hostile takeover was not entirely fortuitous. The one thing that had sustained the Cuban Woolworth's was the steady influx of thousands upon thousands of items imported from America. With the trade embargo firmly in place, and the F. W. Woolworth Company's loss of its monetary stake in the Cuban stores, these shipments were terminated. The stores were never quite the same.

The present status of these eight Variedades is unclear. It is presumed that F. W. Woolworth Company has an active claim on all of their nationalized Cuban properties, just like they had in Germany during Hitler's regime. If Castro, or his successor, ever liberates the holdings, the company will no doubt take appropriate action. In the meantime, the five-and-tens in Cuba can be remembered as fondly as any other Woolworth's chain. Forty years of mercantile history are not easily obliterated, and many Cubans can still remember their earliest visits to the Havana or Santiago Tencent, where colorful dolls, tin soldiers, cars and crayons were the dreams of any child. Some say they can still vividly recall the taste of that delicious American concoction, the frozen Milkyway, or the visions of mouth-watering piles of candies piled higher than their heads. They recapture stolen moments in the air-conditioned Tencent during Cuba's summer months, and trying out that odd but fun, device called the hula-hoop. All these memories, and countless more, remain part of the Woolworth's legacy in Cuba.

TIME CAPSULE MEMORY

"Woolworth Managers at Gunpoint"

One of my Woolworth's colleagues was managing a big Havana store during the Castro takeover. He told me that one day, his Cuban "floorwalker girl," suddenly headed toward him, forcibly flanked on either side by two muscular revolutionaries sporting crossover chest bandoleers and enough gunpowder to kill everyone within four miles. Without preamble, they pointed their guns at the store manager and demanded the keys to his store. In menacing tones, they informed my fellow American that he was to go home, gather his family and get the hell out of Cuba. The floorwalker was forced to translate, but the message was clear regardless. It was time to say adios, Cuba!

—Recalled by a former Woolworth's district manager

Mexico And South America:
F. W. Woolworth Co., S. A. de CV, Mexico

Thirty years after the first five-and-dimes were established in Cuba, the famed Red-Fronts made their debut in Mexico. In 1954, Woolworth President Robert C. Kirkwood sent ambitious T. L. Crump (who had been in charge of the company's New York operations) to Tijuana to start the new division. Twelve Hispanic men were chosen to be managers and were quickly whisked over the border to California for training.

In the beginning, many of the products were made in the United States and imported into Mexico for sale. By 1960, however, 97.5 percent of the merchandise sold in the country's eight stores was being provided by 1400 different Mexican suppliers, which was a considerable boon to these business owners. Of the 650 employees working for F. W. Woolworth Co., S.A. de CV, Mexico, over ninety percent were native Mexicans. Three years later, there were a total of ten stores in place, the most expansive being the Red-Fronts in Tijuana, and in the Lindavista section of Mexico City.

By 1979, there were twenty-four Mexican holdings, and Woolworth's had also expanded into Spain and opened seven stores there. That year, under the leadership of Martin Merritt, managing director of Mexican and Spanish subsidiary, the company embarked upon a major renovation of store facilities and merchandise. They stocked more lines of sporting goods and novelty items than ever before, hoping to capture the growing market of teenagers with expendable income.

The American-owned holdings of F. W. Woolworth Co., S.A. de CV, Mexico, continued to show modest profits through the 1980s. However, the import policies and sporadic unrest in both Mexico and Spain proved draining. The Spanish division was finally sold off in the 1980's. The details of the Mexican holdings are vague, but it appears that in 1997, F. W. Woolworth Co. sold its remaining twenty-seven Red-Fronts to Control Dinamico, S.A. de CV.

F. W. Woolworth's "Down Under": The Australian Market

The Venator Group currently maintains a strong retail presence in Australia. More than twenty years ago, the F. W. Woolworth Co. started testing out a variety of shoe stores there, including Kinney, Susie's Casuals, and Williams. Business in Australia proved to be immensely profitable, and today, the Venator Group owns or controls interest in hundreds of specialty establishments "Down Under," including its profitable Footlocker stores.

However, the largest retail chain in all of Australia is Woolworth Limited. While I was writing *Remembering Woolworth's,* several of my friends who had traveled to Australia brought me back mementos and photographs of the Woolworth's stores there. They had presumed, as many people do, that the Australian Woolworth Limited was one and the same with our American company, especially given the the familiar red letters of the Woolworth Limited logo. The fact is that there is no direct proprietary connection between the two Woolworth's chains, but a little digging uncovered a strong historical connection.

Back in the 1920s, when the founders of Woolworth Limited were just starting out in the variety store business, they purposely capitalized on the success of their wildly popular overseas counterpart. The company's prospectus originally read "Wallworths Bazaar Ltd." but the founders soon decided that this name was too cumbersome and blatantly opted for plain "Woolworth." (Reportedly, this came about only after it was verified that American Woolworth's had no immediate plans to open Red-Fronts in Australia.) The founders then went a step further, and copied the style of the American mastheads, including the use of the color red in its logo and the design of the store's counter displays. American Woolworth's

"The Cuban Tencent in the 1940s and 1950s"

In my hometown of Cienfuegos, the Tencent was situated in La calle San Fernando (San Fernando Street). In the 1940s and '50s, I remember that, at night, a group of young men would hang out in front of the store to wait for their girlfriends. The store was in the middle of the block, had two entrances, three big show windows and the peculiar sign of Woolworth's. Inside, it had cubicles to show off the merchandise, and women inside the cubicles, dressed very neat, gave the service to the public. The store was always clean and you had not to ask for prices because everything was marked. During the time when the yo-yo was popular, the Tencent had a weekend show on the street with a professional man that played the yo-yo and taught different tricks to the people. The Tencent's yo-yo was the best on the market then!

Later on, I lived in Habana, where the main Tencent was on the corner of Galiano & San Rafael Streets. That corner was known as "La Esquina del Pecado" (The Sin's Corner) because the men used that central corner to make love dates. That corner was crowded all the time, with people and traffic. The Tencent had access from three different streets, and there was a wide "portal" (porch) running from the beginning up to the end of the street, on both sides, giving shade from the sun and protection from the rain.

The store was always clean and neat, it was air-conditioned and excessive with illuminations. A large cafeteria served all kinds of sandwiches, food, soda, ice cream, pizza (my favorite) and pie a la moda. The store opened at 8 a.m., closed at noon, open again at 2 p.m. and closed 6 p.m.—six days a week. Only the cafeteria stayed opened during the lunchtime 12–2 pm. Most of the lights on the store were off in that period. Across the street from the Tencent was the high class store "El Encanto," famous all around the world. "El Encanto" was destroyed by a sabotage fire after Revolution sometime in the 1960s. In that site, a park was built. I left Cuba in 1967 and went to Spain. I came to USA in 1968. It was long ago but I still remember the Tencent. —Miguel A De Dios, N.J.

was not quick enough on the draw when it came to trademarking the Woolworth name, and so Woolworth Limited of Australia continued on unhindered. Another historical connection can be found in the Australian's overwhelming response to bargain-priced merchandise, especially in the fledgling days of Woolworth Limited. The first ad (and handbills) which appeared in 1924 for "Woolworth's Stupendous Bargain Basement" in Sydney, boasted:

> "A handy place where good things are CHEAP. Really CHEAP. The CHEAPEST possible. Come and see. You'll want to live at Woolworths! From 9 in the morning till 9 at night. Woolworth's will sell what you want and sell it CHEAP."

This huge Woolworth Ltd. "Metro" store in Sydney, 1998, often causes confusion among North American tourists, who often presume it is related to the former American stores of the same name. There is no connection, but the founders of Woolworth Ltd. purposely took on the familiar American "Woolworth" name back in the 1920s to boost sales. The Venator Group (formerly the Woolworth Co.) does, however, operate hundreds of specialty and shoe stores in Australia, including Footlocker.

People responded so enthusiastically to this ad that the opening turned into a cause celebre. The next day, the papers reported that, "a wild rush of bargain hunters converged on the premises and met in violent collision, many fainting as a consequence, and the staff lunch room was converted to an emergency casualty station!" The scene was strongly reminiscent of Frank Woolworth's wild Red-Front debuts in Washington, D.C., New York City, and Liverpool.

Woolworth Limited of today bears no resemblance to the fledgling company of the old days. It has been transformed from a small variety store to a super store, more along the lines of an American Cosco or Wal-Mart. And so, even without the direct connection, the Woolworth name lives on in Australia, and the Venator Group's hundreds of shoe and specialty store holdings there reinforces the modern-day retail connection between the United States and Australia.

The Mystery Of Woolworth's In Cyprus

Along with Woolworth Limited of Australia, the popular F. W. Woolworth & Co. of Cyprus also generates retail confusion.

North American visitors to the beautiful Island of Cyprus are often pleasantly surprised to see the "Woolworth's" name on red mastheads in that country, again, often presuming that these stores are directly affiliated with the American chain. In this particular case, there is a thread of a legal connection, because by virtue of an agreement, F. W. Woolworth & Co (Cyprus) Ltd. has retained the use of the internationally-known name "Woolworth"—but that is where the connection ends. F. W. Woolworth & Co (Cyprus) Ltd. opened its first store as a purely Cypriot company in Nicosia in April 1974, and was acquired by the N. K. Shacolas Group in 1985. Today, it is the largest retail sales organization in Cyprus, operating six large, modern department stores.

The Many Faces Of Woolworth's International

The meaning of "Woolworth's International," dating from the 1890s to the present day, clearly encompasses a broad perspective. Along with its traditional Red-Fronts, the F. W. Woolworth Co. expanded globally with specialty chains like Kinney, Champs, and the San Francisco Music Box Co.

It is also important to note that Woolco, the company's mass-merchandise, discount department store chain, also played an important role in increasing the company's international scope. F. W. Woolworth Co. debuted its first Woolco in Columbus, Ohio, in 1962, and later that same year, the first Woolco opened up in Windsor, Ontario, Canada. Within a short time, there were over 100 Woolcos, and 10 Woolco catalogue stores operating in Canada. Woolco was popular in England as well; thirteen Woolco stores were operating in the United Kingdom by 1979.

The Woolco subsidiary became so prominent, both in North America and abroad, that in 1975, the Woolco and Woolworth's stores were consolidated to form one large General Merchandise Division, with

Beautiful, upscale Woolworth's store on the Island of Cyprus, 1998.

W. Robert Harris elected as its first president. Even after the Woolco stores in the United States closed down (in 1982), Woolcos in other parts of the world remained open for years afterward.

The company's Red-Fronts and specialty stores located in island resorts also fared exceedingly well. Until the end in 1997, Red-Fronts in the Virgin Islands, the Caribbean and Puerto Rico enjoyed a steady trade of tourists and locals. The U.S. Virgin Islands and Puerto Rico also hosted Kinney Shoe stores, another former subsidiary.

With the exception of Canada and the British Isles, a good deal of the company's global expansion occurred after the passing of Frank Woolworth in 1919. But the seeds for all of the company's international ventures were planted during his lifetime. Frank had the courage, and foresight, to take risks in unfamiliar, uncharted territories, and because of this, he beat hundreds of his competitors to the punch. During an interview for this book, one former Woolworth executive quipped that if Frank Woolworth had been alive to witness our first Americans landing on the moon, he would have quickly set in motion plans to expand his Red-Fronts to the solar system, venturing "where no retailer had gone before."

Chapter Seven

Transition:
From History to Nostalgia

"Frank Woolworth won a fortune, not by showing how little could be

sold for so much but how much could be sold for little."

—*New York Sun*, April 1919

The Passing of the Chief

During the years 1916 to 1919, Frank Winfield Woolworth vacillated between periods of great pride and deep despair. The pride set in each and every time he saw yet another F. W. Woolworth Co. masthead open in a major American city, or on the day he witnessed the completion of his "skyscraper" in Watertown's public square, where it had all began in 1873. When despair took precedence, Frank would immerse himself in more building. He made sweeping enhancements to his already stunning Woolworth Building in New York. He commissioned his own grandiose mausoleum at Woodlawn Cemetery and dedicated a new Woolworth Memorial Methodist Episcopal Church of Champion, New York, in memory of his parents. Meanwhile, over on "Millionaire's Row," he remodeled his estate at 990 Fifth Avenue to include an expansive marble entrance hall and a gothic-styled library.

Of all the building projects of his twilight years, his most ambitious was that of erecting the second "Winfield Hall" in Glen Cove, Long Island. The original Winfield was reduced to cinders in November 1916, the result of faulty wiring. Within weeks, Frank commissioned Cass Gilbert to design another, this one to be more lavish than its predecessor. Amazingly, the structure was completed within twelve months. It was here, in a fifty-six-room Italian Renaissance fantasy-land set on eighteen acres amidst Long Island's famed "Gold Coast," that the chief spent his declining years.

The music chamber of Winfield Hall was by far Frank's favorite place, a haven designed with perfect acoustics and a multitude of gadgets. With a flick of a switch, the room would darken, and the slow, light sounds of a symphony would be heard. As the music raised in pitch and tempo, brilliant white lights would ignite, accentuated with amber, blue, and mauve. As the compositions changed, life-sized portrait of the appropriate composer, be it Beethoven or Bach, would sweep into view. Frank would lead his guests into the music chamber and proudly watch their reactions as the music room came to life. At other times, he would sit in there alone, crying his eyes out, wishing he could turn back the hands of time.

Woolworth immersed himself in all this building almost as though he was determined to fabricate a protective armor of marble, stone, and music, an armor that could shield him from his own mortality. Of course it could not. His health continued to weaken as decades of lavish fatty dinners, fine wines, expensive cigars, and long work hours finally took their toll. He had the tallest building in the world and he had a palace as fine as Napoleon's, but Frank Winfield Woolworth had lost his emotional foundation.

It is probable that the passing of his closest colleagues and family members contributed to Frank's own relatively early demise. By the summer of 1915, he'd already buried Carson C. Peck and Seymour H. Knox. In January 1916, his general manager, C. C. Griswold died, and on May 7 of that same year he lost William Moore. The most crushing blow of all was the death of his middle daughter, Edna Woolworth Hutton.

Edna was only thirty-five-years old, of gentle but moody temperament, and gifted with a concert-caliber voice. Yet, not even her vast inheritance, her life of pure luxury, or the smiles of her daughter, Barbara, could spare Edna from the continual pain she suffered as a result of husband's philandering. Frank Woolworth had warned his daughter about Franklyn H. Hutton, but Edna had been too starry-eyed to heed her father's counsel. It was not for lack of ambition that Frank Woolworth detested his son-in-law—of this Franklyn Hutton (and his brother E. F. Hutton) had plenty. Both male Huttons were successful in the brokerage business and both had chosen their wives shrewdly. Edward F. Hutton had wed Marjorie Post, inheritor of the Post cereal fortune, and Franklyn had snared one of richest heiresses in the world in Edna Woolworth. The trouble was, that Franklyn Hutton also had insatiable appetites for liquor, gambling, and women. It was the latter that Edna's romantic heart could not bear.

The end came in Edna's suite in the Plaza Hotel in New York City, May 2, 1918. Reportedly, Edna had discovered a letter confirming that Franklyn had another steady mistress, regardless of his promises to turn over a new leaf. In response, Edna took an overdose of poison and died, dressed in her favorite white lace dress. Tragically, it was her own five-year-old daughter, Barbara Hutton, who found her mother in this state. In the weeks ahead, the newspapers reported that Edna Woolworth Hutton had died from mastoiditis (an ear aliment) but those closest to her knew better. Amidst his grief, Frank had the sense of mind to pay off various officials to hush up the truth. Little Barbara was bundled up and brought back to her grandfather's estate in Long Island, until the family could decide what to do with her. If all of this tragedy wasn't enough, Frank's granddaughter, Gladys Helena McCann, also died that year. As Frank grew increasingly tortured by his losses, his wife Jennie didn't even notice the surrounding turmoil. By then she was so senile that she enjoyed only fleeting moments of awareness, and Frank and his surviving daughters, Helena and Jessy, were forced to have their mother declared legally incompetent.

Back at the executive offices of the F. W. Woolworth Company, things were progressing at a rapid pace, in spite of the challenges of World War I. With Carson Peck gone, and Frank suffering increasing physical and emotional instability, Hubert Parson had been chosen to fill the void.

Parson, who'd started out with the company as a teenager, was recognized as a business and mathematical wizard, but he was not well liked personally. Fortunately for Parson, he had the chief's undaunted loyalty (Woolworth always thought of Parson as the son he never had), a fact which eased some of the potential tensions among Parson's colleagues. Under Parson's leadership as vice president, beginning in 1915, the company continued to grow. Sales for 1917 increased to $98 million, and that same year, a reported 900 million people passed through the doors of the Red-Fronts. In 1918, the company reached the "1,000th store mark" with the opening of its large dimestore on fashionable Fifth Avenue and Fortieth Street in New York, across from the New York Public Library. Parson's business acumen certainly pleased Frank Woolworth, and allowed the chief to rest easier when he could not personally attend to important business matters.

However, Parson's private life did cause Frank a fair amount of unneeded stress. Parson had been visibly trying to outdo his mentor for years. After Woolworth bought a large mansion on Millionaires Row, so did Parson—instructing the famous decorator, Helwig Schier, to make sure Parson's home at 1071 Fifth Avenue was even more elaborate than the chief's over at Number 990. If Woolworth bought a brand new automobile, then Parson would, too—complete with uniformed chauffeur. At first these antics amused Frank Woolworth, but as Parson's dreams of grandeur began to cloud his judgment, the situation changed.

In June 1918, Hubert Parson purchased Shadow Lawn, a palace in West Long Branch,

New Jersey, close to the resort Asbury Park. Shadow Lawn had been used as a summer house for the American presidents, including Woodrow Wilson. Parson paid $800,000 for the mansion, with the hopes of presenting his wife, Maysie, with a proper summer cottage. As a special perk, Shadow Lawn was larger and more elaborate than Woolworth's estate in Glen Cove. Perhaps sensing that Parson's extravagance was destined to be the younger man's downfall, Frank Woolworth shook his head. "I will be blamed for this," moaned the chief.

Meanwhile, the Woolworth empire continued to rise in size and net worth, as its head steadily declined.

It was inevitable—the passing of the chief—but when it finally happened it still left millions of people in a state of suspended disbelief.

His teeth were his undoing. Over the years, Frank Woolworth had developed a morbid fear of dentistry, a paranoia which had increased after he learned that dental problems were one of the reasons for the death of his old friend, William Moore. Frank's doctors warned him that his teeth and gums must be surgically remedied, and steady treatments instituted, lest severe septic poisoning would set in. Frank disregarded their warnings and his infections raged on.

Frank Woolworth's last work day in his Empire Room in the Woolworth Building was April 2, 1919. Feeling under the weather, he left the office early for his Fifth Avenue home, but still managed to take care of some paperwork the following morning. By the time he reached Winfield House that Friday, Frank was complaining of a painful sore throat and experiencing severe chills. He went to bed directly after dinner, but his fever raged all weekend. On Sunday he was actually unconscious for several hours. The doctors saw the seriousness of the situation, attributing it to septic poisoning, along with gallstones and uremia. Frank's daughters were summoned to Winfield Hall. His wife, Jennie, remained unaware, quietly seated in her rocking chair.

Frank awoke and rallied for a short time, but on Monday, he fell into a deep state of unconsciousness. He died at 1:50 A.M. on Tuesday, April 8, 1919, five days before his sixty-seventh birthday. The word spread like wildfire in the business district of New York: The King of the Five-and Dimes was dead.

On April 10, Frank Woolworth's body was carried to New York City, where an emotional service was held in the Music Room of his Fifth Avenue mansion. The F. W. Woolworth company offices were closed for four days as employees tried to come to terms with the passing of their chief. Even S. S. Kresge, one of the all-time rivals of Frank Woolworth, closed the Kresge five-and-dimes for an hour.

Although Frank had commissioned a private mausoleum in New York's famous Woodlawn Cemetery, it was not yet completed, so his body was placed in a private vault in another part of the grounds. In time, however, Frank would be laid to rest in the impressive Woolworth memorial in Woodlawn, a resting-place shared by hundreds of luminaries such

as La Guardia, Jay Gould, William Dodge, Pulitzer, and Hammerstein. Frank's daughters, Jessy and Helena, as well as Frank's "unofficial son," Hubert Parson, were the named executors of the Woolworth estate. They learned that the only legal will was the one Frank had handwritten back in 1890, before his maiden trip to Europe. The document bequeathed all of Frank's riches to his wife, Jennie, who was now incompetent. Frank had had his lawyers draw up a new will, but he'd carried it around for months before he died, and never signed the document. It took a long time to clear up the confusion. Frank Woolworth had died a millionaire many times over; his personal property alone was worth $29 million, with additional private real estate totaling $847,000. He also owned twenty-five percent of the Woolworth Company's common stock (another $13 million or so) and had paid for the $13.5-million Woolworth Building outright. He left behind two mansions full of priceless artifacts and artwork; his cigars alone were worth hundreds of dollars apiece. Since Jennie was still alive, and would remain so for another four years, Winfield Hall remained temporarily intact, but the Fifth Avenue mansion was mortgaged to pay for the eight million dollars worth of estate taxes. As Frank's daughters grappled with the estate, the executives at the Woolworth Building met to decide the best strategy for carrying on.

F. W. Woolworth's Moves Into the Modern Age

With the passing of Frank Woolworth in 1919, only three of the original founders survived: Charles Woolworth, Earle Charlton, and Fred Kirby. Charlton and Kirby remained directors and vice presidents, Charles Woolworth became chairman of the board, and Hubert T. Parson rose to the ranks of company president. Together, these men led the F. W. Woolworth Co. away from World War I, through the Great Depression, and on to the company's fiftieth anniversary. In 1929, the company boasted 1,825 Red-Fronts and $303 million in sales. When Hubert Parson retired in 1932, Byron D. Miller stepped into the role of president. During Miller's reign, the ten-cent price limit on merchandise was increased to twenty cents. This was a major step in bringing the F. W. Woolworth Co. into the modern age. Over the next few decades, many of the traditional concepts that Frank Woolworth had spearheaded continued to be implemented, but the company did change their marketing strategy. Ads for F. W. Woolworth Co. stores and products started appearing regularly in magazines and newspapers. Commemorative books were issued beginning in 1919 and continued to be issued ever major anniversary through the 100th in 1979. Color catalogs and mail order became commonplace. (There was even a brief foray into radio and television sponsorship.) In 1962 alone, president Robert Kirkwood approved some 40 million print lines of paid advertising. Paid advertising was one area that Frank Woolworth had always resisted, but the world was changing fast, and the F. W. Woolworth Co. executives knew they had to keep up with the times. They continued to accelerate their promotion and opened more Red-Fronts and specialty stores. By the mid-1960s, the name "Woolworth's" was known all over the world.

Woolworth Trivia Box

The First Ten Presidents of the F. W. Woolworth Co. and the Years They Reigned

1. Frank W. Woolworth (1879–1919)
2. Hubert T. Parson (1919–1932)
3. Byron D. Miller (1932–1935)
4. Charles W. Deyo (1935–1946)
5. Alfred L. Cornwall (1946–1954)
6. James T. Leftwich (1954–1958)
7. Robert C. Kirkwood (1958–1964)
8. Lester A. Burcham (1965–1969)
9. John S. Roberts (1970–1974)
10. Edward F. Gibbons (1975–1977)

Noticeably absent among the lists that made up the company ranks throughout the twentieth century are the names of the children and grandchildren of Frank and Jennie Woolworth. Frank was survived by two daughters and six grandchildren but, as biographer James Brough pointed out, "the inheritors of his millions behaved as though they preferred to forget how it had all been made in nickels and dimes, the same source as the dividends that flowed in every three months, as dependable as a tide table." Although Woolworth's daughters, Jessy and Helena, served on the board of directors for many years, this was more a perfunctory privilege. Not one of Frank's descendants took an active interest in the daily operations of the company. Instead, they pursued elaborate lifestyles, which, in some cases, were their undoing. Jessy Woolworth Donohue's husband, James Sr., and her son, Jimmy, committed suicide. Both men lived fast lifestyles, indulging in liquor, gambling, drugs, social climbing, and a preference for young chorus boys. Jessy's other son, Woolworth (Wooly) Donohue enjoyed the high life, especially given his marriage to Gretchen Wilson Hearst of Virginia, the former wife of John Randolf Hearst. Jessy Donohue was the most exuberant of all Frank's daughters; she purchased several private railroad palace cars, including one called *Japauldon,* which she gave to her husband on a lark. She lived in Wooldon Manor in Southampton, Long Island, and had a Palm Beach mansion called Cielito Lindo. Jessy's tastes ran to Russian sables and expensive jewelry. She died in 1971.

Barbara Hutton, born 1912, the daughter of Edna and Franklyn H. Hutton, grew up to

Woolworth heiress, Barbara Hutton welcomes her family to Paris for her wedding to Prince Alexis Mdivani in June 1933. *Left to right:* Wooly Donahue, Mrs. Irene Hutton (Barbara's step-mother), Jimmy Donahue, Jessy Donahue, Barbara Hutton and her father, Franklyn Hutton. Mdivani was the first of Barbara Hutton's seven husbands.

become one of the richest women in the world, and one of the unhappiest. After her mother Edna's suicide, her father, Franklyn ushered Barbara off to a series of boarding schools until she came of age and inherited almost $50 million. Barbara married seven times, but died virtually alone in 1979. She did have one son, Lance Reventlow (from her marriage with Count Kurt Haugwitz-Reventlow), but Lance had died tragically in an air crash in 1972. He was thirty-six.

Frank's eldest daughter, Helena Woolworth McCann, lived a more sedate and gracious life. The McCanns spent much of their time in their country home, Sunken Orchard, located in exclusive Oyster Bay, Long Island. Helena and Charles also devoted much of their time to fund-raising events, and for a short period, Charles McCann served on the board of directors for the F. W. Woolworth Co. Helena died in 1938. Of her three surviving children, Frazier was a gentleman farmer in Connecticut; Constance married Willis Roseter Betts Jr., and Helena married Winston Guest, a well-known polo player. All of the McCann children were considered generous. In 1963, for example, Frazier and his sister, Helena McCann Charlton, were the major contributors of the Woolworth Center of Musical Studies in Princeton, New Jersey, which they named in memory of their grandfather. However, neither Frazier, Constance, nor Helena became involved in the F. W. Woolworth Co. business.

Instead, the line of ascension at the Woolworth company was composed of the descendants of Frank Woolworth's partners. Charles Woolworth served as board director until his death at age ninety in 1949; the final thirty years of his service the most productive and noteworthy of his career. His sons, Fred and Richard were involved with the company for many years thereafter. Carson Peck's son, Fremont, became a director, and another Peck acted as vice president. Allan Kirby, son of Fred Kirby, and Fred Kirby II also played a role, as did Seymour Knox Jr. and Seymour Knox III. Two generations of Charlton men also followed tradition. By 1993, however, the year of the first wave of Woolworth's Red-Front closings, not one descendant of any of the founders were sitting on the board of directors.

And what of Frank's unofficial "son" Hubert T. Parson? Hubert and his wife Maysie continued their spendthrift lifestyles, with grand homes in Manhattan, Paris, and "Shadow Lawn" at the New Jersey shore. In 1927, Shadow Lawn burned to the ground and had to be completely rebuilt. In doing so, Parson lost control of his dreams for grandeur, and his finances. He spent $10 million on the estate's 96 new rooms. Shortly after it was completed, he lost the property. (In 1939, the estate deeded to the Boro of Long Branch for nonpayment of taxes at the nominal bid of $100.) When he reached the age of sixty, the traditional (but flexible) "retirement" age for Woolworth's executives, the board did not ask him to continue on. Parson died, a broken man, in 1940. Today, Shadow Lawn is the administrative office of Monmouth University, and meticulously maintained. In a fitting scenario, it was used as the set for Daddy Warbuck's mansion (allegedly of Millionaires Row in Fifth Avenue) for the movie *Annie,* but Parson's real-life home on Millionaires Row was lost during the Great Depression.

Of Frank Woolworth's legacy, his Fifth Avenue complex was torn down in 1925, replaced by apartment houses. The Woolworth Building was sold in 1998, and its historical preservation remains uncertain.

Hubert T. Parson's estate, Shadow Lawn, was purposely designed to outshine the mansions of his mentor, Frank Woolworth. The grand foyer pictured above was featured in the film *Annie* (1982).

The priceless antiques of Frank's Empire room were long ago auctioned off, except for the few in storage. Winfield Hall still survives, however. It is presently owned by a large pharmaceutical company, and still remains, as author Monica Randal said, "The grandest of grand North Shore palaces. [It is] a house that would have dazzled Gatsby himself."

The vast 118-year-old history of the F. W. Woolworth Company was transported into the realm of nostalgia when the last of the Red-Fronts were closed in 1997 and the name of the company was changed. And although the newly structured Venator Group continues to be a force in the business world, it is a company focused on the future; its current executives prefer not to dwell on, or even remind people of, the company's past. In spite of this, strong memories of what Frank Woolworth and his partners created still exist in the minds and hearts of millions of people. Along with these remnants from the past, we have also been left with words of wisdom from the Merchant Prince himself. A few years before Woolworth died, a reporter asked Frank to summarize the secret of his success. After much ado, he finally came up with seven business tips, which, when reviewed these ninety years later, still stand the test of time.

1. Of course you will be discouraged. But keep on.

2. If you believe in an idea, give it a chance. Some of my first stores failed because I placed them in the wrong part of town. There's always a right location. Find it.

3. Everybody likes to make a good bargain. Let him. Small profits on an article will become big profits if you sell enough of the articles.

4. I believe in doing business by and with cash. Large credit is a temptation to careless buying.

5. Supervise details, but don't allow them to absorb you. Don't waste the time of a high-prized organizer on a clerk's job.

6. I prefer the boy from the farm to the college man. The college man won't begin at the bottom to learn the business.

7. There are plenty of opportunities today. Many young men fail because they are not willing to sacrifice. No one ever built a business on thoughts of having a good time.

Much has been written about Frank W. Woolworth over the years, attempting to unravel the complexities of the man, and the merchant. But one of the most poignant of all came from writer Frank Crane, who, back in 1919, said of Frank Winfield Woolworth: "All his wealth was built up from nickels and dimes. He saw the vast dynamic of multitudes. [Yet] it is not because of the money he accumulated that we honor him, it is because he did things; he was a creator, a maker; in him also was the unconquerable flame."

PART THREE

REMEMBERING . . .

THE STORES!

Chapter Eight

Those Fabulous Lunch Counters!

"Approximately 1,900 food retailing operations in Woolworth and Woolco stores across the U.S. serve over a million customers a day in settings ranging from stand-up snack bars to cafeterias and coffee shops with waitress service."

—F. W. Woolworth Co. 100th Anniversary Booklet, 1979

A Little Soup With Your Parakeet?

Where in the world could you pick up a spool of thread, a tub of car wax, and, if so inclined, a green parakeet, and then dash over a few aisles for a bowl of steaming vegetable soup? At F. W. Woolworth's of course!

It seemed like they were always there, the long lunch counters and twirling red vinyl stools; a capped waitress ready to serve up a grilled cheese sandwich or ice cream soda after a five-and-ten shopping spree. Tantalizing signs lined the back wall, heralding the daily fare: steaming coffee, malted milk shakes, apple pie á la mode, baked muffins, pizza, tuna salad with a pickle wedge, banana split house boats, fresh-squeezed orange juice, even chicken chow mein on a bun.

For cost-conscious consumers, Woolworth's eateries were a great boon. When the company's first official "Refreshment Rooms" opened in 1910, nothing on the menu cost over ten cents, and until World War II, hungry patrons could still get a complete meal for a quarter. It was great bargain, and remained so even after inflation made coffee 50¢ a cup, and a plate of scrambled eggs and home fries skyrocketed to $1.50.

From the beginning, resourceful managers made sure that regional favorites were

Woolworth's lunch counter, c. 1945, Red Bank, N.J.

available. In Georgia, one could enjoy a thick slice of peach pie; in Puerto Rico, a bowl of rice and beans; and in Tennessee, a heaping plate of biscuits and gravy. One of Santa Fe's best sellers was Frito Pie, a blend of spicy chili sauce, beans, and cheese, served on a bed of crunchy Frito corn chips. Indeed, when, after sixty-two years, the Santa Fe Plaza site closed in 1997, the locals were very upset. The mayor was no exception; for years, several times per week, she had enjoyed this exclusive Woolworth's lunch treat, which had been dreamed up by a resourceful Woolworth employee. Reluctant to let the era of the five-and-dime pass, several private citizens purchased the building where Woolworth's once existed, and reportedly there is now a small five-and-dime section still serving up tasty Frito Pie.

F. W. Woolworth variety stores were always located in a central area, making a trip there ultraconvenient. If you were en route to work during a frigid New England winter, you could always slip into F. W. Woolworth's for a cup of hot coffee and an English muffin; or, if in Hollywood, you could escape the heat with a cool orangeade. From coast to coast, Woolworth's snack bars were ready to invite you in.

TIME CAPSULE MEMORY

"Me and Gram"

When I was a child I used to go to the Woolworth's near my house in Dover, Delaware to buy doll clothes with the money I saved. It was wonderful when my grandmother from the Bronx visited and took me, without my brother and sister, to have a special lunch at the counter. I often had grilled cheese, but the main treat was two pieces of chocolate cake with vanilla ice cream between them and topped with chocolate sauce. I don't know what was the best part—being alone with Grandma, the thrill of eating on a stool at the lunch counter, or the great ice cream dessert!

—Ronna B. Feldman

Overseas, Woolworth's in Ireland was the perfect place to enjoy shepherd's pie after shopping for the children's school supplies. The runaway favorites in pre-Revolution Cuba included American pizza, Coca Cola, and cream-filled doughnuts. Many West German towns did a bustling lunch-hour business in bratwurst, sauerkraut, and beer.

In its heyday, Woolworth's counters were so busy during breakfast and lunch that there were often long lines. Considering the plethora of restaurants that now line our city streets and highways, it might be hard to imagine that type of crowd gathering in a plain old five-and-dime store. Yet, the fact is, it took a while for McDonald's, Burger King, White Castle, and Taco Bell to corner the market. Between 1970 and 1995, fastfood restaurants increased by 159%, but before 1970, F. W. Woolworth bakeries and luncheonettes (as well as the counters of rival five-and-dimes) were often the only reasonably priced, fast-service eateries in town.

During the 1960s, Woolworth's also introduced Harvest House restaurants in American shopping malls, and Red Grilles in their Woolco stores. By then, approximately eighty percent of F. W. Woolworth variety stores were equipped with some type of eatery. Some had small counters seating ten, while others could seat over 300. There were stand-up counters, sit-down counters, full-fledged cafeterias, bakeries, and simple soda fountains. Denver, Colorado, was home to one of the largest Woolworth's in the world, and appropriately, the largest food center. That particular site offered a gigantic cafeteria that was a precursor to the familiar "food courts" of today's shopping malls.

All combined, this resulted in the need for millions of burger patties, cheese slices, potatoes, and maraschino cherries, which enabled the F. W. Woolworth Company to reign as one of the largest purveyors of prepared foods in the world for half a century.

When I interviewed former patrons for *Remembering Woolworth's,* the vast majority of responses concerned food. It was soon evident that these ran deeper than simple memories of grilled frankfurters or a handful of walnut fudge. For many families, especially those living in rural communities between 1930 and 1960, eating at Woolworth's on Saturday afternoon was a tradition. It was part of the weekly lifestyle, right up there with Sunday church and Monday wash day. Often, the lunch counter took on the role of a central meeting place for members of the community, or a place of solace for the elderly. Across America, and overseas, the local Woolworth's luncheonettes became a community within a community.

The red twirling stools of Woolworth's were always busy during lunchtime in this Midwestern city, c. 1939.

Across America, Woolworth Luncheonettes and Restaurants Were Popular Places to Relax After a Shopping Spree.

There's a more contemporary feel to this mall-based Woolworth's restaurant in Virginia.

Denver, Colorado's Chuck Wagon food court could serve 700 people at a single sitting. The area contained a large cafeteria, a luncheonette with stools and booths, waitress service, a take-home baked-goods center, a gourmet deli, and a fruit juice facility.

Gossip, Love, and Scandal on Main Street, U.S.A.

The F. W. Woolworth lunch counter was a place to meet friends after school, to swap office gossip, or to learn who just dyed their hair platinum blond or who had a new baby. It was a place to dash in during lunch hour to replace your snagged stockings, then buy a bag of fresh-roasted peanuts or potato chips on the way out. As depicted in the movie, *Come Back to the 5 and Dime, Jimmy Dean, Jimmy Dean* the counters were a favorite gathering place for teenagers in the 1940s and '50s.

The local Woolworth's lunch counter often blossomed into a veritable "love central," the ideal place to meet the man or woman of your dreams. Hundreds of women met their future husbands while employed as Woolworth's waitresses. Sometimes, the young men were regular soda fountain customers; in other cases they were Woolworth's stockboys enjoying an afternoon snack break. And, many Woolworth's managers (who were almost exclusively male, even well into the 1970s) first became enamored of their significant other while watching her serve up portions of "Adam and Eve on a Raft," decked out in that fetching apron and cap. On the other side of the counter, teenage boys and girls would share ice cream sodas, gazing dreamily into each other's eyes.

During leaner times, when America was plunged into the Great Depression and World Wars, these memories also portrayed silent sacrifice. Many a struggling mother took her child to a Woolworth's counter for a sandwich and slice of apple pie while she slowly sipped a cup of tea. It wasn't until years later that those children realized their parents didn't order food for themselves as well, because they couldn't afford even that simple luxury. In small and large towns alike, siblings would routinely pool their money for a heaping dish of vanilla ice cream, served in a silver dish, topped with whipped cream and a maraschino cherry.

Of course, it was not always calm at the counters. There was that memorable day in 1938 when a waitress in Chicago got so mad at her beau for flirting with a pretty lunch counter customer that the waitress dumped an entire ice

---

TIME CAPSULE MEMORY

"Lunch Counter Tableaus"

I remember the popcorn machine, just inside the door, of the big Woolworth's on Connecticut Avenue in Washington, D.C.; its lights bright, and buttery popcorn spilling into the glass box . . . the white paper bags, nickel popcorn smelled so good, left your mouth salty and your hands greasy. And the lunch counter! At the lunch counter you could sit on leathery stools and order from a menu. Hot dogs and milk shakes and a new drink called Coca Cola . . . coffee with cream in little pitchers, ice cream . . . doughnuts, the shiny glazed kind and the white powdered confectioner's sugar kind. Red catsup and bright yellow mustard on the counter, along with glass bowls filled with tiny cubes of sugar. Hurried men sat at the counter, grabbing a piece of pie and coffee; tired women sat at the counter, feet throbbing and resting on top of their shoes; wrinkled brown shopping bags beside them, having salad and iced tea. —Elizabeth Contessa Heine

cream float over his head. One former patron from Kansas recalls a Saturday afternoon when a fellow citizen, totally overwrought because her pet representative for town council president did not win the election, caused a messy scene at F. W. Woolworth. When the winning opponent sat down at the lunch counter for a midday meal, the irate citizen dashed behind the counter, grabbed the drinking dispenser hose, and soaked the poor man from head to toe.

In retrospect, it seems as though those Formica counters, with their laminated menus, were always part of our Main Streets. But in fact, food did not appear in Woolworth's, in any shape or variety, for many years after Frank Woolworth opened his first successful store in 1879. (This is rather curious, considering Frank Woolworth's legendary personal appetites.) The actual lunch counters, bakeries, and soda fountains, which were responsible for so much of the chain's popularity, evolved rather slowly, throughout the decades of F. W. Woolworth's history.

Woolworth's "Food" Firsts: Candy, Soda Water, and Ice Cream

The first official food sold at a F. W. Woolworth was neither chicken soup, grilled hot dogs, nor ice cream—it was candy.

Back in 1886, shortly after Frank moved from Lancaster, Pennsylvania, to a small office on Chambers Street in Manhattan, he did two notable things. First, he devised and placed the historic "Diamond W" trademark on his door, and second, he began beating the pavements in search of cutrate bargains. One of the bargains he was seeking was candy, but every reputable confectioner he visited quickly sent him packing. Woolworth didn't have the capital, or the need, to buy candy in great bulk. He wanted to start by test marketing candy in his established stores, and that meant a purchase of just a few hundred pounds. Further, all of his "partner-managers," including Satterthwait, Hesslet, Wood-

WOOLWORTH'S
Fountain and Lunch Departments Offer

FOODS...Prepared from the purest, freshest ingredients the markets provide.

SERVICE...Quick — efficient — courteous.

PRICES...Woolworth's low prices prevail.

One of our many Values
ROAST TURKEY DINNER

Roast YOUNG TURKEY with Giblet Gravy
Parsley Dressing • Cranberry Sauce
Fresh Buttered Vegetable
Creamy Whipped Potatoes
Hot Cloverleaf Roll and Butter
25 Cents Complete

worth, Knox, and McBrier, were skeptical about selling perishable goods, especially in a five-and-ten store. There'd been a recent scare when irresponsible candy makers had used toxic ingredients to color their hard candy, and the market for hard candy was lax. Fine chocolates were always popular, but much too expensive. Fortunately for the future of the company, Frank's partners relented, and decided to encourage the chief's pursuit of candy bargains. But there was yet another impediment to Frank's dreams of satisfying America's sweet tooth: the jobbers.

Woolworth was not a man who liked to waste money, and he knew if he secured his merchandise through jobbers, that was exactly what he would be doing. In those days, the East Coast jobbers were the supreme middle-men. They purchased material and perishable goods directly from the manufacturers, and purposely kept the turnaround prices to merchants extremely high. The same rule applied to candy. Small chain owners like Frank Woolworth didn't have a chance, especially with current wholesale candy costs running between 25¢ and a dollar per pound. He wanted to sell candy retail for 5¢ per *quarter* pound, and he wanted to eliminate the jobbers and buy direct from the manufacturers. Woolworth believed that, if the idea caught on, everyone would benefit by making a profit on repeat, quantity sales. The problem was, whenever he proposed this scenario, large merchants and small, private candy makers alike would laugh heartily and hand him his hat.

Frank was not, however, a man to give up easily. One afternoon he was strolling down Wooster Street, west of Broadway, when he walked into the tiny shop of a confectioner named D. Arnould. For the hundredth time in months, Frank boldly shared his idea, expecting Arnould to scoff, or at least tell him to deal directly with a jobber. Arnould did neither. Instead, he told Frank to come back the following day. When Frank returned, he was pleasantly surprised when Arnould showed him several varieties of candies that could be sold for 20¢ a pound. The profit margin would be minuscule, but Arnould agreed it might just pan out.

That day, Woolworth made his first wholesale candy purchase: five hundred pounds of mixed chocolates, chocolate creams, marshmallows, and fine hard candies. He chose five of his eight stores to test-market the new item, with each

---

TIME CAPSULE MEMORY

"A Former Candy Girl Remembers . . ."

Working at the Woolworth's candy counter was an exciting experience for a girl of fifteen back in the 1940s. It was my very first job, World War II was just about over, and the Red Bank store was filled with GI's just returning home. They were handsome and anxious to flirt with the Woolworth's counter girls and we enjoyed it! When I was hired, the manager said I could eat as much candy as I wanted. This was a shrewd and effective ploy, because after a few days of eating chocolate I never wanted to eat another bite! I remember I was given a little hammer to break small pieces of candy off this huge five-pound block. The candy counter was always one of the busiest places in the store. The aroma of all that candy was wonderful!

—Marie Ring, Middletown, N.J.

30

Sweet Suggestions from Woolworth's

Famous candies by Schrafft's . . . covered with rich
milk chocolate. In this sweet-tooth delicious selection,
at your nearest Woolworth's Candy Department:

Operas—delightful miniature creams
Montevideos—luscious creams, walnut-topped
Ice cream drops—sizeable, succulent creams
Vanilla caramels—choice and chewy
Nougatines—soft, spongy, sugary
Maple cream walnuts—creams with walnut meats
Chips—crunchy molasses filling

25¢ quarter pound   **95¢** full pound

SCHRAFFT'S
CHOCOLATES

Heaps of hard candy for
Christmas! It's as much a tradition
at Woolworth's as it is in your
home . . . to have heaps of hard
candy on hand. For everyone
loves bowls brimming and stockings
bulging with these colorful,
delicious sweets.   29¢
pound

By Bonomo-Korday Co.,
Peerless Confectionery Co.

A myriad of chocolate-brands, including Schraffts, were available in all the Woolworth's stores, but some treats were exclusive to particular regions. One type of hard, cherry-filled candy was only sold in Philadelphia, and "Peach Buds" a hard-shell peanut-butter-filled candy, were only available in New England.

store being allocated one hundred pounds apiece. He advised his dubious managers to display the candy on attractive glass trays, settled atop the rough hewn shelves, and to watch for the delivery of their newly purchased weight scales. Signs were made up reading: "Candy, 5¢ a quarter pound."

The following Saturday, the stores simultaneously started selling candy. By that evening, every last piece was gone. Woolworth smiled smugly when he heard the news. He'd had one of his "feelings" that candy would be popular: Who could possibly resist a chocolate treat for a few pennies? Back in New York, Mr. Arnould, the man who had taken a chance on Frank, started making a tidy profit, as customers in Pennsylvania, upstate New York, and Trenton, New Jersey, demanded more and more candy. As the F. W. Woolworth syndicate expanded from a handful of stores to hundreds, Arnould's Wooster Street company also expanded, and eventually found housing in a great factory on Canal Street. Several other candy makers, who had been struggling along selling lemon drops and bon bons to jobbers, became direct distributors to Woolworth. Many of them, including Arnould, became fabulously wealthy in the process. In those days, it paid off to attach oneself to Frank Woolworth's star—even if others believed his ideas were out of this world, or that he was out of his mind. In the ensuing years, manufacturers of everything from Christmas garlands to stationery would forgo the middle-men and deal direct with Woolworth. As a result, they too became millionaires. In the meantime, it didn't take long to figure out that the closer he kept his candy to the front door, the better his profits. The tantalizing aroma and vision of chocolate would lure people in to sample a quarter pound, then continue shopping for other articles. Candy fast became one of the features of Woolworth's, especially around the holidays.

When Frank opened up his first Brooklyn store on Fulton Street in 1885, he invested extra money in the candy display, installing four incandescently illuminated showcases. This type of lighting in a five-and-ten was considered revolutionary, and it worked to impress. With the displays in place, he focused on his employees. Woolworth set high standards for all his counter girls, who made up the majority of his workforce, but the candy girls were under special scrutiny. Since he couldn't be everywhere at once, Woolworth hired Charles G. Griswold as store inspector. Griswold, who was quickly dubbed "Old Eagle Eye" by the managers, wrote this report about one store's candy display:

"Shades and mirrors clean but the shades on the lights were an exception. The candy girl wore one of the dirtiest aprons I'd seen for some time and her hair looked like 'sloppy weather.'"

To which Woolworth promptly responded:

"Glad the inspector called the manager's attention to the untidy appearance of the candy girl. I wish to impress on every manager to put the neatest, cleanest and most attractive girls behind your candy counter, as it surely helps to increase sales."

And so, they did, from thereafter.

By the turn of the new century, many more varieties of confections had been added, making the candy center impossible to resist. Customers were treated to a colorful menagerie of lemon drops, lollipops (or "lickers"), novelty candies, mints, bob bons, jelly beans, chocolate-covered pecans, and fudge of every kind. The candy counters eventually expanded to full-blown candy and nut centers, and, during the 1950s, to centers with modern glass candy carousals. Snacks such as hot roasted peanuts and popcorn soon enhanced the sweet center. Some people still recall buying fresh-roasted potato chips for twenty-five cents a shopping bag, savoring every bite of the chips' crunchy, salty, greasy decadence.

Without a doubt, one of the biggest boons to Woolworth's candy business was chewing gum. Commercial chewing gum, in one form or another, had been around since the Civil War era, but around 1914, this little item reached new levels of national popularity. Woolworth was ready to meet the demand, and added it to his candy orders. In 1919 alone, the year of Woolworth's death, he'd sold 14 million packages. These numbers increased steadily as Prohibition took form, the years when clove-flavored gum (which hid the smell of alcohol on the breath) became the rage of genteel and working classes alike. By 1950, the company was reporting candy and gum sales of 250 million pounds per year.

TIME CAPSULE MEMORY

"Roasted Potato Chips, Five-and-Dime Style"

Before we were married, my husband and I used to go to the Woolworth's on Newark Avenue, in Jersey City, New Jersey, which was always a very busy store. My favorite treat there was hot-roasted potato chips. I can still remember the aroma of these crispy chips. The potatoes were sliced paper thin and then roasted in a large glass square machine, similar to a popcorn machine. They were really large potatoes, and so the chips were sometimes the size of your hand! You would get them by the pound (for 25¢ a pound, I think) and the server would place them in a small brown shopping bag. By the time you got down the street, the bottom of the bag was all greasy and so were your hands. These chips were wonderful and I have never seen these anywhere since.
—Mrs. Elaine De Risi, N.J.

Candy had made such a big splash in 1886 that Woolworth speculated that other types of foods and refreshments might also please his customers. He experimented over the next twenty years. Unfortunately, not every attempt at merchandising food was successful.

The first major disappointment occurred in 1897, when Frank introduced a limited line of "Woolworth's Diamond W Pure Foods" in five stores. The particulars of this venture are unclear, but it is presumed these were simple canned or bottled goods that Woolworth had produced exclusively for his Red-Fronts. The "Pure Foods" concept enjoyed a flurry of success, but was discontinued in 1899.

The second strike was hit shortly after the turn of the century, when a "phosphate soda water counter" was opened in Woolworth's Newark, New Jersey, store. The carbonated chiller didn't catch on and was soon discontinued. Several years later, in 1907, E. Z. Nutting, the enterprising manager of the Market Street, Philadelphia, store suggested a combination soda water fountain and simple snack counter. This experienced a level of success, but

Woolworth Trivia

In 1950 alone, the Red-Fronts sold 250 million pounds of gum.

not enough to merit long-term support from the chief, who glumly acknowledged the soda water fountain as yet another failed venture.

It certainly seemed as though the refreshment idea was a lost cause, when the tides unexpectedly started to change. On May 13, 1910, ice cream cones were test-marketed in several of the busier sites, with Horton Company furnishing modern refrigerators. The frosty treat quickly caught on, as did the idea of the unknown manager who proposed selling hot dogs at lunchtime, along with that refreshing American favorite, root beer, which was drawn from an oak barrel atop the counter. The concept of selling refreshments in a variety store finally seemed potentially profitable. The question was, how far should his company go to make this venture fly? By then, Woolworth's little syndicate had become

F. W. Woolworth & Co., a corporation with 268 stores and eight district offices. Frank was already making millions, but a few extra million in food sales couldn't hurt. He and his corporate circle assessed the situation and decided that, in order to make this notion really take off, they had to do it in a big way. They wanted to lure in even more customers, and what better way than making sure the customers didn't even have to leave the store for lunch? Woolworth also thought that the idea of a full-service restaurant was original enough to steal some thunder (and press time) from his arch competitors, Kresge and McCrory. By then, these five-and-dime men were purposely renting space on the same streets where F. W. Woolworth & Co. stores had once ruled in solitary discount splendor. It was time to take action, with no expense spared. He decided to create the first ever, fullscale restaurant in a five-and-dime.

> **TIME CAPSULE MEMORY**
>
> ## "Sweet Treat"
>
> Back in 1952 when I was thirteen and living in Fairview, New Jersey, my girlfriend and I would do our holiday shopping in the Big Apple. We'd always save 15¢ for a soft ice cream in a glass at Woolworth's. You could get either vanilla topped with chocolate syrup (my favorite) or vanilla topped with strawberry syrup. Today I have a candy scale that I purchased at a garage sale. The woman said it came from Woolworth's when it went out of business. It sits on my living room coffee table, reminding me of the glass partitioned counters, the smell of wood, and the wonderful affordable items displayed throughout the store.
> —Marilyn Rietzel

The First Woolworth's "Refreshment Rooms"

On August 31, 1910, the first official F. W. Woolworth & Co. eatery opened on 14th Street, New York City. Managed by J. U. Troy, it was known as the Refreshment Room, a phrase Woolworth had picked up in England. This original restaurant was a far cry from the Formica-counter decor of later Woolworth's luncheonettes. The room was located in the rear of the store, in a space measuring 27 x 60 feet. The dining area featured sixteen Carrera-marble glass-topped tables and a forty-foot glass-topped counter. Behind the scenes, modern kitchen equipment hummed. The aroma of fresh flowers wafted throughout the dining room, where customers were served by uniformed waiters and waitresses who had been strictly instructed "to please." The dishes were china, the tablecloths were linen, and beautiful artwork filled the walls.

Frank quickly duplicated this Refreshment Room concept in Lancaster, Pennsylvania. He opened his in-house restaurant the same day, in October 1911, that he premiered his new and improved five-and-ten store in the Woolworth Skyscraper on the corner of Queen Street and Grant. On opening day, 37,000 Lancasterians came to the new Woolworth's to shop, and another 3,279 patrons were served free "sampler" meals on opening

Frank W. Woolworth (seated far left) and a table of local dignitaries gathered together for the grand opening of his elegant "Refreshment Room" in Lancaster, Pennsylvania, 1911.

day. One of the overriding favorites was fried oysters; harried waiters served over 5,400 portions. Roth's Orchestra played the "Woolworth March," along with popular songs of the time, such as "Let Me Call You Sweetheart" and "Shine On, Harvest Moon." VIPs from the F. W. Woolworth Company, as well as from the state of Pennsylvania, joined Frank W. Woolworth in celebrating his latest spectacle.

Like the stores themselves, Frank's Refreshment Rooms boasted "no item over 10¢." Restaurant sales that first day in Lancaster were modest, a mere $29.95; partly because many people came just for the free food selections and did not order anything else from the regular menu. By the weekend, though, sales had skyrocketed, especially since the press had covered the event and word of mouth spread quickly.

Frank Woolworth soon opened up similar Refreshment Rooms across the country. If a store did not have the square footage to accommodate such a grand establishment, then he compromised with a smaller restaurant, or a standup counter, which was an early version of today's take-out emporiums.

By 1928, the company was proud to announce that 90 million meals per day were being served in Woolworth's coast to coast.

Frank Winfield Woolworth
(1852-1919)

Charles Sumner Woolworth
(1859-1947)

Frank first designed the famous Red W logo in 1886. A blue variation of the W was designed for the company's centennial celebration in 1979.

LEFT: Woolworth's earliest five-and-dimes were small, simple, sidewalk level store fronts, such as this one in York, Pa.
RIGHT: In 1900, the Merchant Prince erected his first wholly-owned, six-story "skyscraper" in Lancaster. It featured two floors of merchandise, an elaborate chandeliered Refreshment Room, and floors for executive offices. On the roof, nestled between the golden poles, sat an English-styled garden and a full Vaudeville stage!

Many people do not realize that Frank's first "nickel and dime" trade was not conducted with actual coins, but primarily with post-Civil War paper money called shinplasters.

Frank Woolworth shocked New York's upper crust when he first opened a five-and-dime on posh Fifth Avenue.

This Woolworth's in St. Petersburg, Florida was typical of the style of Woolworth stores prospering during the 1930s and 40s.

S-82—On the Green Benches along Central Ave. St. Petersburg, Fla. "The Sunshine City"

By 1929, eighty percent of Woolworth's had refreshment rooms or lunch counters. The Salt Lake City, Utah store boasted the longest counter in the region.

During the company's hey day, landmark towns like Scottsdale, Arizona and
Atlantic City, New Jersey drew record-breaking crowds.

Capturing a Country

AT the time *Woolco* Cottons were first introduced to the women of America, less than two years ago, the preference was for foreign-made cottons. Today *Woolco* Cottons are in the greatest demand—the sales are simply enormous. Women everywhere now *prefer*

Woolco QUALITY CROCHET and EMBROIDERY Cottons

This is so *because Woolco* means smooth-working, fast-color cottons—no "roughing up" or "kinking."

These famous cottons—which are superior, in our opinion, to any you can buy, foreign or domestic, are sold exclusively in the Woolworth 5- and 10-cent stores—more than 950 of them *everywhere*. Next time

you want to do an exceptionally fine piece of work—try *Woolco*.

If you are not near a Woolworth store, send your order, at the price quoted plus postage (at the rate of 3 cents a large ball and 2 cents for 3 skeins) to F. W. Woolworth Co., 490 Washington Street, Boston. Circular and color list on application.

F. W. WOOLWORTH CO.
(Prices quoted are for stores in the United States only)

One of Woolworth's most popular features was its plethora of decorations and favors
suitable for holidays and special events. The above photo shows the wedding
and bridal shower, c. 1935.

OPPOSITE PAGE: Woolco-brand cottons, yarns, and all manner
of sewing materials remained best-selling items for decades. Due
to Frank's distaste of "wasting money" on paid advertising, this
elaborate 1917 magazine ad represents one of the few published
before Frank Woolworth's death in 1919.

The magnificent Grand Arcade lobby of the Woolworth Building. Since 1913, it has been one of the most frequented tourist spots in New York City.

Stunning architectural features in the Woolworth Building lobby
include this "Labor & Commerce" stained-glass mural. Reportedly,
the woman's face (center) is a likeness of his beloved mother,
Fanny McBrier Woolworth.

WOOLWORTH BUILDING
NEW YORK

Frank Woolworth's mahogany and gold gilt executive
desk was an exact replica of the desk of his hero, Napoleon
Bonaparte, which Frank saw during a visit to Napoleon's
Palace in Compeigne.

The sixty-story Woolworth Building opened
to great fanfare in 1913. Frank Woolworth
paid 13.5 million in cash to create his
"Cathedral of Commerce," which reigned
as the tallest building in the world
until 1930.

Today, five-and-dime nostalgia collectors are seeking out everything from old coin wrappers to celebrity items to Christmas catalogs.

Wooleys' Post-War Luncheonettes

After World War II, most of the lavish Refreshment Rooms were replaced with lunch counters and luncheonettes. Along with Formica counters, the company started to introduce special in-house promotions, like the Banana Split Balloon gimmick. Customers would pop a balloon from a line of balloons that were strung overhead. Inside each balloon was a small strip of paper. The customer paid whatever price was written on the paper, and sometimes, if they were lucky, the huge banana split "House Boat" was only a penny. One former customer from Wisconsin remembers taking the used ice cream container home with her and using it as a bathtub for her Barbie doll; her brother used his as a vessel for his G.I. Joe figurines.

Other F. W. Woolworth food promotions were created specifically to meet the needs of America's agricultural community. For example, if farmers found themselves with a surplus of products, they would work with Woolworth's to devise a "Dairy Month" or a "Vegetable Week." So, for certain periods, regional Woolworth's would add a supplemental menu, featuring, for instance, tomato soup, fried tomatoes, tomato sandwiches, and any other tomato concoction the company could dream up. In fact, it was a surplus of turkeys that triggered the popular "year-round" turkey dinner at Woolworth's, a meal that had been traditionally served only during the Thanksgiving holidays.

At the forefront of all this activity were the Woolworth's waitresses, who sometimes doubled as cooks in the smaller sites. These waitresses wore company-issue uniforms, aprons and caps, and had to be very good at their jobs in order to keep up with the steady lunch business. Like other food purveyors across America, they developed their own "food lingo." The waitress (only rarely a waiter) would jot down an order for two poached eggs of toast and then yell back to

TIME CAPSULE MEMORY

"The Pick-a-Balloon Game"

My childhood Woolworth's was in Long Island, New York, and I remember the store as being huge with displays of amazing items, everything from bobby pins to goldfish. The big attraction was the lunch counter where they had food unlike what I was served at home—thin hamburgers on white rolls, hot dogs, on soft buns, greasy grilled cheese sandwiches and best of all, banana splits "pick a balloon" game. I recall this from when I was around 3 years old; it is 40 years ago but it is etched in my memory. —Jill Nussinow

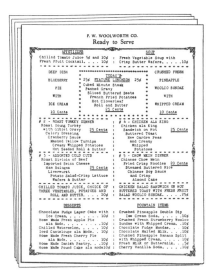

Special Promotions

F. W. Woolworth Co. often dreamed up special food promotions to help farmers deal with crop surpluses. These
photos show examples of dairy and turkey promotions
during the late 1930s.

the cook: "One order of Adam and Eve on a Raft, pa-leese!" Some lunch counter lingo, like "BLT" and "mayo," eventually became part of the everyday culture in homes. However, there were many phrases that remained characteristic of five-and-dime lunch counters and local diners. Peggy Trowbridge, who runs an Internet site (http://www.homecooking.miningco.com) called *The Homecooking Guide,* recalled her early experiences at Woolworth's, a place where, "almost as much fun as eating the ice cream was listening to the waitresses in their starched pink uniforms placing orders with the cook in their own special language and then trying to figure out what in the world people were ordering!"

A discussion of the F. W. Woolworth's lunch counters would not be complete without mentioning some of the loyal customers who graced those red stools. There are countless stories of customers who ate at F. W. Woolworth's every week for years, sometimes every day for decades. *The Woolworth News* (Spring, 1993) reported that Mrs. Dora de' Venau stopped in Store #1674 in New York City for thirty-five years. Every morning, en route to her job at the Boys and Girls Club of America, Mrs. de' Venau ate breakfast at

Lunch Counter Trivia

A sampling of the food lingo used in F. W. Woolworth, and other lunch counters

ADAM AND EVE ON A RAFT: **two poached eggs on toast**

BABY, MOO JUICE, SWEET ALICE, OR COW JUICE: **milk**

CROWD: **three of anything**

DRAW ONE: **coffee**

FIFTY-FIVE: **a glass of root beer**

GENTLEMAN WILL TAKE A CHANCE: **hash**

GROUNDHOG: **hot dog**

HOUSEBOAT: **a banana split, made with ice cream and sliced bananas**

IN THE ALLEY: **serve as a side dish**

MIKE AND IKE OR THE TWINS: **salt and pepper shakers**

MURPHY: **potatoes**

NOAH'S BOY: **a slice of ham**

WRECK 'EM: **scramble the eggs**

—Source: Peggy Trowbridge

that particular Woolworth's, and when she was out of town, she found Woolworth's luncheonettes in other cities so as not to break her tradition.

In Suffolk, England, one customer visited the same Woolworth's for over fifty years. According to a 1989 column by Andy Parker for *The Daily Press,* the customer's name was Henry Lee, who at that time was eighty-three years old. Henry started going Woolworth's luncheonette in the mid-1930s. By 1989, he was still attending, but he was grumbling about the price of coffee ("Sixty-six cents for a cup of coffee? If these people had lived through '29, '30, and '31 they would understand the value of money."). Coffee prices aside, Henry Lee, and scores like him, patronized the Suffolk store like clockwork. Where else in town could they still be served fountain sodas in classic-shaped Coca-Cola glasses, and thick foamy milkshakes made fresh to order?

The End of an Era

The Woolworth food centers and luncheonettes that opened between 1963 and 1997 were more streamlined and less quaint than their predecessors. These were modern food facilities, geared toward a population always on the go, who demanded top quality "fast food" at traditional Woolworth's prices. Full-service Woolworth's cafeterias opened by the hundreds in shopping malls, with large, tailor-made restaurants incorporated into the design of equally giant Woolco stores. To help meet the demand, F. W. Woolworth Co. increased the number of executives and managers involved with its food service industry, as well as the number of Woolworth's trucks carrying perishables to the stores. Yet even with the debut of these new and improved "modern" food facilities, there still remained hundreds of the old-fashioned lunch counters, left virtually unchanged from the day they opened before World War I. A visit to one of these lunch counters, usually found in more rural towns, offered the customer a pleasant trip back in time, and the warm smile of a crackerjack waitress who proudly boasted she'd been with the company for over thirty years.

In the summer 1997, the last of the Woolworth's luncheonettes and cafeterias started

Signs like this one in 1997 were, for many, a symbol that the age of the
five-and-dime was officially over.

closing down in North America, along with the last of the Red-Fronts. Not surprisingly, the food service employees were among the first to be laid off, their final responsibilities being to shut down the cooking facilities and equipment, and pack away timeworn menus and dishes. Many veteran waitresses and waiters took their Woolworth's aprons and caps with them when they left—a bittersweet reminder of the thousands of cups of coffee they'd served to steady customers, and the earfuls of gossip shared by locals en route to work or play. During this course of the final shut downs, some Red-Front managers used the eerily vacant lunch counters and stools to display final sale merchandise. Along with boxes of sewing needles and costume jewelry, they offered up mementos such as root beer glasses and metal ice cream dishes from the lunch counters. Customers who arrived too late for one last grilled cheese sandwich were met with the following sign, propped over the old soda dispensers: "Sorry. *Closed.*"

There is one lunch counter, however, which was spared.

Part of the counter from the Greensboro, North Carolina, Woolworth's store is now on display at the Smithsonian Institute in Washington, D.C. This particular Formica icon has a special significance beyond the nostalgic, living in the realm of one of most tumultuous periods in America's history.

Woolworth's In Turmoil: The Lunch Counter Sit-Ins

The student-led sit-in at the Woolworth store in Greensboro was the beginning of the largely youth-led social reform movements of the 1960s. Four 17- and 18-year-old African American students inspired a generation of Americans in the pursuit of equal justice and equal opportunity.

—Smithsonian Online, http://www.si.edu/i%26d/sitins.v2.4.html

On February 1, 1960, at 4:30 P.M., four African-American college students walked into their local F. W. Woolworth store in Greensboro, North Carolina, and forever altered American history. They achieved this by asking for a cup of coffee, and were told, "We don't serve Negroes here." Instead of leaving, the students stayed there until the store closed that evening. And so was launched the first extended, nonviolent racial discrimination sit-in of its kind in a restaurant, the first such protest to make national headlines. After it was all over, neither America nor the F. W. Woolworth Co. would ever be the same.

The students in this scenario, dubbed by the media as the "Four Freshmen," were Ezell A. Blair, Jr., Franklin E. McCain, Joseph A. McNeil, and David L. Richmond. They were all enrolled at nearby North Carolina Agricultural and Technical College (A&T). Driven by their own frustrations with racial inequality, and encouraged by a local business owner

"The Four Freshmen."

named Ralph Johns, the teens decided that Woolworth's was a symbolic and central place to begin expressing their discontent.

By 1960, the F. W. Woolworth Co. had firmly established their slogan as being "Everybody's Store." In fact, Woolworth's did cater to everyone, when it came to welcoming people into their stores to purchase merchandise. But the rules sometimes changed at the lunch counters. Most of the East Coast lunch counters had been integrated for years, but the restaurants in the South, especially the Deep South, had two sections for food service: one for the "coloreds" and one for the "whites," often with crude signs posted to this effect located near the food service areas. North Carolina was considered a moderate Southern state when it came to discrimination, but it still smacked strongly of old "Jim Crow" attitudes, especially when it came to service in movie theaters, motels, and restaurants. In 1960, the Four Freshmen knew full well they were entering the Elm Street Woolworth's with the intent of violating regional tradition. They knew they were expected to bypass the long, bustling lunch counter reserved for "Whites," and proceed to the nearby counter area set aside for "Negroes," where they usually ate their meal standing up, or, as was the local preference, took their food outside. But this particular sunny winter day, they did not abide by the rules. They felt compelled to take a stand against the dehumanizing racial discrimination that had pervaded their town for too long.

The first day, the four students sat quietly until the Woolworth's store closed that evening. They left with a promise to return the next morning with the entire A&T College black population. Except for one lone reporter who was denied entry to the store, there was no media involved. There was no fanfare and no violence of any kind. Two police offi-

cers entered the store for a short time, but they ex-
changed no harsh words with the protestors. For the
handful of community members who heard about the sit-
in, including Mayor George Roach and local newspaper
publishers, the episode was considered a minor nuisance
and the general consensus was that it would all go away.

There was, however, a semblance of immediate concern on the part of Woolworth's manager, Frank "Curly"
Harris. Harris was a die-hard Woolworth's company man;
he'd started with the company in 1923 and was proud of
his career achievements, and his orderly, shipshape Elm
Street establishment. The lunch counter itself was responsible for a healthy share of the store's profits, and Harris
knew that trouble was amiss in his variety store paradise.
That afternoon, he contacted an executive of the F. W.
Woolworth Co. about the episode with the students, and
was told to sit tight and wait to see what happened. The

Frank "Curly" Harris was manager of the
Elm Street, Greensboro, Red-Front during
the sit-ins, which began February, 1960.

company did not want anyone arrested and wanted to avoid violence at all costs. The umbrella policy of the F. W. Woolworth Co. since the 1930s had been to cater to all Americans,
regardless of race, color, and religious affiliation. Yet the *unspoken* policy was to abide by
the wishes of local store managers (based on the particular traditions of their geographical
region) when it came to serving food to minorities.

The next morning, the silent protestors were back, accompanied by other members
of the A&T student body, for a total of twenty-seven men and four women. Once again, the
neatly-dressed students entered civilly and placed their school books on the lunch
counter. They asked the waitresses for service, were denied, and then continued to sit.
This time the local citizens started gossiping, and Curly Harris realized that his busy lunch
hour trade might be seriously affected.

It was soon evident that this problem was not just "going to go away." The Four
Freshman, along with their friends, returned to the Woolworth's lunch counter like clockwork in the morning, and didn't leave until closing time. Over the ensuing weeks, various
strategies by Frank Harris and his immediate superiors were used to deter the black students' efforts. The store's hours were limited, the actual time the lunch counter was open
was decreased, and piles of merchandise were even placed on the stools to deter them
from sitting down. For most of this period, the strategy was simply to try to ignore the
black students. At one point, the Woolworth's regional manager blatantly denied the Elm
Street store was discriminating at all: "We haven't refused anybody," he told the press.
"Our girls have been busy and they couldn't get around to everybody." In a more aggressive move, groups of local white teenagers were strongly encouraged (some say by local

"The Lunch Counter Experience That Changed My Life"

I grew up in Columbia, South Carolina, in the 1960s. During high school break one year, my cousin and I decided to go shopping downtown. I had inherited the light skin of the family; she was born with an enviable olive complexion that tanned deeply. We stopped into the local Woolworth's, sat down at the lunch counter, pulled menus from the napkin holders, and waited our turn. After about fifteen minutes, we realized that although others at the counter had been served, we had not even been asked what we wanted. The counter help was clearly staying at the far end of the counter, risking only furtive glances our way. We realized that the waitresses thought we were trying to break the racial barrier. Blacks were not allowed to eat at that Woolworth's. Embarrassed, and unsure what to do (we couldn't explain that we were white) we slunk out of the dime store, unfed and intimidated. I had inadvertently stepped into the shoes of Southern blacks and I truly empathized, for the first time. The experience turned me into an activist, rallying for civil rights. I learned, first-hand, what discrimination and prejudice felt like—merely because I wanted a soft drink at F. W. Woolworth's in 1961. —Bobbie Christmas, GA.

Ku Klux Klan leaders) to enter the store early and take up all the seats before the black students arrived. This latter tactic backfired the moment that three white girls, college students clearly sympathetic for the cause, sat down at the lunch counter, and then gave their seats to three black students. This set a precedent followed many times by students during the course of the sit-in.

As the weeks stretched out into months, the usually peaceful city of Greensboro turned into a site of turmoil as everyone, from the town council down, passed the buck as to who was responsible for settling this issue. Behind the scenes, the F. W. Woolworth Co. started tentative negotiations, pressured, in part, by the media attention, which had evolved from local to county to state coverage, until it reached national proportions. In New York City, and other cities with integrated lunch counters, both black and white Woolworth's employees, patrons, and university students staged their own nonviolent protests in support of the Greensboro pioneers. Most of these protests were small, disorganized and short-lived, but chants such as, "One, two, three, four, don't shop at the Woolworth store," became increasingly disconcerting to Woolworth Company executives and public relations representatives.

The Greensboro sit-in continued for almost six months. The protestors used a rotation system, allowing one group of students to rest while another took their places at the lunch counter. At one point, the F. W. Woolworth's in Greensboro was actually closed down, but the undaunted protesters simply took their protest to the segregated Kress five-and-dime lunch counter down the street. They were back at Woolworth's as soon as it reopened. To his credit, Woolworth's manager, Frank "Curly" Harris, tried his best to avoid any type of aggressive ousting; he never even issued any type of formal trespass complaint. Nonetheless, tensions were escalating and everyone knew that something had to be done before things got out of hand.

A seemingly mild incident that started with four teens was now a cast of thousands.

Excerpt of the text of the letter written to the president of the F. W. Woolworth Co. in 1960:

Dear Mr. President:

We the undersigned are students at the Negro college in the city of Greensboro. Time and time again we have gone into Woolworth stores of Greensboro. We have bought thousands of items at the hundreds of counters in your stores. Our money was accepted without rancor or discrimination and with politeness toward us, when at a long counter just three feet away our money is not acceptable because of the color of our skins. This letter is not being written with resentment toward your company, but with a hope of understanding . . .

We are asking that your company take a firm stand to eliminate discrimination. We firmly believe that God will give courage and guidance in the solving of this problem.

Sincerely Yours,

Student Executive Committee

The Four Freshmen, in cooperation with local merchant, Ralph Johns, wrote a letter to the F. W. Woolworth Company President Robert Kirkwood requesting action. Ralph Johns was an interesting man, a Caucasian, rough and tumble radical who owned a clothing store near the black section of Greensboro. Years earlier, Johns had achieved notoriety as the "World's Greatest Gate Crasher" by worming his way into every major boxing fight of the Golden Age, and then, somehow, getting into the photographs with all the winners. The salad days of sneaking in to see Joe Lewis and Jack Dempsey were long over when "Ruffles" Johns arrived in North Carolina in the mid-forties. Johns had always been sympathetic to human interest causes, and although many Greensboro whites despised him for it, he encouraged local A&T students to take a strong stand against segregation. During the sit-ins, Johns remained behind the scenes, offering advice, rallying local leaders for support, and holding onto a spare bankroll—just in case the students got arrested and needed bail.

The letter composed for Robert Kirkwood was short and to the point, asking the company to take a strong stand to eliminate discrimination. As the company muddled over the best way to respond, and the American press capitalized on the growing unrest, the Greensboro community leaders started taking polls to gauge community response. Only seven percent of the town responded, and even then with mixed feelings. Spiritual and academic black leaders were also unsure as to the best way to resolve the issue, conscious of everyone's desire to avoid violence. It was a difficult and complex chapter in the history of Greensboro, and indeed, in the history of America in general.

While local leaders and Woolworth's big wigs danced a two-step between concern and uncertainty, the students and their growing mass of supporters continued to hit this modest F. W. Woolworth's store in the place it hurt most—in the pocketbook.

Manager "Curly" Harris had calculated that during the first week alone, sales in his store were down $6,000., and had increased as the sit-in continued. (By the end of the year the store would lose over $200,000.) The protest eventually spawned a public boycott,

"The Civil Rights Movement in My Own Town"

In the early 1960's, my friend Karen and I were shopping in downtown Pensacola. It was a typical Saturday outing, until we walked into the Kress store and saw a mob of angry blacks, protesting discrimination there. Being raised in the South, segregation was a way of life to us. I never understood exactly why, but there were signs posted everywhere, in restaurants, theaters, and bathrooms, marked "white only" or "black only." Standing near the five-and-dime that day, we watched as several blacks pushed through the "whites only" dining area. In response, angry white customers shouted horrible, cruel words at the protesters. The managers screamed, "Get those niggers out of my store!" That night on the news I learned all about the civil rights movement being led by Martin Luther King. I had witnessed one of the historical sit ins, which had originated at the Woolworth's in North Carolina. Finally, there was justice! It was an event which changed my life, and our country forever.

—Linda Olson, Florida

which really helped turn the tides. Too much money was being lost to continue on this way, and the reputation of the F. W. Woolworth Co. itself was in serious jeopardy.

In the end, it was a combination of the determination of the student protestors, strong media coverage, shifting community sentiment (in the protestors' favor), and economic pressure that led to a peaceful resolution.

On July 25, 1960 at 2:30 in the afternoon, the first three African-Americans were "officially" served food at the Elm Street Woolworth's lunch counter. They were not the Four Freshmen, but three black Woolworth's employees. As per a hush-hush agreement between the local media and the Woolworth's manager, no advance publicity heralded the event. In terms of media spectacle, it was rather anti-climactic.

But it was far from anti-climactic for the students who had started it all. Ezell A. Blair, Jr., Franklin E. McCain, Joseph A. McNeil, and David L. Richmond had persevered, eventually winning enough support to achieve their goal. That week, the four students, along with 300 more African-Americans were served at the Woolworth's Red-Front, and business was soon back to normal at Frank Harris's store.

From July 1960 on, F. W. Woolworth's five-and-dimes tried to enforce the equality issue in all their stores. The key word here is "tried." In nearby Winston-Salem, North Carolina, for instance, the manager did not agree to the order for desegregation, and actually resigned rather than allow Negroes to sit at his store's lunch counter. (The Woolworth Company quickly replaced the Winston-Salem manager with a more open-minded man.) More disturbing scenarios occurred over the ensuing months. In Woolworth's stores in Tampa, Florida, Nashville, Tennessee and at the Hampton Institute, the initially nonviolent sit-ins got out of hand, and hundreds of people were wounded. One afternoon in Nashville, unruly whites yanked blacks off the lunch counter stools and beat them up; the police then arrested the blacks. It took several years before all the Red-Fronts were truly desegregated, in part because the company's directors, including President Kirwood, were reluctant to take an aggressive stance. During the 1960 annual meeting in Watertown, New York, Kirkland told stockholders that, "Dealing as we are with the deep-rooted convictions of the people of the South, it is hardly realistic to suppose that any company is influential enough to suddenly change its thinking on this topic." Even after the passing of the 1964 and 1965 Civil Rights Acts, which banned segregation in all public accommodations, there were still hold-outs among private proprietors in America. In time, of course, all public and private facilities were legally desegregated—a fact which can be traced back, in large degree, to the Woolworth's sit-in in Greensboro, North Carolina.

There is an ironic important postscript to this story. Although an important milestone was reached in Greensboro in July 1960, the entire incident could have been resolved much faster. In May of that year, F. W. Woolworth Co. executives had told "Curly Harris" that he could desegregate when he felt it was the "right time." The decision was left up to Harris, with the company's full support. But Harris didn't want to desegregate when the throngs of A&T students were still in session, and he purposely waited until school was out for the summer and the protesting crowds had slackened. It is probable that he, and several other major white community leaders, feared some type of unruly gathering of African-Americans at Woolworth's would cause problems. However, there was no fuss and furor when desegregation in Greensboro was finally announced. As the local paper stated: "Negroes did not request service en masse. They came as individuals and they were served as individuals. The sky did not fall."

Since July 25, 1960, there have been several anniversaries of the successful Greensboro event, the most noted occurring in 1990. "On February 1, 1990, four middle-aged men sat down at the Woolworth's lunch counter in Greensboro and had breakfast," wrote Miles Wolff in *Lunch at the 5&10*. "No reporter had been present to cover that first sit-in. In 1990 the four were surrounded by reporters and onlookers. The 7:30 A.M. meal was telecast live locally and nationally."

The men were served by two of the waitresses who had been told to deny them service thirty years before. Food and drinks were offered at the old 1960 prices. Ralph Jones returned to the event, along with Dr. Warmoth T. Gibbs, who had been president of A&T in 1960, and a team of Woolworth corporate executives and public relations men. Joseph McNeil, Franklin McCain, Ezell Blair Jr. (by then Jibreel Khazan), and David Richmond each discussed their lives since 1960. Accepting the limelight with great humility, David Richmond said: "Heroes we are not. So many people shaped us. We pay homage to you. Do not celebrate us as heroes. You are the heroes. You know who you are. God bless you."

As part of the ceremony, the corner of Elm and Sycamore Streets, where the Woolworth's was located, was renamed "February First Place."

"Sitting for Justice": The Smithsonian's Woolworth's Exhibit

William Yeingst, a curator for the Smithsonian Institute in Washington, D.C., was watching television on October 13, 1993, when he heard that that the Woolworth Corporation planned to close over 900 stores in a nationwide downsizing move. For Yeingst, like millions of other people, this announcement stirred up personal memories of the old five-and-dime, but it also reminded him of the key historical events that had taken place at Greensboro's lunch counter some thirty-three years before.

According to an issue of Smithsonian Online, that week, he tracked down the manager of the Elm Street (Greensboro) Woolworth's and learned that the site would be closing in just three days. Yeingst asked if the lunch counter was still intact. The manager replied that indeed it was, and that in fact it had remained virtually unchanged since the time of the sit-in. Yeingst decided he wanted to preserve that lunch counter, along with other artifacts of the sit-in, as part of the Smithsonian's American history collection.

Yeingst joined forces with another Smithsonian curator, Lonnie Bunch, and together they traveled to the Woolworth Building in New York to meet with Aubrey Lewis, then vice president for corporate relations. "We stressed to Mr. Lewis the historical significance of the sit-in," recounted Yeingst. "The counter would be held in trust for the American people, forming a lasting record of one of the most significant events in recent American history. The symbolic power of the lunch counter would help the museum interpret not only the history of the civil rights movement, but also aspects of recent Southern history, Woolworth's role in American business history, and the process of urbanization in the South."

After a series of lengthy discussions, the F. W. Woolworth Company tentatively agreed to the proposal. There was, however, one important catch. They would not proceed without joint approval from the Greensboro community. As soon as possible, Yeingst and Bunch flew to North Carolina and met with members of the Greensboro city council, employees of Woolworth's, and representatives of the African-American community. The meetings went well, and the curators were becoming more optimistic. The next step was to meet with members of the Sit-In Movement Inc.

The Sit-In Movement was a local organization composed of African-American residents with a vested interest in preserving the Woolworth's Greensboro store. They had hoped to convert the site into a national civil rights museum. The Smithsonian representatives supported the organization's plans for a museum, and offered advice to help them secure funding and resources. But they also requested that some of the artifacts be donated to the Smithsonian, enabling the museum's six million yearly visitors to view, and remember, that critical era. Yeingst and Bunch had already studied the Woolworth's site and its internal structures. They were interested in acquiring four stools, a section of the lunch counter, mirrors, the soda fountain, and a section of cornice.

A satisfactory agreement was reached with all parties. The F. W. Woolworth Company, along with the Greensboro Sit-In Movement, would receive national recognition for their donation to the Smithsonian; the members of the Sit-In Movement Inc. would also continue with their own local museum plans.

There was great excitement and flurry of activity on Elm Street the day the dismantling began. Under the supervision of trained Smithsonian preservationists, Woolworth workers carefully dismantled the objects. The Greensboro community also assisted, and their carpenter's union donated their labor for the cause. Among those who gathered to watch, were several people who were there that winter and spring three decades before, when Greensboro had been thronged with protesters and media. Finally, the crates holding metal and Formica icons of that turbulent period were shipped to Washington D.C. Through a generous grant from TROY Systems, Inc., and additional support from the Futron Corporation, the exhibit became a reality.

TIME CAPSULE MEMORY

"Heartfelt Moments"

I grew up in a rural community in the 1950s, so going to the five-and-dime (a few miles away) was always a big treat for me. My mother worked very hard, and was only off on Sundays and Mondays. Sundays would invariably find me seated beside her on a church pew, and just as religiously, on Mondays we would sit together at the Woolworth's counter and enjoy a ham sandwich with lettuce. It was the only time that I felt I had my mother's undivided attention, and the Woolworth's lunch counter became a shrine for me. My precious mother is now gone, but I could never pass the old stores without reliving those special childhood memories. —Susan Graham, VA

The Smithsonian decided to name the exhibit "Sitting for Justice."

The exhibit has been available to the public since 1995, and the Greensboro lunch counter is now part of the Smithsonian Institute's National Museum of American History collection. The counter portion of the exhibit is flanked by newspaper articles and photographs of the sit-in's participants. It presently resides in the building's main hallway, which connects displays of the Star Spangled Banner and a monumental sculpture of George Washington. According to Smithsonian curator, Lonnie Bunch, "We felt that it was important to have an icon of race that cried, in the words of poet Langston Hughes, 'I, too, am America.'"

Each F. W. Woolworth's counter across America held a special, unique meaning for its former occupants. Where in Greensboro, North Carolina, the significance is primarily historical, there are other cities which remember their lunch counters as the place where personal histories were made. Whether they were seniors sipping a cup of hot coffee on a cold winter afternoon, or children popping balloons in the hope of winning a food prize, the patrons of Woolworth's took their experiences to heart. The lunch counters, perhaps more than any other aspect of the Woolworth story, have generated the most nostalgic memories.

Chapter Nine

A Store For All Seasons

"For sixty years Woolworth's has been steadfast in the belief that Santa must not pass by so much as one chimney when his reindeer prance over the roof tops of America. How much of this glad Christmas scene is of Woolworth's making? How much of it was made possible by the loose change in Santa's purse? More Christmas joy for more homes is the miracle wrought each year by Woolworth's!"

Sixty Years of Woolworth souvenir booklet, 1939

A Winter Wonderland for the Working Class

Just as millions of people recall their experiences at the Woolworth's lunch counters, so do they recall the old Red-Fronts during the holidays, especially during the December holidays.

"December is our harvest time," Frank Woolworth once told his managers. "Make it pay!"

And they did.

For good or ill, the F. W. Woolworth Co. played a large part in commercializing Christmas, forever altering the seasonal shopping patterns of the working class. This trend started out rather innocently in the 1880s, when Frank introduced his customers to the American version of a new "ready made" tree trimming called a Christmas Ball. One thing led to another, until the aisles of his Red-Fronts were filled with additional "ready-made" goodies such as garlands, Christmas choo-choo trains, simulated evergreens, and elaborate nativity sets. Following World War II, plastic was introduced on a wide scale, adding an entirely new selection of gaudy, colorful, inexpensive items to decorate the home and entertain the masses. To make certain that people knew about this plethora of minutiae, the company started distributing holiday catalogs, jammed with descriptions of the latest gift fads (such as adjustable metal roller skates) and the old stand-bys (such as shaving lotion). By the 1950s, F. W. Woolworth was a firmly established holiday haunt for bargain hunters, as the Red-Fronts had become more bazaar than dimestore. A casual stroll through the aisles offered a pleasant though sometimes overwhelming assault on the senses, full of the vivid colors, sounds and aromas of a cut-rate Winter Wonderland.

And everywhere you looked, you would see the familiar sign: "Welcome to America's Favorite Christmas Store."

Come December, the display windows were transformed into a kaleidoscope of red, green, and gold. The Thanksgiving pumpkins and paper Pilgrims were stored away in favor of silver bells, holly-decked wrapping paper, and spray-on snow.

Store managers pulled out all the stops to entice shoppers inside, where employees bustled to and fro between counters to help Grandma find the perfect woolen scarf for Grandpa, and a bottle of *"Evening in Paris"* for sister Judy. Dads could be seen carrying out large boxes of Christmas lights and ornaments, destined for the family evergreen, moms in tow with enough glittering tinsel to decorate a city block. In the larger Woolworth's, a piano player was often seated in the back, playing rousing renditions of "Jingle Bells" with the hope of selling sheet music. In the smaller stores, piped-in melodies of "Silent Night" made certain everyone maintained the proper holiday mood.

The candy counters brimmed over with every type of delectable treat: festive ribbon candy, boxed Schrafft's candies, pounds of cream Operas, walnut-topped Montevidos, and candy canes as large as your arm. And the toys! Why, the children had never seen so many toys in one place! Everything from Plasticville towns to giant coloring books to fuzzy stuffed bears filled those walls, and baskets of tops, rubber balls, and tiny cars lined the

---

Welcome TO AMERICA'S CHRISTMAS STORE

As the blessed season approaches once more, you may recall one of the most thrilling of your childhood adventures...a Christmas shopping trip to Woolworth's! That may have been long ago or not-so-long ago...but we can speak as an old friend of the family when we say, "Welcome, once more, to Woolworth's at Christmas."

THIS IS OUR 75TH CHRISTMAS! Every Christmas season has found ever new wonders at Woolworth's, but in this 75th anniversary year we have outdone ourselves...to heap our counters high with the most exciting Christmas assortments in our history...all value-priced in the Woolworth tradition.

TAKE TIME TO EXPLORE EVERY AISLE! The pages in this book show only a small fraction of the 1954 Christmas selections at Woolworth's. See them all! Nearly every counter is laden with gift suggestions, because we've planned it that way. Why not make an exploratory tour of all the aisles, notebook in hand, to fill out your gift list? Browse for an hour or as many hours as you like. You don't have to buy a thing until you are good and ready! And of course bring the children—you remember what a trip to Woolworth's meant to you at that age!

USE WOOLWORTH'S LAY-AWAY PLAN! Choose all your gifts now—for the family, for friends, for the home—and just a small deposit will hold them for you. You can make selections early, while assortments are plentiful...before stores are filled with last-minute crowds. Ask any Woolworth store for details of the Lay-Away Plan.

IF YOU LIKE THIS BOOK...if you find it helpful in your Christmas shopping, won't you please mention it to your Woolworth store manager? He will appreciate it, because he will then know that he is serving you as he wants to. Tell him, too, if you have any suggestions that might increase the usefulness of the book to you. And let your friends know that they may obtain copies of it in any Woolworth store.

TO YOU AND ALL YOUR FAMILY, a warm holiday greeting from Woolworth's. May your Christmas be merry, and your New Year happy and prosperous. With this wish, Woolworth's expresses sincere thanks for your patronage during the past year. It is your good will, and that of all Woolworth patrons, that has made our 75th anniversary year so successful.

OUR COVER. The scene, from an original painting by Paul Rabut, shows the Public Square of Watertown, New York, on an afternoon before Christmas. In Watertown the young Frank W. Woolworth conceived the idea for the type of store that was to make his name famous. In 1873, he clerked in a store on the site of the present Woolworth Building, which is visible in the picture. On the building is a plaque with the inscription, "Birthplace of 5 and 10c Business." This building in Watertown houses the Principal Office of F. W. Woolworth Co.

Gifts from Woolworth's

Merchandise in this book on sale at most Woolworth stores.

Copyright 1954 by F. W. Woolworth Co. • Designed and Produced by Lynn Baker, Incorporated, Advertising

Printed in U.S.A. by Alco-Gravure

TIME CAPSULE MEMORY

"Christmas in Kansas"

My fondest memories of Woolworth's in
Hays, Kansas, center around Christmas
shopping. When I was eight or nine years old,
I was given a dollar to spend. I learned to shop
carefully, always getting good value for
my money. I bought Tangee lipstick, boxes of
cotton handkerchiefs, lilac-scented talcum
powder, bars of shaving soap and Evening in
Paris perfume. To this day, I can recognize the
scent of Evening in Paris! —Joan McAfee

bottom row. When the adults weren't looking, little brother would grab a Red Ryder toy rifle off the shelf, press the trigger and gleefully listen to the *click-click-click,* while sister pushed the belly button on a Baby Gurglee latex doll to hear its unique version of *waa-waa.* In both instances, the result would be the same—the loud utterance of the phrase so sweet to a Woolworth's managers' ears: "Mommy, Daddy, I *want* this!"

Fortunately, it was often possible that those toys would indeed show up under the tree on Christmas day. Woolworth's reasonable prices and the vast selection enabled the financially challenged family to partake of the season of giving (and spending) in style. If the purse was a little thin, no matter. Woolworth's offered a convenient layaway plan; just pay as you go, and by Christmas or Chanukah, the treasures would be yours.

All of this was a boon to the working class, who, until then, could only stare longingly into the beautiful display windows of higher-priced department stores. Now, struggling parents could surprise their children with more than just a handful of walnuts and a tangerine in an old darned Christmas stocking. F. W. Woolworth, along with subsequent dime-stores across America and overseas, worked to level the seasonal playing field.

The art of securing the season's most popular items was one of Frank Woolworth's specialties, and in fact, he was one of the first merchants in the world truly to understand how important it was to feed the frenzy of popular culture and interest, especially the interests of children.

After Frank died in 1919, his successors carried on this toyland tradition, assuring tidy profits for Woolworth's stores across the globe. Gene Autry toy guns, Lone Ranger lunch boxes, "make-your-own" Styrofoam ornaments, Shirley Temple paper dolls, Lana Turner cutouts, mood rings, Cabbage Patch dolls, Flintstones' Color-forms, Nancy Drew books, or Beatles records; whatever caught the youth of America's winter fancy was prominently

displayed at F. W. Woolworth's five-and-dime stores.

This holiday extravaganza was not, of course, limited to products for children, neither was it limited to the United States. Wherever in the world there was a Woolworth's variety store, the patrons were assured of seasonal bargains for every age group. A Yuletide trip to Woolworth's in Germany would offer a stunning selection of glass ornaments, and in Mexico, the December favorites were Christmas piñatas, often hung from the ceilings, swaying from the breeze of a *Casablanca*-style fan.

Patrons of the United Kingdom's Woolworth's stores had a particular penchant for Christmas crackers, which can best be described as tubes covered in paper, which one grabs by either side and pulls. One is then rewarded with a loud pop, and often, a surprise. Although these never really caught on in the United States, Christmas crackers have been best sellers in the U.K. almost from the minute that Frank Woolworth opened his first "three-and-six pence" shop in Liverpool back in 1909. These crackers still come in a mind-boggling array of colors and styles, from simple red foils and holly, to "luxury crackers" available in "Merry Christmas" and Poinsettia designs, often sold along with matching napkins and candles. Generally, the more expensive the set of crackers, the more valuable the gift inside.

Whether you were shopping in London, Scotland, New York City, Montreal, or Havana, the holiday season was always a special time of year at F. W. Woolworth's. It probably seemed as though this discount wonderland was always there, ready to help you find the perfect present for everyone on your Yuletide list. But although it didn't take Frank Winfield Woolworth long to capitalize on the bonanza of the holidays, it did take several decades for F. W. Woolworth's to establish itself as America's quintessential Christmas store.

Gold Tinsel and Tree Ornaments: 1800s Style

During his very first Christmas as a proprietor in Lancaster, Pennsylvania, back in 1879, Frank Woolworth immediately grasped the power and potential profits of seasonal shopping. In those days, most of the items on his counters were more useful than fun, and other than occasional silk ribbon, they were not very glitzy. Still, Woolworth made his display windows as festive as possible, and successfully sold off his current stock, including those troublesome "stickers" (slow-selling notions) that never seemed to move at any other time of year. By 1880 he had already started to master his role as the country's bar-

---

TIME CAPSULE MEMORY

"Happy Chanukah, Mom and Dad!"

It was in the Woolworth's in Astoria, NY, back in the 1950s, I would wile away the time pondering the treasures of the stationery section, pouring over the enticing display of makeup, and making friends with the birds. It was the place where I bought my last childhood doll, a two-foot-high bride doll which still sits in its box in my closet. It was also the place where, as a child, I bought my parents their very first Chanukah gifts . . . toothbrushes!

—Donna Z. Steinhorn

German-made Lauscha ornaments were first introduced to F. W. Woolworth stores in 1890. During World War II, when the German ornaments were unavailable, American manufacturers began reproducing their delicate, colorful style.

gain Santa. The windows were lavishly decorated. Wreaths were hung inside and out, and the first American-made colored glass ball ornaments were introduced and sold out in two days.

These were the simple "Meyer & Schoenaman" tree ornaments, and although they were not nearly as lovely as their European counterparts, they were a far cry from the traditional homemade popcorn beads and bows. Several years later, tinsel garland made its debut. Woolworth had stumbled across a tiny factory in Philadelphia, where an immigrant named Bernard Wilmsen was turning by hand a small machine which changed imported German gold tinsel into garlands. Woolworth knew these would be hot Christmas items and offered to buy every garland in the place, along with a cache of simple hand-painted American tree ornaments. At first, Wilmsen refused, protesting that he only dealt with jobbers, and besides, all of those decorations were promised elsewhere. Woolworth would not be daunted and persisted until Wilmsen gave in. In return, Woolworth promised he would keep buying from Wilmsen for life. He kept his word. Many years later, in 1939, Mr. Wilmsen recalled the day that changed his life: "Mr. Woolworth had at that time only a few stores, but I grew with Woolworth. I have sold them

at least $25 million worth of Christmas tree orna-
ments, in one year alone $800,000 worth. At first
we imported tinsel from Germany. Since the war, I
make it myself. Today, at the corner of Haegert and
Jasper Streets I have a big factory. I have 225
people working to fill Woolworth's orders. We sell
to all, but Woolworth's was first. I am the oldest
Woolworth's [ornament] supplier." Wilmsen, like
many other once struggling manufacturers, became very wealthy due to his faith in young, pushy
Frank W. Woolworth.

Perhaps more than any other Christmas decoration, it was the imported German ornaments
that caused the greatest stir with Woolworth's
American customers. In 1890, during his first trip
to Europe, Frank stumbled upon trimmings the
likes of which his Yankee eyes had never seen.
These were the beautiful Lauscha tree ornaments,
crafted of blown glass and quicksilver, which folklore has it were invented by a poor German glass-
blower who created a collection of small glass
balls to hang on his family's tree. Along with elaborate balls, there were hollow ornaments in the
shape of pine cones, fruit, flowers, animals, birds, and Santas. During his lifetime, Frank
made millions selling these particular ornaments for a nickel and a dime apiece.

It wasn't just German Christmas ornaments that made 1890 a banner year for Frank
Woolworth. He also made sure he capitalized on the "McGinty" craze, when the singer
Maggie Cline had made a huge splash with her rendition of a song called "Down Went
McGinty." So, along with McGinty sheet music, Woolworth made sure he stocked McGinty
toy balloons and McGinty watches. Woolworth bought the watches at eight dollars a gross
(just over 5¢ a piece), sold them for a dime, and watched with satisfaction as they quickly
vanished from his shelves.

Behind the scenes, Woolworth pushed his managers relentlessly during the holidays, dashing off memo after memo, full of advice and orders. He was absolutely paranoid
about employee theft, and told his managers to guard every nickel and dime as if it were
their last. In 1892, he was on a real tear, as illustrated by this General Letter:

*"Give your stores a holiday appearance! Hang up Christmas ornaments. Perhaps
have a tree in the window. Make the store look different. This is our harvest time.*

"Hark the Herald Angels"

Setting up for Christmas was always a big job at Woolworth's, but we managed to have a lot of fun doing it. In one store where I was a stock boy in the 1960s, our assistant manager, a fellow with a great sense of humor, was setting up an end-cap display of Nativity Figures and stables. He did a terrible job and the manager made him change it three times. When his solemn Nativity scene was finally accepted, he announced that he had made up a special tape on a message repeater. These were before the more modern tape recorders, and they were short loop tapes on which you could record a sales pitch.

Intrigued, we all waited for his tape to run. The button was pressed and we heard the following song: "Hark the herald Angels sing, 29 cents for the newborn King, and for ju-ust 10 cents more, you can get a camel that lies on the floor!" Of course, he couldn't use it, but everyone got a good laugh out of it. It was moments like those that broke up the tension and gave all the hard-working Woolworth's employees a chance to laugh and enjoy a few moments of camaraderie. Although it was off-beat humor, I think even old Frank Woolworth would have chuckled.

—Robert Bennett, former stock boy

Make it pay. This is also a good time to work off stickers or unsaleable goods, for they will sell during the excitement when you could not give them away at other times. Mend all broken toys and dolls every day. Also, watch your clerks and customers to see they do not steal. When the store is crowded, don't allow any boys or girls in the stores at all, unless they are with parents, as most of them come in on purpose to steal. The cashier needs your watchful eye, as it has been the experience of at least one store every year to lose large amounts through the cashier's dishonesty. Remember, the cashier has the best chance of all to steal."

The Christmas season of 1892 was his most prosperous to date, and the profits just kept on climbing over the ensuing years. As the new century dawned, Woolworth had fifty-nine stores with annual gross profits exceeding five million dollars. In 1899, his Christmas trade alone amounted to a half million dollars. That particular year, he even departed from his Scrooge mentality by initiating a Christmas bonus system. Employees received an additional $5.00 for each year of service, with a limit of $25. Of course, there was a catch:

> *"Pay this present just before Christmas or the day after. Our object is to secure the services of our clerks at a time of the year when competitors are tempting them with higher wages."*

Perhaps realizing that his empire was running nicely without him, he decided to spend the holiday with his wife, Jennie and his three children. Although his family was probably thrilled, Frank had a different take on the matter.

> *"For the first time in twenty years I spent the night before Christmas at home. It's the last time I'll do so. I'd probably be of little service to any store, yet it is pleasanter to be in the fight at the last moment than to wait at home in suspense."*

The Grinches that Tried to Steal Christmas

Despite all the successful years, F. W. Woolworth Co. executives were sometimes called upon to muster up every ounce of inventiveness to salvage seasonal profits. Between 1879 and 1930, America suffered at least nine economic depressions that caused the demise of many retailers across America. F. W. Woolworth Co. was never one of the depression casualties, but the company had to work double-time during these periods. Buyers would be sent out to scour the countryside looking for holiday items they could sell to a financially strained public, yet still make a small profit. One of the most marked challenges occurred in the summer of 1914, with the onset of World War I. Frank and Jennie Woolworth were in France when the war broke out and were consequently marooned in Geneva for weeks before sailing home. This caused a fair amount of apprehension and inconvenience, but that was the least of the merchant prince's problems. By then, Frank had begun to rely on European imports for some of his most popular lines of merchandise. He had bustling German warehouses in Bavaria, Sonneberg, and Thuringia, and French offices in Paris and Calais. All were closed for the duration of the war and suddenly the harbors were closed. With the Christmas season just months away, Frank Woolworth knew he had to act fast.

D.M.C.-brand imported British crochet cotton and knitting wool were among his fastest-selling commodities, and because of cheap labor costs, they were also high-profit items. Sales of all manner of sewing materials would routinely increase before the holidays as people across the country made seasonal scarves, coverlets, and quilts for their family members. By 1915, the supply of D.M.C. products were dwindling down to nothing, so Frank Woolworth wisely induced an American mill to try to duplicate these goods. Thus was launched the famous Woolco cotton line, which soon attained immense popularity. After the War, British sewing supplies, such as needles and snaps, were once again available for import, but this time around they were released under the Woolco brand name. The Woolco name itself eventually became a familiar brand name in Woolworth's stores world-wide, and fifty years later, it became the name of the company's Woolco store division.

Through fast-thinking and definitive action, Frank Woolworth had turned lemons into lemonade.

A similar strategy was used to replace the suddenly scarce German celluloid dolls and Christmas tree ornaments. Woolworth backed a domestic manufacturer to create a copy of both, and just in the nick of time, millions of American-made tree ornaments and dolls were available to holiday shoppers. World War II was even more devastating for Woolworth's holdings overseas and stateside. Many of Woolworth's largest suppliers and manufacturers stopped creating their standard retail products in order to manufacture war-related products. Tariffs, import problems, escalating prices, and government restrictions on the sale of certain goods all combined to make the Christmas seasons between 1941 and 1944 potential financial disasters. Ironically, the hardship of being forced to do without certain key items worked to spawn many entirely new industries. For example, the very Lauscha German Christmas ornaments that had once been responsible for millions in Woolworth's seasonal profits were virtually replaced by the American-made counterparts. However, these original Lauscha trimmings have not been forgotten, and these days, they are extremely collectible, some of the rarest bringing hundreds of dollars apiece. Many of the old molds and original techniques have been resurrected by German glassblowers to meet the demand for traditional (and historically accurate) Christmas ornaments.

F. W. Woolworth's saw a moderate decline in net profits during the war years and the various depressions, but the company soon bounced back, even stronger and richer in the purse than before. The Grinches that tried to steal its Christmas profits were no match for the inventive F. W. Woolworth Company, which somehow always seemed to overcome adversity.

A World of Bunnies, Shamrocks, and Candy Hearts

"For every day is a holiday at Woolworth's! Fun-loving Americans . . . six or sixty years young . . . crowd the counters . . . thrilled with the delightful finds—the favors and the foolishness—full of the spirit that makes you want to blow whistles and ring bells and make noise. Woolworth's is here to meet your needs, for every holiday and every special event!"

That's the way the F. W. Woolworth Company described itself back in 1939, and they weren't exaggerating. Christmas was just one slice of the mercantile pie. New Year's Day was the official close of the Yuletide season, the signal for the busy bees at Woolworth's to put away the Santas and noisemakers and bring out the Valentine hearts.

One of the company's slogans was, "Woolworth's calendar—like yours—is dotted with dates for good times!" And they did their best to make certain the customer's good times translated into healthy profits. In rapid succession, one holiday after another was featured from coast to coast: St. Patrick's Day, Easter, Mother's Day, Father's Day, Memorial Day, Fourth of July—all within the first six months of the year.

F. W. Woolworth's was always in seasonal transition, which was a boon to patrons but a challenge to the managers, stockboys, and display artists who had to transform the stores' themes, often in record time. It seemed as though they'd just dragged out the large boxes of shamrocks when it was time to the drag out the Easter baskets. If it was any consolation to those hard-working men and women, the steady flow of patrons appreciated their efforts. Children and adults alike thought it was a just plain fun to stroll down Woolworth's aisles during the company's heyday, and choose a special gift for a loved one, or a set of thematic paper plates and matching cups for the family's annual Fourth of July picnic.

There was never any doubt as to which holiday one was dealing with, because each was marked by its own personal brand of colors and seasonal items. After New Year's Eve, the Valentine's Day ritual burst forth with a flurry of red, pink, and silver. This was the time for Woolworth's customers to choose

EASTER EXCITEMENT . . . Easter baskets, jelly beans, greeting cards, gifts, candies, favors, typical of the seasonal specialties you'll find at Woolworth's.

ST. VALENTINE'S DAY . . . Woolworth is well stocked with Cupid's aids—hearts, favors, placecards, paper napkins, souvenirs—cards, amusing or sentimental.

the perfect romantic greeting card for their sweethearts, to purchase boxed Whitman candies, to select an inexpensive but colorful corsage or piece of costume jewelry. And everyone remembers those tiny candy hearts with messages such as "I love you" and "Please be mine."

When the winter snow started to melt it was time to transform Woolworth's Wonderland from Valentine's red to St. Patrick's Day green. The counters suddenly brimmed over with shamrocks, leprechauns, and "I'm Proud To Be Irish" tee-shirts and ties. There were even special "lucky" green collars for the family cat and dog.

Next on the agenda was Easter, a fantasyland of pink, pale yellows, and white. During the Lenten season, customers could choose from tasteful religious cards to bright Easter baskets filled with chocolate bunnies and wrapped in colorful cellophane. Everywhere you looked, there were piles and piles of jelly beans, and the perennial favorite: yellow marshmallow "peeps" chick candy.

For many Americans, Easter was also the time of year to get dressed up for church, enjoy the local parade, and then return home for an elaborate family feast. In response, the

F. W. Woolworth was there to meet its patron's needs on Halloween and every holiday.

larger Woolworth's stores added expansive clothing sections where one could purchase Buster Brown shoes, black patent leather Mary Janes, a boy's first suit and tie, or a girl's frilly pink-and-white dress. The sewing department was stocked with the makings of Easter bonnets; offering special sales on silk, flowers, and ribbons, netting, feathers, and bows. Just inside the front door, the Easter Bunny was ready to take a photograph with the toddlers.

Behind the scenes, the Easter season offered its own set of labor challenges. Most people do not realize that until the early 1960s, the Woolworth's "filled" Easter baskets were personally assembled, one by one, and all large novelty candies and chocolate eggs were decorated by hand by Woolworth employees. To accomplish this Easter magic in a timely fashion, managers often used an assembly line approach, which started as early as mid-January when the first jelly beans arrived at the stores. The employees also made up other novelty items. Remember the old toy wooden paddles with the attached rubber ball on an elasticized string? These paddles were decorated with candies and small toys, then wrapped in cellophane for sale

TIME CAPSULE MEMORY

5&10

"Easter-time in Massachusetts"

Every Easter, my mom would take me to our local Woolworth's in Boston and buy me a new hat and white cotton socks trimmed with dainty laces to go with my home-made Easter dress. The socks and the hats didn't cost very much (under a dollar) but I felt like a million!

—Nancy Miller

during Easter, Christmas, and other holidays. Come summertime, plastic sand buckets were filled with beach toys, coloring books, and crayons, then tied with ribbons. Again, every bucket was assembled individually by a Woolworth's employee.

After Easter, people would head to their local Red-Front on Main Street for that special gift for Mother's Day and Father's Day. Greeting cards flew out of the store by the millions, as did bottles of Blue Waltz perfume and Old Spice aftershave. Of course, sales of Blue Waltz were not restricted to Mother's Day; this popular, inexpensive scent (along with Evening in Paris) was often purchased as the "first perfume" for young girls, and remained their favorite scent for years to come.

Both Memorial Day and Fourth of July offered color schemes of red, white, and blue. Not surprisingly, flags were the best-sellers, along with thematic paper plates, cups, and napkins to spruce up Independence Day picnics.

As the hazy days of summer gave way to falling leaves, Woolworth's customers, and employees, turned their thoughts to autumn.

> **TIME CAPSULE MEMORY**
>
> **5&10**
>
> ## "The Holidays at Woolworth's"
>
> Kids loved F. W. Woolworth's, especially during the holiday seasons, like Valentines Day, Easter, Fourth of July and Thanksgiving. Christmas was extra special because of all the toys. Halloween was special too. Woolworth's always catered to the holidays with delicious candies and an abundance of merchandise. My friend once sold three small papier maché lanterns in a yard auction that were purchased at Woolworth's back in the early forties. They still had the Woolworth's price tags on them: fifteen cents apiece. They sold for $50 each! A thin cardboard witch riding her broom, originally twenty-five cents, brought in $45 and a fifteen-cent cardboard cat went for $35! —Donn Hornung

Autumn Specials: Back to School, Halloween, and Thanksgiving

The parents usually started making out the "school lists" in late August, while the children were outside trying to get in one last kickball game before their precious summer vacation ended. September meant "back to school" for millions of children, and for F. W. Woolworth's, it meant a bonanza of special sales. Back in the 1870s, Frank Woolworth only offered the basics, such as small chalkboards and pencils, but by 1930, the stationery section of the stores offered a profusion of items to help the younger set learn their ABCs. There were marble composition books, pencil tablets and boxes, Waterman's ink, pen points, mucilage, and looseleaf paper. Soon, colored pencils and mega-packs of crayons were added to the mix, along with jars of that creamy white school paste which one applied with a stick that was attached to the lid. To school children across America, the white paste looked good enough to eat, and it often was!

The fabulous fifties heralded an explosion of new school products. World War II was over,

> **Woolworth Trivia**
>
> During 1929, 4000 miles of pencils and 300 miles of pen points were sold during the Back-to-School season at F. W. Woolworth's

"The Old Easter Jelly-Bean Flares"

Back in the early days, before everything came to stores pre-packaged, it was our job as Woolworth's employees to make-up hundreds and hundreds of Easter baskets. We were also given the task of decorating and "painting" the candy novelties. We used a small brush to coat every single chocolate Easter novelty with a special non-toxic edible lacquer. (The lacquer helped protect the chocolate from heat and allowed the decorative icing to stick better. It would also make you as high as a kite if there wasn't ventilation where you did it!) I have vivid memories of this particular holiday job, dating back to the time when I started working for the company in the late 1940s. All of the larger Easter Chocolates (like tall bunnies and larger egg treats) would come in to us individually boxed. We would then set up an Easter assembly line. We would open up each carton, pull out each bunny or egg box, paint it with the lacquer, and let it dry. One of the more talented female associates would then do the actual decorating, using the type of sweet candied icing that people use to decorate birthday cakes. She had a lot of materials to work with, including several boxes of pre-made sugar based flowers, leaves etc., that she would stick on each novelty. Some of the candies really came out beautiful. We used a similar assembly line approach with making up the Easter baskets. The Easter Basket job would start as soon as the first shipments of jelly beans arrived in January or February. The first task was to make up what the employees called "jelly bean flares." These were created by taking a small colorful cellophane square and wrapping it around an ounce or so of jelly beans, which was then tied with a ribbon. At the same time, hundreds of ribbons and bows were also being pre-made (at first by hand and later by a simple machine). These were all used to help decorate the Easter baskets. This practice continued through the 1950s and 1960s until it was decided it was too labor intensive. It's too bad, in a way, that the tradition of custom-made baskets and chocolate novelties was stopped, because they were really a lot nicer than most of the pre-packaged holiday merchandise we get in stores today.

the import business was back to normal, and television was introducing children to all manner of exciting products. Suddenly, plain old brown wrap lunch bags were a thing of the past, and thematic lunch boxes with matching Thermoses were all the rage. Every boy wanted a "Hopalong Cassidy" or "Davy Crocket" lunch box to hold their peanut butter sandwich, and every girl wanted a clear plastic pencil case that closed with a nifty zipper and was decorated in dainty flowers. And, many people recall the first time they saw that wonder of wonders, the "three-in-one" retractable pen, that could dispense different ink colors: red, blue and green. For decades, Woolworth's also sold heavy leather book satchels with buckles and straps. However, children growing up in the late-1970s and beyond enjoyed the advantage of more lightweight book gear. The contemporary youth of America headed down Golden Rule Lane carrying modern versions of knapsacks. These practical carry-alls were first introduced in simple, solid colors, but soon Woolworth's offered knapsacks decorated with characters such as Power Rangers, X-Men, Barbie, and Rainbow Brite. The thought of leaving the glorious days of summer for the toils of the schoolroom was not always the most pleasant for children, but the trek to Woolworth's to purchase yearly supplies was fun for one and all. Many families made this trip a special event, allowing the children to select their school supplies, then treating them to an end-of-vacation ice cream. Before you knew it, the kids were on the school bus, the parents were reveling in blissful silence, and the Woolworth's employees were at it again, setting up for Halloween.

Aside from Christmas and Easter, Halloween was the largest holiday in terms of sheer net sales and the variety of specialty merchandise available to consumers. The Halloween season at F. W. Woolworth's had its own special brand of magic, a magic characterized, of course, by orange and black. In the candy arena, customers would buy tons of sweet orange pumpkin candies, candy corn, black licorice sticks, striped Juicy Fruit gum, and bite-sized, foil-wrapped chocolates—all destined for the bags of trick-or-treaters who would soon be arriving on neighborhood doorsteps.

The aisles were jammed with boxes of prepackaged "Collegeville" Halloween costumes, including perennial favorites such as clowns, cowboys, ghosts, and fairy princesses. For those making up their own costumes, there were wigs, makeup, mustaches, rubber noses, hats, and the occasional fang. Ever conscious of the parties that accompany Halloween, Woolworth's was ready with orange-and-black paper plates and flatware, candle centerpieces featuring ghosts and goblins, plastic serving platters in the shape of witches, and yards of wispy streamers to hang from the ceiling. During the 1980s, all manner of battery-operated Halloween goodies were introduced, adding a more high-tech and often "spooky" feel to the occasion. There were illuminated trick-or-treat bags, ghosts that hung from trees and *booed* when you got too close, window witches that cackled, and

TIME CAPSULE MEMORY

"Shopping for School Supplies in Iowa"

Back in the late 1930s, farmers flocked to our Woolworth's in Keokuk, Iowa, every Saturday afternoon, and in late August, they brought along their kids to shop for school clothes, shoes and school supplies. Small Red Chief tablets were five cents, big ones were ten cents. Good pencils were two for five cents (and you'd better not chew on them, lose them, or let anyone steal them). Ink pens with a cork finger grip were five cents and pen points were two cents. Script ink, in black, blue, green and red, was ten cents a bottle which had a little lip so you could dip your pen point and not get ink on your pen or fingers. Coloring books were five cents, and crayons cost ten cents for a box of sixteen. A 100-sheet pack of typing paper was only fifteen cents!

—Donn Hornung

skeleton costumes that talked! Another big hit with children was battery-operated antenna gear. These were thin coated wires that fit around the head, like a stereo headphone. At the top, two small "lit-up" orange pumpkins dangled on the end of elasticized wires, bobbling as the child walked. One of the most popular Halloween novelties of all time were the sweet "red wax lips" that you used to put in your mouth, held in place with your teeth, and ate later. In the 1930s these sold for a nickel apiece at Woolworth's, and the company sold millions of them over the years. They are still popular even today.

Next on the seasonal agenda was Thanksgiving, more subdued but still notable. Thanksgiving was the time of year when Woolworth's would offer paper pilgrims, decorative gourds, and Indian corn of every size, and Thanksgiving dinnerware and serving platters inlayed with turkey designs. As with every other holiday, Thanksgiving was an extremely busy time at the local five-and-dime, with long lines at cash registers and customers crammed into the aisles looking for bargains. It was somewhat disconcerting when you banged your Woolworth's red canvas carry basket into that of a fellow patron's in the crush, but the prices (especially during the days when everything cost a dime) made it all worthwhile.

Setting Up House: Five-and-Dime Style

Although not technically a "holiday" for the masses, the tradition of heading down to Woolworth's to purchase brand-new household goods was a memorable part of many people's lives. For the entire span of its 118-year history, and throughout every season of the year, F. W. Woolworth's catered to working-class newlyweds setting up house. Company catalogs made it crystal clear that the business of brides and grooms were welcome. "F. W. Woolworth's," its 1939 booklet boasted, "is where you can find, under one roof, the thousand and one things that make a house into a home!" An additional bonus was "the marvelous host of kitchen utensils in shining array that would make a homebody of a girl who never boiled an egg."

F. W. Woolworth's "Back to School" Sales Through the Decades

For School

Excerpt from 1919 catalogue lists general merchandise for children, as well as school supplies such as paper and "mucilage."

A wide assortment of back-to-school items were available to customers in 1939.

Countless newlyweds returned from their honeymoons, pocketed what was left of their wedding gift money, and headed to Woolworth's for a post-marital shopping spree. For those just starting out as a couple, one of the most popular sections of the store was the "gadget" department. Here the young, thrifty housekeeper could find corn holders, egg poachers, potato mashers, and metal vegetable peelers that never seemed to wear out. Few could resist the "Faucet Queen," a device which slipped over the faucet and, with a light push of its lever, changed the direct flow of water into a fine spray. Nearby, one could find cake pans, pudding pans, and muffin pans . . . funnels, hand towels, scrub brushes, and steel wool . . . cedar oil polish and mixing bowls. In the early 1950s, there was a big push on Woolworth's "Plastic Ensembles," which were arguably the most practical yet gaudy kitchen accessories ever offered by the company. Plastic Ensembles were vinyl "work-saving" plastic covers, which were available in several patterns, including "Fruit Festival." For a mere dollar, you could buy a five-piece cottage window set that included a sash curtain in a red, green, yellow, and orange fruit pattern. For a few dollars more, you could add an entire line of matching appliance covers, tablecloths, even bowl cover sets. At the time, these Plastic Ensembles sold like hotcakes, especially given the promise that they "wipe clean in a jiffy." Nowadays, they frequently show up at garage sales, and there is a branch of the collector's

A busy Woolco store in Gretna, Louisiana, c. 1979.

market that specializes in these and other 1950s five-and-dime items.

Tableware was always on a newlyweds' list, and Woolworth's exclusive Harlequin brand was often at the top. Harlequin dinnerware came in a variety of colors, including Kraft Blue and Red Majestic. They were priced for the budget-conscious consumer and were always laid out in lovely displays. What customers didn't realize was what the Woolworth's stockboys went through to get that dinnerware to the consumer. The dinnerware (each piece loose) would arrive at the store in giant cartons filled with straw so by the time they finished unpacking, the workers were covered with dust, straw, and dirt, and itched and sneezed for three days! Harlequin dinnerware is also highly collectible in today's retro market.

Another important part of setting up house was cultivation of the new garden. Whether you had a small window garden in New York City, or an expansive landscape in the suburbs, Woolworth's "Gardening Department" had everything you needed to make your garden one of the prettiest on the block. Come springtime, Woolworth's stores would feature piles of seeds, garden tools, and watering cans, right along with its Easter merchandise. During the late 1970s, some of the larger Woolworth's and Woolco stores offered entire landscape and gardening substores; these were especially popular in the United Kingdom.

After the newlyweds settled in to their first apartment or home, their social life usually expanded rather quickly, and Woolworth's was at the ready to equip the young couple for all their social needs. The local five-and-ten was the perfect and most convenient place

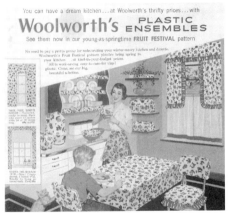

You can have a dream kitchen...at Woolworth's thrifty prices...with

Woolworth's PLASTIC ENSEMBLES

See them now in our young-as-springtime FRUIT FESTIVAL pattern

to stock up on supplies for church bake sales, surprise birthday parties, and bon voyage celebrations. A typical Saturday night in the late 1950s and early 1960s would find couples meeting for Bridge card parties, and to make these events more enjoyable, Woolworth's offered an entire line of Bridge accessories. There were playing cards, special bridge pencils, and card table covers, along with individual match boxes and ash trays which were placed in table corners. Woolworth's also popularized the now familiar "Bridge Mix," its own special mix of candies and salted nuts.

More often than not, within a year or two, a baby was on the way, and the mother-to-be headed downtown to Woolworth's to purchase baby clothes and blankets in blue, pink, and neutral yellow. If her friends and family threw a baby shower for the mother-to-be, it was a good chance they purchased their party favors and gifts there as well.

In their company booklet, *50 Years of Woolworth: 1879–1929,* the F. W. Woolworth Co. bragged that they could supply all of the babys under five years of age in the United States and Canada with most of the things they needed. At that time, they were buying merchandise for over twelve million babies a year!

Mementos of Holidays Past

Many former customers still have some of their F. W. Woolworth holiday mementos tucked away in shoe boxes in their closets, as special reminders of days gone by. It might be the colorful tin that once held holiday cookies, or the set of porcelain salt and pepper shakers purchased to spruce up the Easter dinner table. Others have kept the pair of ten-cent button earrings their child presented to them on Mother's Day, or the plastic orange pumpkin used the very first time out on a night of Halloween trick-or-treating.

The local F. W. Woolworth's, along with other five-and-dime stores, created memories, amusing or sentimental, that would last a lifetime. Many still cling to their memories as relics of a simpler, happier time.

Page from Woolworth's catalogue, "Fashions for Baby," 1956.

TIME CAPSULE MEMORY

"A Gift Given with Love"

I give Woolworth's credit for making one Christmas *very* special. Mrs. Kalioma, a lady who had no children and could afford expensive gifts, asked me which doll I thought the prettiest. Of course, my choice was a beauty with 'real' hair that could be combed and big blue eyes which opened and closed. Santa didn't leave it under the tree, but when the Kalioma's came for dinner there was a long box for me . . . and inside it, my doll! Woolworth's played an important role in my life, not only at Christmas but throughout the year. I grew up in a small town 22 miles from a Woolworth's. Once a month the family journeyed to Ironwood, MI to shop and while my parents shopped for groceries, my sister and I explored Woolworth's. I will never forget those times.

—Hope Abadie

ITEM	DESCRIPTION	RECOMMENDED	WANTED	PRICE
DRESS-UP TIME...				
Socks or stockings		3 pr.		
Soft-soled shoes		2 pr.		
Slips		2-3		
Dresses		3-4		
Boys' suits		2-3		
Training pants		4-6		
Panties, dress (optional)		2		
Creepers or diaper suits		3		
Polo shirts		3-4		
Sunsuits		3-4		
Booties, wool, Orlon or stretch nylon		3 pr.		
Sweaters, wool or Orlon		2		
Shawls		2		
Caps or bonnets		2		
Pram suit (optional)		1		
Buntings		2		
Diaper sets		2-3		
NURSERY FURNITURE...				
Bassinet or carrying basket		1		
Bath table or tub		1		
Crib and mattress		1		
Crib bumpers		1-2		
Nursery lamp		1		
Wall plaques (optional)				
MISCELLANEOUS ITEMS...				
Diaper pail		1		
Tot trainer		1		
Baby record book		1		
Baby hangers		6-8		
Strollers and carriages		1		
Scale		1		

Lay-Away Plan

It's no strain on the family budget when you buy Baby's things at Woolworth's. For a 10% deposit, and no carrying charge, Woolworth's puts aside any item until you want it.

BABY DESERVES THE BEST—THAT'S WOOLWORTH'S PATA-CAKE

Chapter Ten

The Spectacle of Woolworth's

"Great things are far from over. It was not too long ago,

A boy in the country thought that there was more he ought to know,

So he put the farm behind him, Said good-bye to cow and hen,

Then started a great new wonder, Mr. Woolworth's Five and Ten.

What a Notion, what a dream, what an idea, the perfect scheme!"

—Theme song from: "Mr. Woolworth Had a Notion," 1965

Drama and Artistry: Five-and-Dime Style

Frank Winfield Woolworth was the first of the chain store magnates to actively consider both dramatic and sensory impact as vital components of successful ware merchandising. He viewed his business as a stage performance; the product displays his scenery, the employees his actors, the customers his audience. Over the decades, this drama moved out of the confines of the actual stores and into the wider realm of popular culture. The vision of F. W. Woolworth's Red-Fronts, both in the United States and abroad, became so familiar, and the experience of shopping there so ingrained in millions of people's lives, that "Woolworth's" evolved from simple dimestore to household name. Consequently, the Red-Fronts quickly found their way into countless poems, sonnets, parodies, editorial cartoons, and Nickelodeon reels. As you will soon learn, the chief himself once appeared in a silent "flicker"—much to his delight. After Frank died in 1919, the legend of his empire, and that of the five-and-dime concept he had spawned, eventually infiltrated Hollywood, Broadway, Tin Pan Alley, and the air waves. References to Woolworth's popped up frequently in published stories and best-sellers; British author, Barbara Comyns even named one of her

Beginning on New Year's Day 1952, the manager of the F. W. Woolworth in Pasadena, California, and the company at large, sponsored the Tournament of Roses Parade. It was broadcast for years over NBC-TV network. In 1954, it was hailed as the first event ever broadcast in full color.

books, *Our Spoons Came from Woolworths*. The Donahue Sales Corporation, one of Woolworth's oldest suppliers, produced a foot-tapping New York musical review in honor of Mr. Woolworth. It eventually reached the point where the mere mention of a one simple word, "Woolworth," in a song lyric or sentence, instantly evoked a nostalgic response or mental image.

Even Frank Woolworth himself, with his penchant for thinking big, could not have imagined just how far the stores bearing his name would become imbedded into the popular culture. And since "talking pictures" weren't even established yet, he didn't have a clue that eight years after his passing, a musical sound film would be produced bearing his store's name. While some of the fame occurred by accident, Frank Woolworth, from the beginning, did have a semblance of a master plan for celebrity. He set it in motion in 1878 when he saw the frenzy created by his five-cent bargain table in Moore & Smith's Watertown, New York, store.

From the get-go, Frank strived to make shopping at Woolworth's a memorable and newsworthy event. He transformed the working class's traditionally hum-drum shopping expedition into an enjoyable affair. He did so by paying attention to both the aesthetics of his stores and the sensibilities of his customers. With his first few shops in Utica and Lancaster, the priority was simply to buy as many goods as he could afford with his limited capital, get these items out on the counters in record time, and start making a profit. But the moment he had a few thousand dollars to spare, this Barnum of the Dimestores started to focus on artistry, drama and, whenever possible, *spectacle*.

Opening-Day Galas and Special Events

Frank Woolworth was a great aficionado of symphony, opera, theater, and art, and these were the very resources he called upon when weaving aesthetics into his mercantile opus. This was particularly true in the late 1880s, when he initiated the practice of grand opening galas. Such events often featured popular singers or full-fledged orchestras, surrounded by "props" such as swaying palms and aromatic flowers. In later years, he added his Gilded Age "Refreshment Rooms" to the mix. And so, on opening day (and every day) his financially strained patrons had the rare opportunity to dine at marble-topped tables with linen napkins and attentive waiters, while they gazed appreciatively at the surrounding statuary, oil paintings, and wall murals. Best of all, his customers could enjoy such luxuries for a mere pittance. The prices on the food menu were the same as those in the stores—*nothing* was over ten cents. The masses thronged to Frank's opening day sales, and being so impressed with the incomparable bargains and the spectacle of the premier, they became steady, life-long customers of F. W. Woolworth's, just as Frank had hoped.

This impression of heightened drama was not limited to store premiers. After the hoopla died down, the sensory experience continued. There was always the aroma of popcorn to greet you at the door, the visual lure of chocolates piled high on sparkling glass trays, and the comfort of being served by uniformed clerks and counter girls, who were ready to please. Many of Woolworth's turn-of-the-century five-and-dimes even featured talented piano players and singers, thus providing a bit of melodious accompaniment to the background sounds of jingling cash register machines.

Despite all this pomp, Frank Woolworth was not a pretentious man when it came to his chosen profession. He knew full well that he was selling tin shovels for a nickel, not diamond bracelets for thousands of dollars. But he did not believe that cut-rate prices automatically translated into cut-rate treatment or sloppy displays. His merchandise was always arranged in a way as to appear aesthetically pleasing to his clientele. He eventually replaced his stores' original humble pine shelves with mahogany-veneered counters, some with lower glass cabinets sporting brass fittings. Attractive overhead Casablanca fans cooled the bargain-hunting masses, and the silver metal cash registers were scrubbed until they gleamed in the gaslight. This is not to imply that the utilitarian Woolworth's could be considered or described as "classically beautiful," but the old five-and-dimes did have a certain genteel charm. Even after World War I, when all of F. W. Woolworth's Refreshment Rooms were outfitted with new Formica lunch counters, and the quaint wooden counters (and individual counter girls) swapped for modern metal and plastic "self-service" shelving, the stores retained a high level of artistry.

Thousands of Woolworth's managers, straight through to the end of the Woolworth era, dreamed-up sensational promotional gimmicks that lured in record-breaking crowds. Back in the late 1950s, for instance, the ambitious manager of the Menlo Park, New Jersey, store, arranged a two-week sale to sell hundreds of pieces of *original* artwork, some of which were painted by the Old Masters. This certainly wasn't the routine Woolworth's sales event in Edison, a store which usually did its stock in trade in school supplies and kitchen gadgets. Some of the surrounding specialty store owners even criticized the Woolworth's manager for being pretentious and stepping out of his five-and-dime station. He plunged ahead anyway and met with great success. Along with original paintings and expensive lithographs, there were moderately-priced pieces of art to appeal to those with less to spend. The works of artists including Renoir, Van Gogh, and Cezanne made their Woolworth's debut during those weeks, luring in three thousand visitors a day!

Front page of the Summer/Fall 1994 issue of the company's newsletter, the *Woolworth News*, illustrates that Frank Woolworth's sense of fanfare persevered straight into the 1990s. This cover featured "The Great Return" gala of store #1725 in Harlem, New York.

As late as 1994, the atmosphere was festive and hopeful at many regional F. W. Woolworth's stores. In July of that year, "A Great Reception" was held in honor on the grand opening of store #1725 in Harlem, New York City. A ribbon-cutting ceremony, featuring a guest appearance by Seattle Supersonics basketball player, Gus Williams, and free refreshments, was just the tip of the promotional iceberg.

A large parade was staged on Broadway, led by the Jackie Robinson Drum and Bugle Corps, with hundreds of community children sporting "Great Return" tee-shirts leading the way. According to the *Woolworth News,* opening-day sales at the store were overwhelming and continued to exceed expectations. Other 1990s events, ranging from promotional to charitable, included the successful "March of Dimes Walk for Healthy Babies," which involved employees of the Hilo, Hawaii, store, as well as the many health clinics and literacy programs sponsored in inner cities. "Customer appreciation" days were another popular form of creative community service. In Caro, Michigan, the local manager organized a giant sidewalk sale with Woolworth's employees dressed up as circus performers and free refreshments for one and all. Certainly one of the most unusual gimmicks was the display of a 100-pound live catfish in Rhinelander, Wisconsin, which acted as a "lure" for special sporting equipment sales, and raffle drawings for fishing poles, tackle boxes and fish food. All these events were testimony to the spirit of hundreds of Woolworth's employees and managers, who were by then witnessing the first devastating wave of Red-Front closings across America. It also indicates that there were stores making healthy profits, right up until the fateful day in 1997 when all the remaining F. W. Woolworth variety stores were closed down.

Thousands of similar stories can be found in the historical archives of the company. It wasn't until the final months of Woolworth's 118-year history that this charm and spectacle began to disappear. At that point, employees knew their time with the once-great company was limited, and it was difficult to muster up any semblance of enthusiasm.

This spirit of drama and artistry, of dreaming-up creative ideas that would make a splash with millions of budget-conscious customers, was a tradition started by Frank Woolworth over a century before. These days, we take such merchandising events for granted, yawning at the latest ad for a gala sidewalk sale or a 150-story high Godzilla balloon heralding a grand opening. However, in the early days, before the advent of these and other high-tech amusements like video arcades, ten-screen movie theaters and Disneyland, many working- and middle-class Americans looked to their weekly shopping trips to Main Street for diversion. Frank Woolworth capitalized on this knowledge, and in some cases, pulled out all the stops to give his patrons a true spectacle.

The Woolworth's Roof Garden and Vaudeville House

As a poor farmboy growing up in northern New York, Frank was not exposed to much artistry or theater, but his sensibilities rapidly matured after his first venture to Europe in 1890. He didn't waste any time transferring some of his newfound drama into the framework of his American stores. The term "Refreshment Room," for example, was a phrase borrowed from the British, as Frank thought it a much more sophisticated term than "restaurant" or "food hall." The magnificent frescoes he incorporated into his great Woolworth Building in New York reminded him of Paris; the lively "ooompa" and march bands that amused patrons during some of his grand openings in New York and Chicago, were reminiscent of his experiences in Germany and Switzerland. It was in Vienna, however, that his primary artistic passion, which was music, was fueled to near capacity. The performances of Vienna symphonies brought tears to his eyes, so inspiring him that, in later years, he actually imported a piece of Vienna to his Woolworth's store in Lancaster, Pennsylvania. He accomplished this through building "the wonder of wonders," the Woolworth Roof Garden and Vaudeville House.

Frank had premiered his first tiny store at 170 Queen Street in Lancaster, Pennsylvania, in 1879. By the end of 1890, he had replaced this one with a bigger site on 6 and 8 North Queen. Still not satisfied, Frank opened an even larger, more expansive five-and-ten on November 6, 1900, and this was the landmark that added true drama to his emerging commercial empire. Located in a new five-story Woolworth "skyscraper" on the corner of North Queen and Grant, the five-and-dime itself was situated at sidewalk level, with leased offices filling up the interim floors. The store alone was enough to raise eyebrows, with its profusion of merchandise, displays, and employees, but the most spectacular part of all was located high above the sidewalk, in the Woolworth Roof Garden. To get there, patrons would walk through the five-and-dime proper, then take a modern elevator to the top of the building. Upon arrival, they were astonished to find an exquisite roof garden resplendent with exotic greenery and flowers. They were treated to a bird's eye view of the sky-scraper's gold-domed peaks, colonnades, and peristyles, enhanced by colored lights. An observation area offered panoramic views of the city and surrounding countryside. The lo-cal *Intelligencer* reported the Woolworth's skyscraper was so high that "the people ap-peared in the streets below like pigmies."

The highlight of all this rooftop opulence was a large stage and auditorium area, known colloquially as the Woolworth Vaudeville House. It was here that Woolworth intro-duced some of the best entertainment on the East Coast to the growing and heterogeneous population of Lancasterians. Vaudeville was in its prime in 1900, and Lancaster was dotted with flourishing opera and vaudeville houses, including the popular Colonial Theater and Orange Street Opera House. When the week's work was done, whether at factory, retail es-tablishment, or farm, the population would stream to the town's amusement centers to en-joy the acts of current headliners. Favorite performers at Woolworth's Vaudeville House and other theaters in Lancaster included the Four Musical Maids, the Famous Miners', Miss Josephine and Her Quartette of Colored Youngsters, and the "authentic Indian rain dances" of Princess Wan-A-Tea. All of the vaudeville houses, including Frank's Wool-worth's, presented several different forms of entertainment in one night, so along with the songsters and dancers, there were also magicians, ventriloquists, comedians, and acro-bats. Animal acts such as Wesley's Sea Lions provided additional sure-fire crowd-pleasers. One of the more memorable evenings was the night that F. W. Woolworth's featured a gen-uine European symphony orchestra, straight from Vienna. On that balmy weekend in Lan-caster, the sounds of master violinists and percussionists filled the auditorium, allowing Frank Woolworth to bring the music he loved into the realm of the Pennsylvania's working- and middle-class families.

By 1910, vaudeville was already on the decline, as fledgling movie houses and nick-elodeons started showing short silent flickers. Many of the vaudeville houses, in Lancaster and in large towns across the country, started to offer both silent movies and vaudeville performers on the same bill, but it was soon clear that minstrels and acrobats were being passed over in favor of this marvel of moving picture entertainment. Frank Woolworth was never one to balk at changing times, and he was certainly not the type to hang on until the bottom fell out of the market. So, he razed the beautiful roof garden and its auditorium and replaced it with modern offices, which he rented out for top-dollar rates. In 1911, he remodeled the site's sidewalk Red-Front, thus creating the largest ever Lancaster five-and-dime, complete with an exquisite Refreshment Room that specialized in fried oysters. In the rear of the store, one could find a lavish executive office, entered by walking through a plate-glass doorway and past two life-sized, hand-carved lions. Over 35,000 locals and scores of dignitaries attended the grand opening. That afternoon, Frank smugly boasted to one reporter: "We've got some of the best people in town here. Don't it do your heart good?" It was certainly good for Frank's wallet. The day's sales were astronomical, and the media fairly gushed with praise for the porky, silk-hatted Merchant Prince who brought elegance to the world of the five-and-dime. Although they would miss the roof garden for years to come, the Lancaster county patrons were pleased to be gifted with a new spectacle to replace the old.

Woolworth's in Hollywood

By 1916, the sixty-four-year-old Frank Woolworth's health was seriously deteriorating, and he was ordered by his doctors to take a few weeks off for some rest and relaxation. Frank's first vacation preference was Europe, where he loved to bask in the healing waters of expensive spas and indulge in exotic, rich French foods. But World War I was wreaking havoc overseas, making that sojourn impossible. As an alternative, one of his colleagues suggested he visit the Pacific Coast of the United States, a region he had never seen before. Frank agreed and so set out with a large party to take in the scenic mountains and Yellowstone, and tour a sampling of his hundreds of West Coast F. W. Woolworth's stores. In the beginning, Frank attempted to arrive at the stores undercover, but this plan was quickly shelved. Word of his arrival quickly leaked out, both to employees and the press, until his every move became a topic of great excitement with the local media. The King of the Five-and-Dime was finally on the West Coast, and his loyal employees were both excited and proud about this milestone. Indeed, such a hoopla was created that one would have sworn that it was the president of the United States, not the president of F. W. Woolworth's, who was coming to town.

For the entire span of his five-and-dime tour, Frank was greeted with banners, lavish entertainment, executive banquets, and massive crowds. It is unclear exactly how restful this trip was, considering his hectic schedule, but it is documented that one of his favorite experiences of the sojourn occurred in Los Angeles, California. It was there, at the "picture center" known as Universal Studios, that Woolworth experienced the thrill of a lifetime. Frank was invited to Universal for a private studio lot tour, followed by an opportunity to watch the

Silent Movie Trivia

The original backdrop for a major scene in "Poor Little Rich Girl" (1917) starring Mary Pickford featured a "doll-sized" F. W. Woolworth's store. This was one of the first times in film history that a miniature painting was used to create the illusion of a location

filming of a silent movie. Knowing of Frank's great love for all of the dramatic arts, the director asked Frank to step in front of the cameras. He instructed Frank to act the part of a man who had lost his wife in a crowd. His task was to walk across the room, looking for his spouse. He was then to show apparent concern when he couldn't locate her. Reportedly, Woolworth did exactly as he was told, and was lauded by the director for a job well done. For the time being, the name of both film and director is a mystery, but Frank Woolworth certainly documented this event in his famous series of General Letters, which detailed his business and personal adventures for his managers and colleagues. If the Venator Group ever releases its Woolworth archives to the public, the unsolved mystery of Woolworth's debut in the silent pictures will most likely be unraveled.

Another pre-Depression movie that specifically involved F. W. Woolworth's was the 1929 musical, *The Girl From Woolworths*. Frank was gone eight years by the time this film debuted, but he would have probably gotten a kick out of its use of his company's name.

The Girl From Woolworths was one of the earliest feature films to incorporate a "Vitaphone" musical sound score. By the end of 1927, only about 200 movie theaters in the country were even equipped to run such sound (it took several years before talking pictures totally replaced the silents) and for this reason alone, *The Girl from Woolworths* was a special film.

First National Pictures produced this 60-minute musical as a showcase for up-and-coming actress Alice White. In *The Girl From Woolworths,* Miss White portrayed the character of Daisy, a singing clerk in the music department of a Woolworth store. One day, lovely, talented Daisy meets handsome Bill Harrigan at a subway, and they both fib about the nature of their real jobs. Harrigan invites Daisy to dinner at the fabulous Mayfield Club, where the owner promptly offers Daisy a job as an entertainer there. Daisy is ecstatic, but Bill is

This issue of *Movie Magazine*, 1930, offers a double treat for Woolworth nostalgia buffs. *Above:* The cover features Alice White, who starred in *The Girl from Woolworth's* and inside, on page 9, is a rare telegraph from singer Al Jolson, who frequented the famed Hollywood Woolworth's.

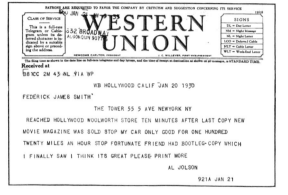

PLAYBILL

NOW PLAYING . . . !

"THE GIRL FROM WOOLWORTHS"

First National Pictures • *Premier: Oct. 27, 1929*

CAST INCLUDED:
Alice White as Daisy King
Charles Delaney: Bill Harrigan
Bert Moorehouse: Dave
Wheeler Oakman: Lawrence
Mayfield
Milla Davenport: Ma Donnelly

PRODUCER: Ray Rockett
DIRECTOR: William Beaudine
STORY: Adele Commandini
SCREENWRITERS: Edward I.
Luddy & Richard Well
MUSIC & LYRICS: Al Bryan &
George Meyer

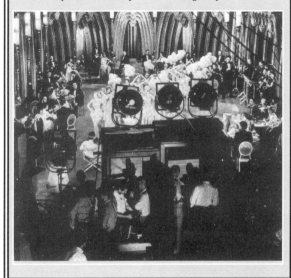

jealous; he wants her all to himself. In the end, Daisy forgoes her career for the love of her life.

The reviews for *The Girl From Woolworths* were mixed. The sets were hailed for their splendor, but the script itself fell short of expectations. The audience did like several of the songs, such as "Crying for Love" and "What I Know About Love." Whatever the reviews, *The Girl From Woolworths* is yet another testimony to just how much the Woolworth's five-and-dimes had become part of America's lifestyle by the 1920s.

A study of *The American Film Institutes' Catalog of Feature Films* uncovers a number of other pre-Depression movies which featured five-and-dime themes. In October 1927, United Artists released *My Best Girl,* a thirty-five-minute silent featuring actress Mary Pickford. *My Best Girl* was the Cinderella tale of a struggling five-and-ten counter girl who falls in love with the owner's son. *Five and Ten Cent Annie* arrived a year later, starring Louise Fazenda, Clyde Cook, and

Cast members Alice White, Charles Delaney, and Rita Flynn

William Demerest in a slapstick comedy about a street cleaner who is head-over-heels for a lovely dimestore salesgirl. In the end, the girl gets her man, and the fortune he inherits from his rich uncle, but not before several perilous adventures.

Another Mary Pickford movie that offers up a bit of historical "Wooley" interest is *Poor Little Rich Girl.* This was one of the very first silent flickers to use a visual backdrop to give the illusion of a location shot. For *Poor Little Rich Girl* (1917), a doll-sized backdrop of a Main Street city block was created, complete with an F. W. Woolworth's 5 & 10. (Ironically, "poor little rich girl" was the same phrase used to define Frank Woolworth's infamous granddaughter, Barbara Hutton in later years.)

All such films capture a part of the Woolworth's tale for posterity. Since F. W. Woolworth's was the first, the largest, and the most famous five-and-dime store of all time, it is likely that even the generic dimestore movie depictions called on F. W. Woolworth's for inspiration.

The Woolworth's Medley:
Sheet Music, Ragtime, and "The Woolworth March"

The moving picture industry underwent great strides during the 1920s, thirties, and forties. Production techniques became increasingly sophisticated until all the silent flickers were replaced with talkies. Elaborate musical sound scores and dance scenes became the norm, spawning big screen singing stars and a surplus of movie gossip magazines. All of this had a direct effect on the type of products that F. W. Woolworth's carried in its stores, and which trends the company followed in its quest for the billion-dollar sales mark. Along with celebrity photos, memorabilia, and Hollywood magazines, F. W. Woolworth's cashed in on the post-1910 popularity of sheet music, and later, into the phonograph album craze.

Actually, nickel and dime sheet music made its Woolworth's debut surprisingly early in the game, late in 1886. During that period, the chief still only owned eight stores (a far cry from the thousands of Red-Fronts operated during the company's heyday) and was showing gross sales of about $100,000 per year. He'd recently moved his offices from Lancaster, Pennsylvania, to New York City and designed the famous Red "W" logo. His stock in trade was still tin pans and sewing notions, but inspired by his love of music, he decided to test out sheet music in several of his Red-Fronts. Four years later, he experimented with the concept of selling sheet music through direct mail. This was F. W. Woolworth's first foray into mail order, and although the idea didn't take off at the time, it opened the floodgates for the company's future catalog business.

Frank's managers were not particularly keen on selling sheet music. They kept trying to tell him that this was a "sticker" item which only sold when a particularly hot song, such as "The Band Played On" or "After the Ball" caught the fancy of the masses. Eventually,

Frank was forced to agree with them and he dropped sheet music from the Approved Manager's Buying List in 1893. One notable exception to this rule occurred in 1896, when demand for "The Merry Widow Waltz" reached such proportions that even Frank's skeptical managers agreed that it was one of the year's "must-sell" items.

In the meantime, Frank indulged his love for music elsewhere by commissioning his own composition called "The Woolworth March." Designed for full-orchestra, the march bearing the King of the Five-and-Dime's name was first played in 1900 during his New York city store premier, then played on throughout the next two decades, from coast to coast, whenever he was hosting a special event. (An updated centennial version was composed in 1979.)

Around 1910-11, the public became enamored with a new form of music called ragtime. Ragtime was not just listening music, it was lively foot-tapping music, and in response, Frank installed a pipe organ in his new Fifth Avenue Red-Front. Tunes like Alexander's Ragtime Band vastly entertained his Manhattan customers but Woolworth wanted them to empty their pocketbooks as well, and it bothered him that his organ player was not increasing sales for any particular item. It seemed a merchandising natural to connect live music with the sale of sheet music, but he needed to figure out how to do it.

Frank muddled over this dilemma for a while, and finally came up with an exciting, novel idea. He hired piano players and singers to perform in his larger stores—not just during grand openings, but *all* of the time. He surrounded them with displays full of colorful, ten-cent sheet music and folios, and instructed them to play or sing any given sheet music tune a customer requested. The idea caught on and Frank once again made mercantile history. Sheet music was placed back on the "Approved Buying List" in 1911.

Soon, sheet music was selling like hotcakes. His customers purchased vocals, galops, love songs, and hymns by the thousands. The music section of Woolworth's rapidly expanded to include accessories such as music stands, metronomes, and small instruments. Aside from ragtime, one of the biggest boon of all was the growing availability of affordable phonographs. Consequently, in 1915 alone, F. W. Woolworth's sold 20 million sheets of music and over 5 million phonograph records. Those numbers more than tripled by 1917, with "I'm Forever Blowing Bubbles" alone selling 2.6 million copies. That same year, patriotic tunes like "Over There" and "Hunting the Hun" were added to the roster of Woolworth's best-sellers.

The cash continued to roll in during the 1920s, straight through to World War II in the 1940s. Hollywood was cranking out musical after musical, and every time a new song reached the Hit Parade, F. W. Woolworth's was ready to oblige. For the price of pocket change, Woolworth's customers could now purchase the sheet music for record-breaking hits such as the Andrew Sister's "Boogie Woogie Bugle Boy," and if they weren't accomplished "ticklers of the ivories," well then, they could simply buy the phonograph album of the same name to play on their home Victrola.

I Found a Million-Dollar Baby in a Five and Ten Cent Store

Once in a while, the very music that Woolworth's was selling, included a reference to its own five-and-dime establishments. "I Found A Million Dollar Baby in a Five and Ten Cent Store" was one example of this. This 1931 hit, with lyrics by Mort Dixon and Billy Rose, and music by Harry Warren, was first introduced to listeners in a review called *Crazy Quilt* featuring Fanny Brice. Four years later, it was interpreted for the musical *Million Dollar Baby,* starring Arline Judge and Jimmy Fay. The term "five-and-dime" could have meant any establishment of its kind, but to this day, most people associate it with F. W. Woolworth's. "Million Dollar Baby" was also one of several phrases used by the press to describe Woolworth's granddaughter (and heir) Barbara Hutton.

Another favorite of the time was a 1928 song called "I Can't Give You Anything But Love, Baby," with lyrics by Dorothy Field, and music by Jimmy McHugh. The Woolworth Red-Fronts were immortalized in one line: "Gee, I'd like to see you looking swell, baby, Diamond bracelets Woolworth's doesn't sell, baby." This tune was recorded many times over, by artists such as Louis Armstrong and Benny Goodman. It was also featured in a 1938 screwball comedy called *Bringing up Baby,* starring Katherine Hepburn and Cary Grant. In that now-classic film, the only thing that a wayward leopard named Baby would respond to was that song. (Cary Grant, by the way, was the third husband of Frank Woolworth's granddaughter, Barbara Hutton.) A more recent hit which mentions Woolworth's is Nancy Griffith's country song, "Love at the Five and Dime," the tale of Eddie, "a sweet romancer" and his beloved "who made the Woolworth counters shine." There have been hundreds of such lyric references through the decades, music being yet another example of how F. W. Woolworth's has found its way into the popular culture.

The celebrity crazes of the 1940s and 1950s also spawned a few interesting five-and-dime collectibles. Several Woolworth's stores, for example, offered record album brushes decorated with pictures of musical artists such as the Andrew Sisters and Guy Lombardo. These were usually given away free as store promotions during grand opening or reopening sales. Some of these record brushes now sell for up to $100 a piece.

Meanwhile, back in the larger Woolworth's stores, hired piano players and singers (who sometimes doubled as clerks) continued to bang out melodies to boost sheet music and phonograph celebrity record sales. These performers weren't paid much money, but they did receive a type of Main Street acclaim. Once in a while, their stint as dimestore performers led to bigger and better things. Scenarios as depicted in the film *A Girl From Woolworth's* (1929), whereby pretty Daisy starts out as a singer/clerk at Woolworth's and is offered a shot at the big-time nightclub circuit, were not that unusual.

One of the legendary crooners of our time, Mel Torme, can trace his roots back to F. W. Woolworth's in Chicago. Both of his parents loved show business, and for a time in the 1930s, his mother worked as a pianist in Woolworth's, playing and singing her heart out for the five-and-dime customers. According to celebrity folklore, Mel Torme was learning these songs while his mother played; she sometimes brought him into Woolworth's to perform a solo. Before the age of five, Torme was being acknowledged as a child prodigy, and by age sixteen one of his original music compositions was selling in record numbers right in Woolworth's, where it all began. The song was "Lament for Love," performed by Harry James beginning in 1941.

Of course, not every musician or singer made it big as a result of a stint at Woolworth's, but for many customers, the memory of music resounding through the store as they shopped for dimestore bargains was a special memory indeed.

For Your Listening Pleasure: The Woolworth Radio Hour

During the late 1940s, the F. W. Woolworth Company made a leap into the national advertising circuit by sponsoring a network radio show called "The Woolworth Hour." Until that time, the company had rarely indulged in any type of paid advertisement, save an occasional co-op ad in a magazine (funded in conjunction with one of the company's product suppliers), or the announcement of a grand-opening sale in a local newspaper. The ever-increasing popularity of radio, with its rapt audience and potential customers, managed to convince company executives to break the "no paid advertising" tradition.

Details about "The Woolworth Hour" are sparse, but we know it was broadcast live on Sundays (after the ball game) in New York City, St. Louis and several other American cities. It was a music program which featured the melodies of popular bands of the time, such as Percy Faith and his Orchestra. Naturally, in between musical selections listeners would hear all about the latest and greatest Woolworth's bargains. "The Woolworth Hour" only lasted for a few years, no doubt terminated as television began to capture the attention of the public.

On-Stage Now! Mr. Woolworth Had a Notion

Along with the film and music references that have surfaced over the decades, there are several notable stage events to add to the Woolworth's medley. After the age of big Hollywood musicals started to fade, along with the Big Band era and radio, America started to turn its attention back to live theater. In the 1960s, New York City bounced back as the supreme showcase for Broadway and Off-Broadway shows of all kinds, as well as for specialized musical reviews. One particularly elaborate stage event associated directly with Frank Woolworth, was a musical review produced by the Donahue Sales Corporation in 1965.

Mr. Woolworth Had a Notion, was a one-night only gala of thematic playlets, songs and dances, held at the Biltmore Hotel Ballroom on Wednesday evening, June 16, 1965.

Written and directed by Michael Brown, with music direction by Norman Paris, this review served double-duty by paying tribute to the long-deceased chief while acting as a lively advertising outlet for Donahue's products. Musical reviews of this type were very popular at that time, being considered an ideal way to promote good will and morale among the employees of the honored company in question, while boosting sales for the supplier. Some of the featured numbers from *Mr. Woolworth Had a Notion* included, "Opening Day at the Five-and-Ten" and the lively "Woolworth Managers' Work Song." Executive producer Theodore P. Donahue was an old pro in the review arena, having already sponsored twenty-five of them for various American companies. The Woolworth's review held special significance because Donahue's father had teamed up with Frank Woolworth as a supplier half a century before in 1915, and the two companies had been bonded ever since.

Hundreds of Woolworth's employees were invited to attend *Mr. Woolworth Had a Notion,* which featured a commemorative record album of the same name. The album listed song lyrics, production team credits, a playbill of performers, and most important of all, the names of select, Donahue-distributed products. In between the cast lists, readers were reminded about the availability of Talon zippers, Simplicity Patterns, Italian white poodle pullovers, and A-line black wool jumpers. Not to be forgotten, menswear was also featured, including the practical "All-weather coat" (available in black and natural) for $16.95, and the classic stand-by, a white button down Oxford dress shirt for $2.99—a complimentary tie available for only a dollar more. Reportedly, *Notion* was a fun and memorable event for those who attended, as was the after-musical review party. Just as a sidenote, the commemorative record album is now very had to come by, and is eagerly sought by Woolworth's five-and-dime collectors.

Fifteen years after the cast of *Mr. Woolworth Had a Notion* played the New York Biltmore, the cast of another show centering around a dimestore made an Off-Broadway premier at the Hudson Guild Theater. *Come Back to the 5 and Dime, Jimmy Dean, Jimmy Dean* was Ed Graczyk's critically acclaimed drama about a group of women who gather around a timeworn Woolworth's lunch counter for a very special, and, as it turns out, very emotional reunion. The gals are there to celebrate the twentieth anniversary of their James Dean Fan Club, which began back in 1955, when their heartthrob was filming the movie *Giant* just a short drive away from the small Texas town's five-and-dime. The original cast included Fannie Flagg and Barbara Loden, with David Kerry Heefner as the producing director. After a thirty-performance trial run beginning February 27, 1980, the project was shelved for two years, then made its all-important Broadway debut at the Martin Beck Theater in February, 1982. This time around, the stars included Cher, Sudie Bond, and Sandy Dennis, with direction by Robert Altman.

Come Back to the 5 and Dime, Jimmy Dean, Jimmy Dean was more "Woolworthesque" than precisely "Woolworth's." Structurally, the tiny dimestore featured in the play was a composite of the many different luncheonettes and Red-Fronts located in rural America

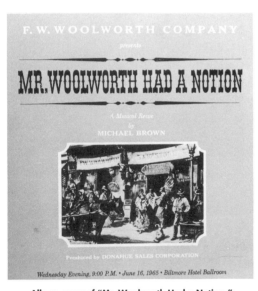

F. W. WOOLWORTH COMPANY
presents

MR. WOOLWORTH HAD A NOTION

A Musical Revue
by
MICHAEL BROWN

Produced by DONAHUE SALES CORPORATION

Wednesday Evening, 9:00 P.M. • June 16, 1965 • Biltmore Hotel Ballroom

Album cover of "Mr. Woolworth Had a Notion."

during the 1950s. However, for the New York Broadway version, F. W. Woolworth Co. and its employees did play an important supporting role. Production Designer David Gropman's period set was composed of an authentic Woolworth lunch counter, complete with twirling stools and drink dispensers. The counter was donated by the F. W. Woolworth Company for the occasion, carefully dismantled from one of its East Coast stores. The entire population of employees of the Woolworth Building in New York was invited to attend the Broadway premier, along with a gala opening night party held at F. W. Woolworth's historic "mother store" on 34th Street in Manhattan. A few former Woolworth's employees also recall the official cast party which was held at Tavern on the Green in Central Park. The play was short-lived, closing two months later, on April 4, 1982.

The same year, a film of the same name was produced, with most of the cast members reprising their Broadway roles for the big screen, including Cher, Karen Black, and Sandy Dennis. Like the play, the film received mixed reviews. The movie was a box office disappointment, but garnered praise for some powerful performances. For those who saw either stage or film version, *Come Back to the 5 and Dime, Jimmy Dean, Jimmy Dean* was a nostalgic reminder of younger days, when hanging out at the local variety store's lunch counter was much a part of a star-struck teenagers' social daily life. (A bit of trivia: the original James Dean played into the Woolworth's saga in a more intimate way than being featured in the play title. Before his early and tragic death in 1955, Dean had a brief affair with Frank Woolworth's grandchild, Barbara Hutton.)

Several other Broadway plays, before and after, have incorporated the old five-and-dime lunch counter settings into their scripts, but *Come Back to the 5 and Dime, Jimmy Dean, Jimmy Dean* was the only one known to actively involve the F. W. Woolworth Company during the course of its production.

It is clear that the renown of F. W. Woolworth's five-and-dimes reached far into the popular culture, finding its way, purposely or inadvertently into film, music, drama, and art. However, the true "spectacle" of the Red-Fronts was rooted in the individual stores themselves. From sea to sea, Woolworth's stores made their mark. They achieved this in a variety of ways: via the architecture of its buildings, the mind-boggling square footage of the sales floor, and by the original displays and promotional gimmicks dreamed up by its managers.

Chapter Eleven

Woolworth's Coast to Coast

> *"Interpreting and satisfying the will and whim of people as consumers was still Woolworth's prime mercantile function . . . By the very nature of their function, Woolworth's stores had to be involved with, and closely identified with, the communities and neighborhoods in which they were located."*
>
> —John P. Nichols, 1973

Which F. W. Woolworth's Do You Remember . . . and Why?

There was a certain uniformity to all F. W. Woolworth's, including the brand-names they carried and their familiar mastheads. However, each Red-Front was also highly distinctive, shaped, to a great degree, by the personal experiences and lifestyles of its patrons, and by the size and geographical location of the store. One citizen might remember Woolworth's as the site of a devastating fire on Main Street, while another recalls the big-city dimestore where her sweetheart (and present husband) proposed to her at the jewelry counter. In some cases, Woolworth's was simply one of many bustling stores in a sprawling mall, in other cases it was "the" community hub, perhaps even thought of by its patrons as "a second home."

Over the decades, scores of people stopped in for sandwiches and hot chocolates at Woolworth's lunch counters, but the circumstances that shaped these events were unique. For an adult, that repast might have been a routine stop en route to work,

---

TIME CAPSULE MEMORY

"A Second Home"

As a small child in the 1960s, our town had a five-and-ten on its main street, which was Mamaroneck Avenue in New York. It was my favorite store. Woolworth's felt safe, like my own home. —Beth Rowan

How Woolworth Helps
Make Home Sweet Home!

while for a child it was a luxury, possible only after saving up a week's allowance. Everyone who shopped at Woolworth's had the same opportunity to purchase Tangee lipstick or Woolco cottons, but the *hows* and *whys* of these purchases varied greatly. Was the buyer a young girl choosing lipstick for her first real date, or a housewife who wanted to experiment with a new color?

Furthermore, the types of people who patronized a particular Woolworth's had a great impact on the store's regional ambiance. A packed-to-the-rafters, Chicago Red-Front frequented by busy executives evoked a starkly different feeling than that of the tiny Red-Front in rural Pennsylvania patronized by friendly, local farmers trying to make ends meet. The personalities and devotion of individual store employees also had an enormous impact. Some stores experienced a steady turnover of new managers, counter girls and stockboys, while others featured the same familiar faces for upward of twenty, sometimes forty years.

During my research for *Remembering Woolworth's,* it quickly became clear that the data I was collecting represented an individualized experience as much as a collective experience. Some of the company's most poignant, even outrageous chronicles are to be found among the personal stories, memories, and experiences of those who shopped in

Northampton Street, Looking West from Center Sq. Easton, Pa.   E-11

Woolworth's, worked in Woolworth's, and on occasion, had their lives drastically altered as a result of their experiences with Woolworth's. This is just as much a tale of the sole manager who gave his all to the Woolworth Company for forty years, as it is the tale of Frank Woolworth and his struggle to create a mercantile empire. Taking this concept one step further, this is just as much the story of hundreds of architecturally interesting, small-town Red-Fronts, as it is a tribute to the Woolworth Building of New York, once the tallest building in the world.

And so, one of the first questions that might be asked is: *Which kind of F. W. Woolworth's do you remember?*

A Red-Front for Every Kind of Town

According to Woolworth Company records, by January 1, 1920, every single town in the United States with a population of 8,000 or more had a Woolworth's Red-Front. Over the years, the company moved into even smaller towns and villages, some with populations of under 4,000. By 1979, the F. W. Woolworth Company had stores in every state of the Union. At its peak there were over 3,000 assorted sizes of Red-Fronts in the United States alone, with scores more located in Canada, Mexico, and overseas. No chain of any kind, including the oldest of all chains, the great A&P Co. could boast that magnitude of geographical presence. Neither did the sum total of all of the five-and-dimes owned by Frank Woolworth's arch competitors (including Newberry, McCrory, Kress, and Kresge) add up to as many stores as owned by the retail giant Woolworth's. Consequently, wherever it was you lived, worked, or vacationed in North America, there was always an F. W. Woolworth Red-Front a short ride away: whether small, medium, or large.

In Woolworth company language, "smaller" traditionally meant sales volume, as opposed to pure square footage. The bottom line was how

TIME CAPSULE MEMORY

"Boyhood Days in Ogden, Utah"

My childhood experiences at F. W. Woolworth Co. made a significant and positive contribution to my philosophy, education and interests throughout my life. Much of my Woolworth experience can be attributed to my wonderful Aunt Barbara Barton and the Woolworth's store in Ogden, Utah. Aunt Barbara started taking me to the movies in the 1930s. On the way there, or after, she would sometimes stop in Woolworth's and buy me Dentine chewing gum or Sen Sen breath fresheners. We would enjoy some ice cream or a root beer at the lunch counter. For my 12th birthday, she bought me a stamp album from Woolworth's. It was a hardcover book and cost $1.00 (no tax) that initiated a sixty-year interest in stamp collecting. I still have that stamp album. She also bought me my first balsa wood model airplane. When I was 13, I got a larger Cessna model airplane for Christmas. That was followed by many models of military ships and airplanes used during World War II, all of them from Woolworth's in Ogden. Now, the record of our cumulative Woolworth's experiences is traveling through space at the speed of light. At this very moment, perhaps an astronomer on some distant sphere is looking at the words, 'F. W. Woolworth' through a super-advanced telescope! —Thomas W. Johnston

Woolworth Trivia

In 1918 alone, a billion persons entered Woolworth's stores and over 820,000,000 bought goods.

"The Smells of Woolworth's"

by Elizabeth Larrabee

Woolworth's was not an empire
inherited by a debutante
named Barbara.
It was a thousand distinct aromas.

Lily of the Valley
and Johnson's hard floor wax
whammed your nostrils upon
the in-swing of the glass door.

Hot chocolate sauce at the fountain.
Over-ripe bananas disguised
in strawberry smothered splits.
A stack of on sale percale
house dresses assaulted from the left
while freshly inked comic books
invaded your senses from racks
placed just right to extract
the one nickel from your pocket.
The nickel meant for the sweetness
that exploded through thinly wrapped
Necco Wafers.

Tangee lipstick—
THAT was Woolworth's.
A sniff of the orange, waxy stuff
was enough to knock you out
and that's what you got for sticking
your nose where it shouldn't be.

many "dollar sales per square foot" were generated over a year's time. But regardless of why they were considered small, these particular dimestores had a special ambiance. If you grew up in Bakersfield, California; Parkersburg, West Virginia; or Melrose, Massachusetts, you probably recall your local Woolworth's as being cozy and quaint. Smaller Woolworth's (especially those in rural towns) typically retained their employees for long stretches of time, and it was not unusual to have several members of one family sharing shifts. The same efficient manager was always there to greet everyone by name, or, in some cases, to double up as the town's local magistrate. Over time, some of these Red-Fronts were remodeled to allow for more sales space, but for much of their long history, they remained markedly intimate in feeling. If you lived near a small Woolworth's, you might not have memories of a long, spacious "Refreshment Room" or cafeteria, but you might recall standing at a tiny formica counter sipping a root beer float. In rural Woolworth's stores that did happen to be equipped with cooking facilities, it was common to enjoy a bill of fare prepared by the same waitress/cook, who for years had used her own delectable recipe for apple pie.

Back in 1911, the smallest Red-Front in America was located in peaceful Claremont, New Hampshire, which generated a sales volume of around $6,000 per year. (This, as opposed to Laconia, New Hampshire's more tourist-oriented Red-Front, which boasted over $35,000.) By 1992, these figures had changed dramatically, with two of the chains "smallest" stores in Fond Du Lac, Wisconsin, and Jamestown, North Dakota, netting an average of $270,000 per year.

The vast majority of American Red-Fronts fell into the "medium" category. They were usually

"Woolworth's Across the Country"

I have been to Woolworth stores in many parts of the country. On F Street in Washington, D.C., the store was large, and the floors were sometimes wet from recent moppings with a big gray-curled mop, which looked like a badly made wig. In Newport, Rhode Island, I was there when Old Town still had wooden sidewalks in front of the store. The one in Honolulu, on the main street in Waikiki was a

Honolulu, Hawaii, store, 1950s

wonder of muumuus, straw hats, and sandals. And the one in old Honolulu, downtown, was close to the Aloha Tower. These stores looked slightly different, but they all had red signs with big gold lettering that said, Woolworth & Co., and old brass cash registers that clanged when a sale was rung up. The drawer would jerk open and the sales clerk would count out your change, and then you left, smiling, holding your five-and-dime treasure. —Elizabeth Contessa Heine

located in towns or small cities which had a main thoroughfare, dotted with a full-range of retail stores, including several different dimestores. Their steady sales, although not astronomical, formed the "bread and butter" of the great F. W. Woolworth Co.

These medium-sized establishments shared some of the qualities of the smaller stores. The local ambiance was still evident and the number of employees was still limited, which meant you probably knew most of them by name. In contrast to the smaller stores, though, the medium-sized Red-Fronts almost always had a food service area of some kind, offering a full menu of items for breakfast, lunch, and early dinner. When you walked into the store, the aromas of fried potatoes and eggs from the luncheonette area would mix with those of freshly-made popcorn from the candy center to create a heady (and memorable) sensory assault.

More space also meant a wider variety of merchandise, which the managers frequently attempted to push via special sales and promotions. In the early days of the company, managers were encouraged to become involved with their communities, therefore, these medium-sized Red-Fronts were often sponsoring charity drives or participating in lo-

"Woolworth in the News: DATELINE—March 4, 1949"

"I remember the Woolworth's in Charleston, West Virginia, for many reasons," wrote Lynn Hartz. "The toys in the basement, and the paperback books . . . and the "rising stairs" [escalators]. But my most impressive memory of Woolworth's was the tragic fire on March 4, 1949."

Ms. Hartz still recalls that horrible afternoon in March 1949, when she (only six years old) was walking home from school in Charleston, West Virginia, and noticed smoke coming from the downtown shopping district near Capital Street. Concerned, she hurried home and asked her mother what was happening. She was told that "the worst fire in Charleston's history" was raging at the local Woolworth's store. All day long, the fire raged on, with numerous citizens and firemen injured, and seven brave firemen killed in the line of duty. The papers reported that the fire had started in the basement and was not immediately detected. Along with loss of life, damages exceeded one million dollars. For residents of that particular West Virginia town, it was a day they would never forget, and a memory that would always be associated with their local five-and-dime.

cal holiday events. If you shopped at one of these Woolworth's, you might also recall strolling toward the back of the store and checking out the latest additions to the pet department.

At the turn of the nineteenth century, stores such as those located in York, Pennsylvania; Trenton, New Jersey, and Newport, Rhode Island, were averaging annual sales of about fifty-thousand and enjoyed a steady flow of traffic. By the 1960s, medium-sized Red-Fronts such as in Freeport, Long Island, or Walla Walla, Washington, were generating hundreds of thousands in income for the company.

The presence, and meaning, of these bustling Red-Fronts took on special significance in times of financial stress. The taxing years of the Great Depression, and of World Wars I and II, caused hardship for millions of people. It was during these periods when the old Woolworth's dimestores shone brightest—at least in terms of Frank's dream to offer the working class "so much, for so little." The Woolworth chronicles are filled with stories of people who relied on the five-and-dimes to get through lean years. Shopping at Woolworth's was often the only alternative for a struggling family who longed to have presents under the Christmas tree, or who needed to create durable, home-made garments from store-bought yarns and cottons.

Along with affordable merchandise, Woolworth's also provided much needed employment. During the 1930s and '40s, many companies were forced to lay off people by the thousands—but not F. W. Woolworth's. Along with wage slots filled by hard-working stockboys and counter girls, scores of jobs were available at Woolworth's warehouses, and in the offices of the great Woolworth Building in New York. Several veterans also told me how grateful (and relieved) they were, to find their old jobs were still available when they returned from military service. For those who remained back home, the local luncheonette was the ideal place to gather together and discuss the war, or to seek solace for loved ones lost. In this day and age of instant communication, organized support groups, and of shopping malls located in even the most remote regions, it might be difficult to imagine a time when the local dimestore was a pivotal source of solace, humorous relief, and social activities. But it was. Donn Hornuk of Iowa captured the feeling of the old days perfectly in his personal account of the five-and-dime era:

> Our F. W. Woolworth store on Main Street, between Fifth and Sixth, here in Keokuk, Iowa, was gone by the early fifties, but I remember it well. Back in the thirties and forties, it filled an important spot in everyone's life, farmers and townsfolk alike. Our Woolworth's store was a great deal more than a five-and-ten. It was a gathering place, inside and outside, for friends who hadn't seen each other for weeks. It was a social event where friends "ran into each other," sometimes literally, under the two long rows of Casablanca fans that tried to cool that hot-as-Hades store during the summer. Lots of laughter, screams of delight, and hugging, lots of hugs and sometimes kissing, but just women did that. On the street in front of the Woolworth's on Saturday night, groups of friends would "jaw" for fifteen or twenty minutes in all kinds of weather. Today, a senior citizen center occupies that building site. Woolworth's not being there brings a dull and distant ache like missing a beloved friend, and it will never be like it used to be. They call it progress. But Woolworth's was like a great mother hen and the customers her chicks.

Following World War II, the United States enjoyed a remarkable period of prosperity. In turn, the local Red-Fronts were ready to take advantage of their customer's new expendable income by offering an unsurpassed variety of everyday necessities.

The Five-and-Dimes of Tourist Centers and Big Cities

Another type of Red-Front, which could fall into either small or medium category, were those based in tourist areas. These five-and-dimes had all the trappings of a typical bargain store paradise, with the additional perk of carrying an endless supply of souvenirs. If the store was located in an historical city, such as Richmond, Virginia, or Philadelphia, Pennsylvania, then these souvenirs were appropriately historic in nature.

TIME CAPSULE MEMORY

"The Atlantic City Boardwalk"

One of my most vivid memories from the old Woolworth's on the Atlantic City boardwalks was a brassy blond selling this wonderful product called VI-DE-LAN. Vi-De-Lan was a hair pomade made with lanolin and Vaseline. The lady, who had this really "poofy" hair, would put on "just a little bit" of the pomade, sometimes hundreds of times a day. Don't know if the stuff made her hair so swell, or if it already was that way. We bought a jar of it and had it in the linen closet for years. After awhile, it separated and became amazingly gross. But of course we kept it anyway. After I tore myself away from Vi-De-Lan lady I went inside Woolworth's for more goodies. The Red-Front in Atlantic City was the one where I bought my treasured '45' record of Peter, Paul & Marys' "Puff the Magic Dragon."

—Geoffrey S. Lapin

The F. W. Woolworth Company often took extra care to make certain that the architecture of their Red-Fronts blended in with the local historical theme. Such was the case in Scottsdale, Arizona, known as "The West's most Western town." The upscale Scottsdale Woolworth's sported an old-fashioned Western motif, right down to the wooden planked sidewalks.

F. W. Woolworth stores operating near the ocean had an entirely different feeling than their suburban or city counterparts. Red-Fronts in the Virgin Islands, the Caribbean, coastal Puerto Rico, and scenic southern California, offered a preponderance of beach towels, sun glasses and tanning lotion. When you walked across the floor, it always felt a bit "scratchy" from tracked-in sea sand, and the smell of salt water permeated the entire premises. One of the busiest, and oldest seaside Red-Fronts of all time was the one on the boardwalk in Atlantic City. During the peak tourist months from May to September, this five-and-dime was literally teeming with humanity. Since the dimestore was flanked by all manner of amusements (from spin-the-wheel games of chance to fortune-tellers) the managers of the Atlantic City Red-Fronts always needed to create their own form of competi-

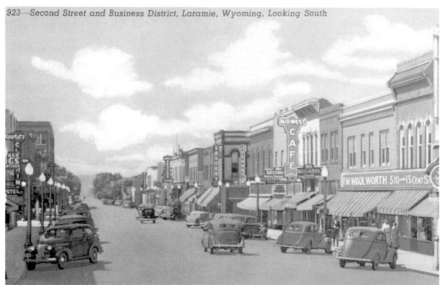

923—Second Street and Business District, Laramie, Wyoming, Looking South

Laramie, Wyoming,
Woolworth's store.

tive amusement. Hence, they featured puppet shows, ragtime bands, "authentic" salt-water taffy sales, and special promotions for products such as "singing Hula Hoops" and "magical" hair lotions. As far back as 1910, store number #104 on the boardwalk was reeling in $160,000 per season.

Each type of Woolworth's store had its own ambiance, and in turn, generated its own type of nostalgia. But the big-city Red-Fronts were in a category all their own; the likes of which will surely never be seen again.

The sheer size of a big-city Woolworth's would be almost inconceivable to those who only shopped in small or modest-sized Red-Fronts. The actual variety, range, and amount of merchandise featured in the company's banner stores was mindboggling. The first high-sales volume Woolworth's stores opened long before the era of Wal-Mart, Sears, or even F. W. Woolworth's own subsidiary, Woolco. Because of this, when one of these mega Red-Fronts debuted, it was a media bonanza. Frank Woolworth opened his first big-city five-and-dimes toward the end of the nineteenth century, in Washington, D.C., New York City, and Boston. From there, the company branched out to cities all over North America.

These large scale Red-Fronts offered almost every type of utilitarian merchandise, as well as thousands of novelty and gift items. Imagine not one but three aisles of toys; party favors piled to the ceiling, rack displays of children's clothing, including Buster Brown shoes and monogrammed baby blankets. Imagine as well, every conceivable kitchen gadget, bathroom accessory, and sewing notion housed under one roof. It was not unusual to see some type of musical or theatrical entertainment going on somewhere in the store, and colorful posters and placards announced special sales wherever one looked. Roaming the aisles of those particular dimestores was like wandering through a bazaar.

One of the world's largest Woolworth's was in Denver, Colorado.

Most of the big-city Red-Fronts featured multiple floors; in the early days these levels were connected by broad staircases, later by "electric steps" and modern elevators. Overhead automated air-tube systems sent money and messages flying from one part of the store to another, and during the summer, beautiful fans overhead cooled the masses. If a customer didn't find anything she wanted on the first floor, it was almost a given she would find something on the next. One Chicago journalist pointed out that, "Woolworth's stores made everybody feel so comfortable that they managed to sell them things they didn't even know they needed until they walked in the door." Most astonishing of all, perhaps, was the fact that until the mid-1930s, one could buy each of these items for a quarter or less.

As the decades progressed, these stores retained their largesse, but the outdated Casablanca fans were replaced by electric air conditioners, and streamlined luncheonettes replaced the quaint and elegant Refreshment Rooms. What Woolworth's lost to antiquity, it more than made up for in variety, especially in the food centers. One former district manager, John Compton, clearly recalled that most large downtown Red-Fronts were equipped with the popular lunch counters with their swiveling stools, as well as with pancake bars, delis, bakeries, fried chicken counters, pizza ovens, corn poppers, and nut cookers.

Which Red-Front was the largest of all? At the turn of the twentieth century, the busiest store in the chain was located in Boston's Scollay Square (now "Government Center"). In 1912, the highest sales volume store was located on State Street in Chicago. The first Chicago store had been originally opened by Seymour Knox (Frank Woolworth's protégé) in the early 1900s and had been bringing in record sales ever since. Another Red-Front worth mentioning was the expansive, modernized site in Denver, Colorado. It had started out as a modestly sized five-and-dime in 1904, but by 1965 it was *huge*. So large, in fact, that postcards were issued proclaiming Denver's Red-Front as the largest variety store in the world. By 1992, one of Honolulu's Red-Fronts had earned the honor of the busiest store in the chain.

In terms of the greatest number of stores operating in one city, both Chicago and New York were neck-and-neck. During the company's variety store zenith, it operated more than 100 Red-Fronts in Chicago, most of them concentrated in the Loop and outlying middle-class neighborhoods. New York City and its five boroughs also had over 100 stores. In both cases, the stores ran the gamut from small storefronts on sidestreets to expansive sites on major thoroughfares. Wherever the subway took you in the Big Apple or the Windy City, there was a F. W. Woolworth nearby to feed your bargain-hunting fancy!

Oh, Those Pet Departments!

From coast to coast, some of the most nostalgic (and humorous) memories of all started in Woolworth's famous pet departments. The general rule was: the larger the Red-Front, the larger the pet department. Due to most state health regulations, the pets had to be a certain distance away from food areas, which usually meant that living creatures were set up in the rear of the store.

A July 17, 1997 Associated Press article pointed out that, "There are no statistics to prove it, but there may not be a baby boomer alive who didn't once own a parakeet, turtle, goldfish, hamster, or baby chick bought there with piggy bank money—and later buried in the backyard or flushed down the toilet."

PENN PLAX
CAT.NO. 0-82
ACTION DIVING SEA - DOG
Woolworth $9.99
ACTION AERATING ORNAMENT
swims to the top-
dives to the bottom!

Both fish and fish toys like this one were best-sellers for decades.

TIME CAPSULE MEMORY

"Talking to the Birds"

The Woolworth's in Fair Lawn, New Jersey had a wonderful pet department. The parakeets were near the rear entrance of the store, near the cashier. My mother always headed straight to the sewing aisle; I raced to the birds. I knew that no color of thread or cloth could ever be as beautiful as the blues and yellows of these skittering delights. The cashier would occasionally complain about the racket they made, but I knew they were just "talking." So I talked back. I chirped, I tweeted, I whistled. And I was certain that the pretty blue one in the top cage was just begging for me to take him home. I passed his request to my mother. I pleaded, cajoled and promised to imitate the lives of the saints forever. Finally, she complied. For under six dollars, I had been able to do the impossible: buy happiness.

—Clare Wharton

Counter girl feeding birds, c. 1937.

TIME CAPSULE MEMORY

"The Great Parakeet Caper"

My mother was a frequent shopper of the Woolworth's in Irvington, New Jersey. I have to laugh when I recall a story she told me that happened in the spring of 1963. My mother and sister, who was two years old at the time, had gone shopping. They were in the downstairs department of the store, and my sister had wandered off. While my mother was browsing around, a woman came up to her, pointed to the ceiling, and asked if my mother knew what my sister had done. When my mom looked up, she couldn't believe her eyes! Perched upon the light fixtures were about six parakeets. She rushed over to where they kept the pets and found my sister, happy as can be, freeing the birds from their cages. My mother couldn't help but laugh. She also didn't want to stick around when the manager found out, so she took my sister by the hand and made a dash for the side door. Once outside, she asked my sister why she had opened the cages. My sister smiled and said she just wanted to play with them.

—Sandy Fergesun

If you shopped at a small or medium-sized Woolworth's, the pet section was probably rather modest; perhaps a few goldfish tanks, a large cage for parakeets, and another for the ever-popular green turtles. However, the big stores had several aisles of pets, amounting to a pet store unto itself. Regardless of whether the pet department was big or small, you knew you were moving closer to it when you started to hear those familiar noises: birds chirping, hamsters scrambling, chicks peeping, and fish tanks bubbling. Piled high beside the cages and tanks you could choose pet accessories such as pet food, leashes, pet vitamins, and, of course, pet toys.

The pet department was a constant source of fascination for children, and a steady source of consternation for employees. All the children had to do was gaze adoringly at the cute little turtles as they climbed over each other's backs, or press their noses against the tropical fish tank to get a better look at the creatures inside—but the employees had to care for all the animals. This required constant supervision, and a lot of time was devoted to cleaning cages and tanks, and feeding the animals and fish. Inevitably, a child, or sometimes an adult, would "accidentally" open a cage door, and suddenly, chaos would ensue in the store. When the parakeets got loose, they would often fly all over the store, landing on the hanging overhead lights. All would be well until they got bored and started dive-bombing the customers at the lunch counter.

Chuck Wilkerson, who worked for the company for over twenty-five years and managed both Woolco and Woolworth's stores, still recalls the day that the hamsters got loose in one Ohio Red-Front. Within minutes, hundreds of hamsters were scattered throughout the store, and several escaped into the ceiling area where they chewed on everything in sight, including the electrical wiring. Getting them back into their cages took hours! Wilkerson also remembers asking one of his clerks to amuse the children by fixing up a twenty-gallon tank with all of the accessories, including colored gravel, little shipwrecks, divers, etc. A sign was then placed on the tank: "Invisible fish." The kids had a great time trying to point out the one they "saw" to their parents or friends. Until the very last, the pet department was one of the favorite stops in the local Woolworth's. There was something fun, even a bit off-beat, about being able to buy a bird or turtle in the same place one purchased toothpaste and frying pans. Even though the green turtles didn't seem to last long, and the parakeets sounded a lot louder when you got them home, millions of creatures were happily purchased at Woolworth's for almost seventy years.

Woolworth's in the News: Strange but True

Back in 1997, when the F. W. Woolworth Corporation announced it would be closing the last of its Red-Fronts, a wave of nostalgic articles and television spots flooded the newspapers and the airways. The vast majority of these were human-interest pieces containing nostalgic recollections of days gone by, articles about particularly historic Red-Fronts, and speculative editorials about the future of the parent company. However, the landmark closing also unleashed a tide of more unusual, sometimes downright strange, memories involving the F. W. Woolworth Company.

For example, there was the time during the fall of 1987 when videotapes containing Superman cartoons were discovered to include fifteen minutes of pornography. According to the *Chicago Tribune,* the pornography was reported to police by a woman who complained that her four-year-old son had watched several minutes of sexually explicit material on a tape that was supposed to contain four innocent Superman cartoons. This caused quite a stir in Chicago, and across the country, and the remaining copies were immediately removed from Woolworth's counters. Naturally, these videotapes became instant "collectibles" to some avid Superman collectors.

In the case of the Superman videotape mishap, F. W. Woolworth was an innocent victim of an outsider's tasteless prank (or mistake), but another story involves a salaried employee of the company. The October/November 1998 issue of the nostalgic *Diamond "W" Newsletter,* published an article which illustrates just how far some Woolworth's managers were willing to go to increase sales. Back in the 1960s, there was a popular rock group called the Monkees, who were starring in a television show of the same name. One manager (the article did not identify him) placed a display ad in the local paper announcing that the "Original Monkeys" would be appearing live in the record department of his Woolworth's store at 9:00 A.M. the following Saturday. Naturally, a large crowd showed up for the event, no doubt some of whom were toting cameras and autograph books. They were thrilled to finally be able to meet the wildly popular quartet of musical comedy stars: Peter, Davy, Michael, and Mickey. Instead, customers were greeted by a huge cage suspended from the ceiling of the record department, containing a group of real live monkeys (as in the hairy variety). Amazingly, after the initial shock and disappointment faded, most of the crowd took the publicity stunt in stride, and indeed, sales did increase that day.

The Woolworth's manager's "monkey prank" was considered, by some, to be a bit unethical, but it was certainly not considered destructive. However, another incident was destructive, as well as being quite peculiar. Back in April 1995, a retired trash collector named Milton Anderson brutally attacked scores of ladies' brassieres in a Denver, Colorado Woolworth's. For some inexplicable reason, Mr. Anderson, armed with a knife, entered Woolworth's (and other stores) and purposely slashed the bras in a violent lingerie attack that lasted several hours. A Woolworth's store clerk found eight such damaged articles, and the report led to Anderson's arrest for criminal mischief. What was really odd about this crime was the fact that the culprit only slashed the right cup of each garment.

Another piece of Woolworth's trivia involving intimate apparel was passed along by former manager, John Compton. "Conventions brought big sales increases for the large downtown stores," said Compton, adding that these conventions were usually scheduled for three to four days. Although there is nothing unusual about that, what is a bit unusual is "what" merchandise items were the hot sellers during these events. One would presume items such as cameras or aspirin would be the largest sellers, but in fact it was underwear. Compton was somewhat surprised the first time this happened, and thought it might be a fluke, but subsequent conventions held in towns where he managed stores (including Louisville, Kentucky, and Rochester, New York) continually required extra orders for upcoming conventions. Mens and ladies underwear were both popular, and one can only speculate on the reasons for the exceptionally high demand.

Finally, one of the most far-reaching and bizarre of all Woolworth's tales involved a simple Social Security card. Back in 1938, a wallet manufacturer (the E. H. Ferree Company in Lockport, New York) made a decision to promote its wallets by showing just how well a Social Security card could fit inside. To prove their point, they decided to insert a sample card in each wallet they sold. Company vice president and treasurer, Douglas Patterson, also thought it would be a clever idea to design the sample card using the actual Social Security number of his secretary, Mrs. Hilda Schrader Whitcher.

Well, the wallet was inexpensively priced and attractive, so the F. W. Woolworth Company purchased several thousand of them for a sampling of their Red-Fronts. Over the next few months, the wallets sold well, more orders were placed, and everyone was happy. Then the trouble started. It seemed that many purchasers of these wallets had adopted the bogus Social Security number as their own. In 1943 alone, more than 5,700 people were using Hilda Whitcher's personal Social Security number! It should be added here that the sample card in question was smaller than the size of a normal legal-issue card, and it even had the word "specimen" stamped across the front of the card. Nonetheless, thousands of people decided, for whatever reasons, to use the number.

In the mess that ensued, the Social Security Commission voided the number and issued Hilda a new one. Amazingly, the sample number was used for years afterward; the commission estimates that over 40,000 people reported it as their own number as late as 1977. Of course, the grand total of all Mrs. Whitcher's "alleged income assets" eventually added up to millions of dollars. Mrs. Wichter, who reportedly took the entire matter in relative stride, did marvel about the fame generated from this incident. She also told reporters that as a result of her alleged income, her friends used to greet her by singing a variation of a popular song refrain from the 1920s: "Here comes the million-dollar baby from the five-and-ten cent store."

So, if you are at a garage sale or flea market and you see one of these E. H. Ferree wallets, with Social Security card intact, do try to buy it! If you do, you'll have an authentic piece of Woolworth's sometimes strange history.

By the way, the number on the infamous Social Security card was:

078-05-1120

Jacksonville, Florida, Woolworth's store.

The Woolworth's experience "coast to coast" was certainly an interesting blend of the humorous, the poignant, the historical, and the bizarre. From the rural Western towns where customers were greeted with a tip of the Stetson and a polite "how-do," to the briskly efficient "May I help you" in the big-city Red-Fronts, there was something special about every single F. W. Woolworth's in America. And what made them most special of all were the Woolworth's employees.

The Heart of the Red-Fronts:
The F. W. Woolworth Co. Employees

It is virtually impossible to get an accurate account of just how many men and women worked for F. W. Woolworth Red-Fronts between 1879 and 1997. Access to employee records is prohibited, and outside sources (such as published books and articles) are not consistent in their totals. It is known, however, that in 1954, F. W. Woolworth Co. employed over 93,000 men and women in the U.S., Canada, and Cuba. By 1979, the year of the company's centennial, that number had jumped to 200,000. (That total also included people working for Woolco and Kinney Shoes, two major subsidiaries of the company.) Given the 118-year old history of Woolworth's, it is probably safe to presume that the company employed close to one million people.

In the beginning, they were simply referred to as "store employees," but in the early 1990s this changed to "Woolworth Associates." Over the decades there have been several in-house publications devoted to the experiences and accomplishments of these employees; notably the *Woolworth News* and *Woolworth World.* The pages of these newsletters contain a wealth of information about the employees lives, their daily routine, and their subsequent retirement activities. There is now a nostalgic, privately printed newsletter called The *Diamond "W."* Publisher Chuck Wilkerson works hard to help former associates relive the old days and recall the special accomplishments of their colleagues.

One thing is clear from reading all of these newsletters: there was a strong feeling of family among Woolworth's employees, especially those who worked for the company before 1985. Further, due to the longevity of the Red-Fronts, and the amount of people who drew paychecks from the big diamond "W," the old newsletters (and the new ones) will never, ever run out of material to write about.

One million employees! One million different lives were affected—in one way or another—by their time working for Frank's dimestore

A
· Newsletter
for and about
ex-Associates
Of the
F.W.Woolworth Co.
And Woolco Stores

1879-1997

Diamond "W" Newsletter

1957 Glenrose Circle
Cookeville, Tn. 38506

Fax: (931) 432-5529   Email: bcards@yahoo.

The nostalgic *Diamond "W" Newsletter* is a wonderful resource for former employees. Write to the address listed for further information.

Sales strategy meeting of the management team of the North Regional Office.

legacy. At the nucleus of every Red-Front lay the seemingly all-seeing, all-hearing figure of the Woolworth's store manager.

The Woolworth's Employee Structure

The F. W. Woolworth Company had a defined employee structure for most of its history. After the executive board and members, a series of regional, or district, managers kept tabs on a specific number of stores throughout the world. At one point, this structure also included merchandise men, assistant district managers, district managers and Woolworth's buyers. The position of a Woolworth's buyer was coveted, and virtually all of them came from the district offices. But the persons ultimately responsible for day-to-day operations were the thousands of Woolworth's store managers.

Ada's Adventure—1920's Style"

In the early 1920's (the time before plastic and brown bags) my mother, Ada, took a sales job at Woolworth's. She'd lied about her age, thinking herself too young to be hired, but she did just fine. She added the items in her head, punched down the cash register keys, and figured out the change. It was the cord that got her! One day, Ada carefully wrapped an item in brown paper, tied the cord, and handed it back to a lady customer. A few minutes later, Ada noticed that the roll of cord was still unwinding. She had forgotten to cut it! She dashed from the counter, scissors in hand, and followed the cord through the aisles, out the door and down the block. At last she caught up with the package, and with the lady (who'd never even noticed). F. W. Woolworth suffered a cord loss profit that day, but a few curious onlookers had followed the cord to see where it had started. Fourteen-year-old Ada had brought F. W. Woolworth's into the streets of New York city—it's first live commercial! —Jan Carol Sabin, Florida

Straight through the 1970s, almost all managers were male, and all of those men started out as "Learners." Learners were the stockboys who started their employment career (usually as teenagers) with the Red-Fronts by baling cardboard, stocking shelves, and sweeping floors. If they were bright and energetic, they had a good chance of moving ahead with the company at a relatively rapid pace. Many Learners eventually made it to the rank of assistant manager, and finally, to store manager.

Store managers selected all the sales employees, stockboys, and "floorwalkers," and coordinated store displays and in-house promotions. Along with being responsible for hiring and firing, salary management, stocking and ordering, the Woolworth's managers also had more "human" (and sometimes unexpected) challenges to deal with. One example of such challenges was the aforementioned pet department, and another involved the store's instant photo booths. Accord-

A Woolworth's manager teaching his "Learner" the ropes, c. 1940.

ing to several managers, these photo booths often attracted crowds of teenagers and, in turn, a rowdy heap of trouble. During the 1940s and '50s, in particular, local students would head to Woolworth's and see how many of them could fit in one booth. Fortunately, their antics were usually innocent, and order was quickly restored before things got out of hand. Several former managers also had the unusual experience of having to oust females who decided to go into the photo booth, take off their clothes and pose nude! If the managers got wind of this, the usual tactic was to unplug the machine and whisper (through the curtain) to the customer that she should take her private posings elsewhere.

Managers of high visibility, or particular historic, stores, such as those in Lancaster, Pennsylvania, Watertown, New York, and the 34th street "mother store" in New York City, also had the responsibility of helping to organize special events during milestone anniversaries of the company. Other managers were involved in large-scale promotions, such as the Tournament of Roses parade in Pasadena, California. Beginning in 1952, and for many years following, the Pasadena Woolworth's store sponsored the parade, in conjunction with the executive office. The Tournament of Roses Parade was the F. W. Woolworth Company's first entry into television sponsorship. The parade was broadcast nationally over the NBC-TV network, and on January 1, 1954, it made television history when a mobile unit was used for the first time to telecast it in full color.

In less celebratory cases, managers such as Frank "Curly" Harris also found themselves plunged into America's own crisis, such as with the Greensboro, North Carolina, sit-ins of the Civil Rights Movement. Others had to contend with fires in their stores, or deal with wage strikes.

All agreed that a Woolworth's manager's life was never dull. The hours were long, and the work was hard, but it is worth noting that by the time of Frank's passing in 1919, some of his managers were making over $15,000 per year, a fortune in those days. Those who had been wise enough to purchase stock several years before, when the company incorporated, made even more. Managers also had the additional incentive to keep working hard until they could take over as regional managers, or even serve on the board of directors, at which time their salaries would increase to hundreds of thousands of dollars. The store managers of the old F. W. Woolworth Company were considered by its chief to be the hope and ultimate resource for the future of the company. And the chief treated them accordingly.

Unfortunately, this was not the case with the women who formed the bulk of his empire: the Woolworth's counter girls.

The Counter Girls

"For millions of customers," wrote author James Brough, "Mr. Woolworth represented a kind of all-season Santa Claus. But had he, in fact, been an image of benignity or something different? Whatever he had made of himself, he was no Saint Nicholas." Indeed, when it came paying his hard-working female wage employees, Mr. Woolworth was an old Scrooge. For all of his outstanding leadership qualities, and his spirit of enterprise, Mr. Frank Woolworth never quite recognized the value of his female workforce.

They were called the "Woolworth Girls" or the "Woolworth Counter Girls," and they made up over eighty percent of his employee ranks. Between 1876 and 1940, the average age span of Woolworth's counter girls was eighteen to twenty-one. They were, for the most part, unmarried, living at home, and involved in their first experience in the business world. They often worked from nine in the morning until ten at night, at which time they positioned their "fire buckets," covered their counters with muslin, and set off for home. The counter girls were considered the lowest form of employee, yet without them there would not have been a Woolworth dynasty.

One of the reasons he was able to run his earliest stores with such tight profit margins was because of his ability to utilize cheap labor. Since he displayed the merchandise openly on individual counters (one for sewing notions, one for candy, etc.) he created a structure whereby the customers made most of their own buying decisions. This virtually eliminated the need for salesmanship, and in turn, it also eliminated the need to find top quality, experienced salesmen. Instead, he could hire scores of young counter girls who had only to look clean and neat (and preferably pretty) and keep the counters organized. Since the prices were fixed (either a nickel or a dime), and these prices were clearly posted near all the counters, the girls didn't even have to be particularly good at mathematics. For this, Frank reasoned, a $1.50 or so a week was plenty.

Beginning in 1879, and for over a decade, the Woolworth's counter girls quietly accepted this policy. They were of the mind (as was their boss) that they were really only working there until they could get married, or because working allowed them to make enough money to feel somewhat independent. But by the winter of 1892, things had started to change. Some of the girls realized they hadn't gotten married and might need a job for a long time. Other girls saw their friends, the stockboys, being rewarded for their hard work with raises and promotions. They also started to hear stories about counter girls at rival five-and-dimes who were making more money. Something, they realized, was not right. And so, they started to rebel. Counter girls from Frank's busiest stores asked for higher wages, and when they were denied, they decided to strike.

In response, on the morning of December 13, 1892, Frank Woolworth told his managers: "One store writes in that all their girls are on strike for higher wages. No doubt they take advantage now while we are so busy, and think we will pay the advance. All such girls you should remember when the dull season comes and give them the bounce."

Frank managed to quell the discontent and carried on. Things still didn't change much for the girls, until one of Frank's main men, Carson Peck, started to intervene. Woolworth greatly respected Peck, and so when Peck advised him to give the girls raises, and to offer vacation pay and bonuses to all his wage employees, then Frank complied. In 1899, Woolworth initiated the first Christmas bonuses: five dollars for each year of service with a limit of $25.00. The counter girls' wages were increased to a minimum of $2.50 per week, with the most experienced earning a little more. But he was still stingy:

"When a clerk gets so good she can get better wages elsewhere—let her go—for it does not require skilled and experienced salesladies to sell our goods," he wrote. "You can get good, honest girls at from 2$ to $3 per week and I would not get $3.50 for any saleslady except in special cases. It may look hard to some of you to pay such small wages but there are lots of girls that live at home that are too proud to work in a factory or do housework. They are glad of the chance to get in a store for experience."

The counter girls from one Detroit, Michigan, store, 1930.

The counter girls carried on, and their numbers increased steadily as the number of Red-Fronts in America also increased. By 1929, at the beginning of the Great Depression and ten years after Frank Woolworth had died, the F. W. Woolworth Co. employed more than 40,000 counter girls. Over the next few years, the current executives of Frank's dynasty were faced with some of the largest counter girl strikes in the company's history. Girls from New York City to the smallest Red-Fronts in Texas took a stand for higher wages. The most organized of these strikes occurred in the big cities, such as Chicago, New York, and Detroit. In 1937, 110 Detroit counter girls actually camped out in the Woolworth's store for days, hoping that if they closed down the prosperous Red-Front, the company would better understand their request for higher wages, as well as their value. Some of the nation's major newspapers made light of the situation; depicting the girls as if they were on holiday, "living in luxury" in the five-and-dime. But the girls ignored the ridicule and pursued their cause.

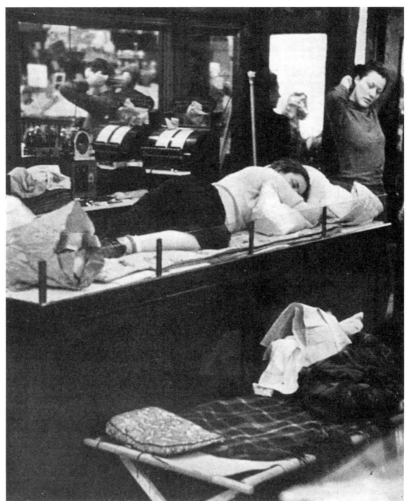

**The Famous
Woolworth's Counter
Girl Strikes of 1937.**

In pursuit of higher wages,
the employees took over
the store for several days,
requiring make-shift sleep
accommodations.

Eventually, the counter girls did win the battle for higher wages, but it wasn't just because of their strikes. They won, in part, because of the negative publicity generated by
Frank's granddaughter, heiress Barbara Hutton. Back in 1930, at the lowest point in America's history, Hutton had garnered the Woolworth's girls' hate when she held a multimil-
lion dollar debutante ball in New York City. Outside, starving people formed bread lines
and stared aghast at the flaunting of wealth and power of the famous Woolworth's heiress.
Hutton's elaborate lifestyle continually made Society headlines, and the counter girls decided that if Barbara Hutton could get millions of dollars from the Woolworth dynasty,
then they deserved a few dollars more in wages. In reality, Hutton's father had sold off all
his daughter's Woolworth's stock years before, but that didn't matter. In the minds of the
counter girls, Hutton had made millions because of her five-and-dime inheritance, and she

"The Day John F. Kennedy Died"

I was working Friday, November 22, 1963, the day President John F. Kennedy was assassinated. It was very quiet in the usually bustling Woolworth's store that night. The people who did come in looked like zombies. Their swollen red eyes, set in blank stares, matched their grimaces of shock. By the next week the store was well stocked with all kinds of pictures of our slain president for sale. Those pictures and memorabilia were replaced with music items, a few months later, right after the Beatles appeared on the Ed Sullivan show and Beatle-mania swept the nation. —Norma Jean Hissong

became the poster child for their discontent. At Woolworth's from the Pacific to the Atlantic, counter girls sang their theme song:

> *Barbara Hutton has the dough, parlez vous.*
> *Where she gets it, sure we know, parlez vous*
> *We slave at Woolworth's five-and-dime*
> *The pay we get sure is a crime*
> *Hinkey Dinkey parlez vous.*

The media pressure became so intense that the Woolworth Co. executives asked Barbara if she could leave the United States and return to one of her mansions in Europe, at least until the heat died down. With Hutton out of the country, they were finally able to retain order at their Red-Fronts. A reasonable wage agreement was finally reached, and the next era of the Woolworth's counter girls began.

During the 1950s, the individual counters of Woolworth's five-and-dimes were replaced with self-service aisles. Former counter girls took on the new role of salesgirl and cashier. Their wages remained competitive throughout the history of the Woolworth Company. By 1954, audio-visual training methods were being used to teach basic business skills, and each long-term employee participated in Woolworth's program of paid vacations, paid holidays, recognition of service events, and the company pension plan.

Gradually, women began to move out of the ranks of cashiers and floorwalkers into management positions. However, straight through the 1970s there were no females employed in the higher executive levels. Fortunately, that began to change in the 1980s.

Hundreds of thousands of employees have stories to share about their experiences with the F. W. Woolworth Company. Some, like Jonathan Hansen, worked only briefly as a stockboy, but since it was his first job he will never forget it. Nor will he forget the wonderful aromas of fresh popcorn and candy of his Maynard, Massachusetts, Red-Front. Other employees devoted half a century of service, making Woolworth's part of their lives, as well as their careers. One of the most touching stories of all is the tale of "Sadie," (see sidebar) who started working at a Woolworth's in Pennsylvania in 1913, and remained there until the day in 1960 when that Red-Front went out of business.

TIME CAPSULE MEMORY

"How Many 'Sadies' Do You Remember?"

by Chuck Wilkerson

The year was 1960, and tucked away in a small mining town in northwestern Pennsylvania, the unpleasant task of closing a Woolworth's 5&10 was in progress. The mood of employees and customers became increasingly sober as the business day drew to a close. The combined service of the store's employees exceeded 250 years. Out of all these fine employees, one stood out because of her good work habits, the excellent upkeep of her assigned counters, and the service she provided to customers. But most of all, she stood out by the dress code she had maintained each and every day. The matronly lady arrived each day wearing a long black cotton dress that came down to her ankles and partially covered high-topped black shoes. She wore a white apron, and her hair was covered by a white ruffled dust bonnet. Before leaving for home each evening, she carefully covered her counters with unbleached muslin, to keep the merchandise free from dust. When asked why she wore what she did, the answer was briskly spoken: "This is what I was instructed to wear when I was hired 47 years ago, and no one has told me any different." Sadie was hired at the tender age of fourteen, and not yet 62, she was too young for Social Security. Sadly, as of December 31, 1960, Sadie didn't have any counters to cover anymore . . ."

PART FOUR

PRESERVING THE LEGACY

Woolworth
STORE HOURS

MONDAY	9 :30am to 6 :00pm
TUESDAY	9 :30am to 6 :00pm
WEDNESDAY	9 :30am to 6 :00pm
THURSDAY	9 :30am to 6 :00pm
FRIDAY	9 :30am to 7 :00pm
SATURDAY	9 :30am to 6 :00pm
SUNDAY	*Closed Forever!*

Chapter Twelve

The Collectibles!

*"Culture, in order to grow, must be fertilized. And it may well be that
the glorious trash of the five-and-ten-cent stores played a large part
in helping to build the Great American Dream."*

—Anita Loos

Reaching out to Five-and-Dime Infinity

Like any other icon that has captured the popular fancy, F. W. Woolworth Co. has established a niche in the ever-expanding collectibles market. The very day in 1997 that the company announced the demise of its Red-Fronts, the prices on related five-and-dime memorabilia started to soar.

That is not to imply that there wasn't a healthy market prior to 1997. In fact, people have been buying and selling five-and-dime items for decades. Knick-knacks that once sold at dimestores for a handful of pennies now bring in hundreds, sometimes thousands, of dollars apiece. The difference is that the old "F. W. Woolworth," logo, the mark of the most famous dimestore of all, will never again appear on new products. This makes those that are already out there even more valuable.

The Woolworth's collectibles market is presently in a state of flux, and will remain so for several more years until it becomes clearer just how much those Red-Front collectibles are worth in the open market. For that reason, you will not find exact price estimates here. It is also impossible to list *all* the Woolworth's collectibles (that would require a separate book), but on the off chance that you are wondering if any of the dusty collectibles in your attic are worth money, this chapter is a good starting point, and will provide you with a general overview of the five-and-dime craze, with a focus on American Woolworth's memorabilia.

The best price references for general five-and-dime memorabilia remain established guides such as *Kovels Antiques & Collectibles*. There you can look up the value of everything from toy trains to colored perfume bottles, and begin your trek into five-and-dime collectibles. There are also several specialty volumes that can provide both insight and enjoyment into this unique era and its products. One of the most fascinating of these is *Dime Store Days*, by Lester Glassner and Brownie Harris (Penguin, 1981), which offers 128 pages of photos of everything from 1940s sunglasses to pressed-paper Santas—all gleaned from the author's personal collection of dimestore merchandise.

One of the first questions people often ask is: *Which items are most valuable?* When it comes to five-and-dime products, some of the most prized collectibles include pre-World War I German tree ornaments, first introduced in the United States by Frank Woolworth in 1890. Other high-ticket items include Bakelite products, pre-1950 Disney memorabilia, Plasticville toy sets, and Golden Age celebrity memorabilia like Joan Crawford publicity stills and Charlie McCarthy greeting cards. Novelty costume jewelry is also very popular, running the gamut from Carmen Miranda "banana" earrings to necklaces bearing the Batman Bat Signal logo. You can also find salt and pepper shakers, ash trays, perfume bottles, sugar bowls, and spoons that were issued in every conceivable color and style.

If you are interested in military items, contemporary dealers are doing a brisk business in a large variety of World War I painted metal army nurses, World War II wind-up soldiers, Tokyo Rose movie memorabilia, and post-1950 plastic military figures. Paper war bonds are also popular with collectors; F. W. Woolworths was the first chain to start selling war bonds during World War II.

The aforementioned products were available at most "five-and-tens" throughout the United States. Along with the established chain dimestores like Woolworth's, there were thousands of small, independent "mom-and-pop" establishments selling sewing notions and trinkets for pocket change. However, given the fact that there were literally thousands of F. W. Woolworth stores, the majority of collectibles that surface in today's market were originally purchased by patrons of the old Red-Fronts.

Beneath the umbrella category of general "five-and-dime collectibles," there are also distinct subdivisions. For example, some collectors prefer to acquire based on the individual five-and-ten company name itself. Therefore, along with Woolworth's collectors, there

are Kress, Newberry, and others. It is not unusual to find the paper price label reading "Woolworths 5¢" & "10¢"or "Knox 5¢" & "10¢" still on the item; naturally, this helps to identify the origin of the piece.

Traveling and fixed "museum" exhibits of such collectibles are becoming more commonplace as America moves away from the once expansive five-and-dime era. These exhibits are colorful and informative reminders of days gone by, and can be helpful in determining the value of that tiny china ring box or paper Halloween ghost that you're been saving since you were a child.

This pair of early 1930s porcelain spoon rests still bear the original Woolworth's 10¢ label.

Woolworth's Exclusives

Among the F. W. Woolworth collecting specialists, there is always a popular demand for "Woolworth's exclusives." These exclusives take on four primary forms:

The first encompasses products made specifically for the Woolworth Company, which were issued by Woolworth's under the guise of a "brand" name. Such was the case with *Woolco* sewing notions and *Herald Square* typewriter ribbons. The Woolworth company itself never personally assumed the role of product manufacturer. Company executives (beginning with its ambitious founder) preferred to make deals with independent manufacturers, hiring them to make products to be sold only in Woolworth's stores. This is a common practice now, but in the early part of the century it was a novel idea, one which Frank Woolworth capitalized on to a great degree. Woolworth brand-name exclusives can usually be identified by the presence of both said brand name (such as Herald Square) along with an accompanying red "W" logo printed somewhere on the products. In other cases, a line of typed print might read: "Only through F. W. Woolworth," or "Sold exclusively through F. W. Woolworth."

Popular-Brand Name Woolworth "Exclusives"

Herald Square and *Woolco* were brand-names exclusive to F. W. Woolworth Co.

The second type of Woolworth's exclusives are those items manufactured by established, popular (non-Woolworth-related) companies and sold as limited run or limited editions through F. W. Woolworth stores. Two highly collectible examples of these would be Mattel's "Special Expressions" Barbie dolls and the Topps Baseball Card packs. A variety of Disney items, as well as comic book character items, were also sold in limited edition through Woolworth's over the years. One of the hottest traded contemporary products are the Hot Wheels limited editions, which came in an assortment of colors. They were offered in two-packs, featuring a Hot Wheels car and a red-and-white Woolworth's truck. Popular brand Woolworth's exclusives can be easily identified because the box or package clearly states that the item is a Woolworth's exclusive or limited edition.

The third type of Woolworth's exclusive includes those items designed to promote a specific Woolworth's store. These were usually given out during a store's grand opening or a store reopening, or to commemorate a special sales event. Hundreds of different store promotions were issued through the decades. They ranged from simple match books listing a particular store, to record brushes (these brushes were used to keep 78 RPM records free of dust and grime) imprinted with the image of a famous celebrity, such as the Andrew Sisters along with an F. W. Woolworth store's address. This particular type of promotion collectible is prevalent among Woolworth's specialist collectors because of the large range of items to be had in the marketplace—sometimes for under $20.00 a piece. These items often appear unexpectedly at garage sales and flea markets.

More contemporary "Special Expression" Barbie Doll" in original box runs between $25 to $50 apiece.

In some instances, several different stores shared the same store promotional item, and in such cases, you will only see the "F. W. Woolworth" name and not an individual store name. These items are trickier to identify as store promotions, and it takes a bit of sleuthing to determine their origin. For example, the Woolworth's multicolored yardstick only stated "Woolworth's" but I was told that it was given out by several stores in the Midwest as part of grand reopening sales. These were also many similar yardsticks that were distributed throughout Woolworth's history.

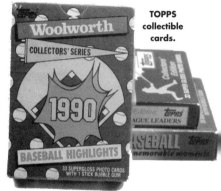

TOPPS collectible cards.

The general rule of thumb is to try to accumulate products that actually state "Woolworth's" or "F. W.

This multicolored yardstick (red, yellow, and blue) is an example of a Woolworth's store promotional item.

"Celebrity" record brushes like this Guy Lombardo item advertised regional F. W. Woolworth stores during the 1940s. Record brushes range in value from $25–$50.

Woolworth" if you are trying to acquire a varied and colorful cache of exclusive Woolworth's collectibles. You might also want to be on the lookout for overseas Woolworth's store promotional items, such as the Woolworth's thimble. This particular thimble came from a London store and includes the phrase: "Right Up Your Street For Value."

The fourth major category of Woolworth exclusives is Woolworth specialty memorabilia. This category is made up of paper memorabilia which relate directly to the company's history (such as anniversary booklets and vintage stock reports), or the life of its founder, Frank Winfield Woolworth. It also includes material products issued specifically as souvenirs (such as Woolworth Building curios) and actual fixtures and signs from Woolworth's five-and-dime stores. Of related significance are Woolworth's advertising posters, and all manner of magazine and print ads.

This category is so vast, and so broad, that it is easiest to assign each of these specialty memorabilia their own sub-divisions.

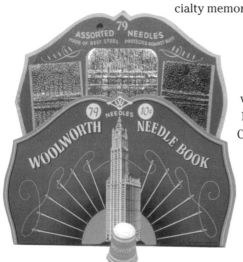

Woolworth Building Collectibles

The Woolworth Building in New York on Broadway, reigned as the tallest building in the world from 1913 to 1930. Not surprisingly, the F. W. Woolworth Company took advantage of this acclaim, issuing hundreds of different Woolworth Building-related mementos. Most were officially licensed by the F. W. Woolworth Company, but there were also assorted

Woolworth Building Needle Book, c. 1925. These colorful needle books designed in red, white, and blue, range in value from $5 to $25.

postcards, for instance, that were printed up by ambitious entrepreneurs and sold for a tidy profit to tourists.

The earliest Woolworth Building collectibles are among those given out to visitors and sightseers who trekked to the observation tower near top of the building, beginning in 1913. Some of these mementos were

Woolworth Building stereograph, c. 1913.

also available in the Manhattan-based Woolworth's stores, as well as through local non-Woolworth gift shops. One of the most prized mementos of all is a jeweled powder case. This was given out during the first few days the Woolworth Building was opened, and it is extremely rare. The lion's share of Woolworth Building collectibles date from 1913 to the mid-1940s, at which time the tower was closed to visitors—but one can still find a few miscellaneous items dating from 1945 to 1997.

Woolworth Building collectibles can be found in the form of postcards, salt and pepper shakers, commemorative coins, posters, wooden boxes, hand mirrors, needle books, and more. Those issued between 1913 and 1930 often include the phrase: "Tallest Building In The World." This helps to date the item. In cases where this phrase is omitted, it becomes more time-consuming and challenging to date and value the piece.

The one thing that all of these souvenirs have in common is the image of that regal sixty-story edifice, printed or embedded somewhere on the item.

Another pricey collectible is the Woolworth Building cast-iron bank. These banks routinely sell for $50 to $250, and are much sought after by Woolworth's specialty collectors and general novelty bank collectors. I have seen at least three different versions of

One of the rarest of all Woolworth Building collectibles is this "jeweled" powder set issued in 1913. In excellent condition, it sells for between $250 and $350. This is the ad that one dealer used to sell the item on an online auction.

GRAND OPENING GIFT

WOOLWORTH BUILDING

Attention Ladies... Had you been there in the early 1900's... on that great day in history, the Grand Opening of the Woolworth Building in New York City, you too would have received one of these!

A RARE treasure indeed! These just don't come along everyday!

Original, powder, and rouge cakes are inside and UNCRACKED, original puffs are there too! Mirror is PERFECT! Minor corrosion inside, around cakes Outside is beautiful, all original, stones in place, finish is BEAUTIFUL!! Measures Approx. 2-1/4" across the top, by 3/4" high when closed. When all sections are extended, the length is 5-1/4". A true beauty! Hinge is perfect and strong. Clasp works perfectly, snaps shut tight!

High bidder to prepay cost+ S/I
...did I mention... overall condition is EXCELLENT!
Questions? Please, email me! Thanks for looking!

LEFT: Example of a Woolworth Building cast-iron bank, c. 1930s. It came in a variety of styles and sizes through the decades. Prices range drastically, based on age and condition, from $25 to $300. CENTER: Examples of Woolworth Building pewter salt & pepper shakers. RIGHT: "Silver Shoe," one of the most unique Woolworth Building collectibles, measures only about 4 inches long and has the Woolworth Building etched into the tongue of the shoe. The marks on the sole read: "J.B. 515."

this bank, and one can presume there are several more versions of varying detail and size.

In the realm of most unusual Woolworth Building collectibles, one would have to include the polished silver shoe, which features the building cast into the tongue of a ladies high-heeled shoe!

Postcards of the Woolworth Building have been in plentiful supply for eighty-five years, and these are also popular with collectors. The postcards run the gamut from simple black-and-white sketches to colorized drawings to photos, and can be purchased from anywhere from $5.00 to $30.00 apiece. Most Woolworth Building postcards are found in the standard 3x5-inch size, but at least one was issued which measured three feet tall.

Souvenir booklets and pamphlets are yet another category of Woolworth Building collectibles. These were given out to visitors of the building, and range from the more contemporary trifold paper flyer to elaborate full-color booklets.

One of the most attractive and informative of these booklets is "Above the Clouds and Old New York," with text by H. Addington Bruce, which was published in 1913 specifically for distribution among the visitors to the Woolworth Building. It includes a detailed history of the actual site of the building in Old Manhattan, as well as information about the building's many architectural wonders. It is lavishly illustrated and a must-buy for serious aficionados of Woolworth's history.

Perhaps most unique of all Woolworth Building memorabilia are the paintings and sketches rendered by artists, famous and obscure, who sat outside the building to capture the beauty of the structure for posterity. Countless sketches no doubt still lie gathering dust in basements and storage rooms across the world, but several have made it to the marketplace. In the realm of noteworthy artistic collectibles one should also include the preliminary sketches of the Woolworth Building as rendered by its architect Cass Gilbert.

FAR LEFT: **Souvenir coin, 1925.**
LEFT: **Souvenir coin (solid brass)
issued during 1988. A similar
coin was issued during the
company's 100th anniversary
in 1979.**

Several of these have been reprinted in Woolworth Building booklets, but the originals are worth many thousands of dollars and are rare indeed.

Lucky treasure hunters might also stumble upon the limited edition hardcover book called, *The Dinner Given to Cass Gilbert by Frank W. Woolworth, April 24, MCMXIII.* This beautiful red leather-bound hardback contains the speeches and addresses of key players in the construction of the building, as well as those men who paid glowing tribute to architect and financier that memorable evening. The book offers a wealth of data, with everything from the guest list (800 male dignitaries) to the seating arrangements and menu. Photographs of Woolworth, Gilbert, and Louis Horowitz (the builder), are interspersed throughout. It is believed that this was produced after the dinner and presented only to the 800 attendees, plus additional select executives. The book is extremely rare and has been sold upwards of $200 per volume.

F. W. Woolworth Company Anniversary and Commemorative Publications: 1919–1979

Some of the most entertaining and most available Woolworth specialty collectibles are the anniversary books that were issued by the company beginning in 1919. These were top-quality publications, using only the finest of then-modern printing methods. They all include a brief history of the company and its founders, and pages of illustrations which capture the Woolworth's five-and-dime of a particular era. Some are hardcover with color illustrations; others are paperbound with primarily black-and-white or sepia-toned illustrations.

Souvenir booklets were issued during the company's fortieth (1919), fiftieth (1929), sixtieth (1939), seventy-fifth (1954), and one–hundredth (1979) anniversaries. The fiftieth anniversary booklet had two parts. The first was an undersized "Golden Book" concentrating on Frank Woolworth and his fellow founders, while the second was a small 6x4-inch red-covered companion, the *Home Shopping Guide,* which listed many of the company's most popular five-and-dime products of the late 1920s. The *Home Shopping Guide* was freely distributed among Woolworth's stores throughout the country.

The sixtieth-anniversary booklet from 1939 was also issued in a limited edition of 100

red leather-bound copies, stamped in gold, which were personally signed by Charles Sumner Woolworth, who was still an active member of the board of directors at that time. My personal copy of this rare edition includes a typed note from E. C. Mauchley of the executive office in New York City, which indicates that the general distribution of the sixtieth-anniversary (non-leather bound) booklet was scheduled to begin October 21, 1939.

By the time of the centennial in 1979, the anniversary booklets were not as elaborate as their vintage predecessors had been, but they still offered a wealth of historical and contemporary information about the company. There was also a special paper supplement issued during the eightieth-anniversary year, titled "The Woolworth Story: 80 Years of Progress." This was an 8x10-inch, green fold-out which featured excerpts from a *Christian Science Monitor* newspaper series about F. W. Woolworth Co. It also includes interesting photos and facts about the British Ltd. Woolworth's.

Another source of company history are the annual stock reports. These are most valuable to researchers seeking financial information, or pictures of the largest or most productive Woolworth's stores.

RIGHT: Company
promotional
booklets, such
as the "Fortieth
Anniversary
Souvenir 1879–
1919," are popu-
lar collectibles.
FAR RIGHT: Origi-
nal sketch of the
Woolworth Build-
ing by artist
A. E. Poore.

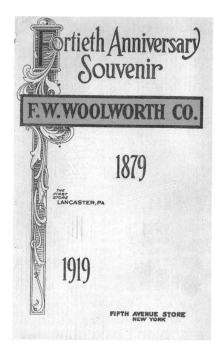

These F. W. Woolworth Co. anniversary booklets and stock reports are affordable collectibles that range anywhere from $5 to $60 per item. Autographed copies of Woolworth booklets bring in even more. A Frank Woolworth autograph alone is worth $150—a fact that would have surely tickled the chief.

Lunch Counter Memorabilia

Do you still have the apron and cap that you wore as a Woolworth's lunch counter girl in the 1950s? Did you pick up a dozen authentic root beer glasses when your local Woolworth's went out of business? Is there a tin "Coca Cola 10¢" poster hanging in your rec room? Do you own a portion of the F. W. Woolworth lunch counter that was used in the Broadway show, *Come Back to the 5 & Dime, Jimmy Dean, Jimmy Dean?* If so, then you already have a jump on the lucrative Woolworth's lunch counter collectibles market.

As of this printing, the most popular and actively trading articles were vintage advertising signs promoting everything from banana splits to grilled cheese sandwiches. Some are constructed of tin, some of cardboard or plastic; some are faded, some have catsup stains on them, some look like new—but they are all extremely popular among collectors.

Authentic Woolworth's lunch menus are also enjoying a brisk trade. The pre-1940 menus are rare, in part because they weren't designed for longevity. But beginning in the early 1950s, the menus were often laminated or coated with a protective material, allowing them to last through ensuing decades. There were many different types of Woolworth's menus. An ambitious search will uncover Woolworth's cafeteria menus, luncheonette menus, take-out bakery menus, and those wonderful "special of the day" flyers and cards that were used in conjunction with the regular menu. There are menus from the standard F. W. Woolworth eateries, as well as from Harvest House Restaurants, Woolworth's Grille's, Chuck Wagons, and other variations the company tested out over the years.

One of my favorite finds was a poster that appeared in the Havana, Cuba, Woolworth's in the mid-1950s. Loosely translated it reads: "Why cook? Visit our new deli department and buy your meals. The list is for take-out to your home." In general, European or South American luncheonette memorabilia commands higher prices in the American market. American Woolworth's menus run between $10 to $60, and considerably more for pre-World War I menus in good condition.

This menu came from an F. W. Woolworth's lunch counter in Kentucky.

Not everyone is satisfied with a simple menu, however. I once saw an entire lunch counter, intact, with a row of red stools and a bevy of soda and ice cream dispensers, for sale on the Internet during an online auction! The minimum bid was $2,000 and the buyer was responsible for shipping.

Of course, most people cannot easily splurge on the cost of buying, shipping, and installing an entire Woolworth's lunch counter in their homes, and so they often settle for the less expensive items. Utensils, glassware, silver and glass ice cream dishes, and Woolworth's-themed paper placemats are all popular. If you're lucky, you can find the pre-1920 china plates that were used in the larger Woolworth's Refreshment Rooms. Some of these have surfaced bearing the Woolworth's name or logo lining the rim, or along the back of the plate. Woolworth's lunch counter memorabilia continues to be the most sought after of all the Woolworth's specialty collectibles.

Store Signs, Fixtures, and Carry-Alls

If you happen to have an authentic "F. W. Woolworth 5 & 10¢" store sign hanging over your family bar, then you are fortunate indeed. You might also consider getting it insured, considering that the prices for these vintage gems can go as high as $3,000. Among the rarest and most coveted are the c. 1890–1915 mahogany signs that once decorated the outside of the stores, many of which include Tiffany glass highlights and gold leaf lettering. Frank Winfield Woolworth spared no expense when he came to placing his name on a masthead. In the beginning, he settled for simple, pine hand-painted signs, but as soon as he made his first million, he pulled out all the stops.

Vintage Woolworth's signs are truly a piece of Americana. They are available in a wide assortment of sizes and styles. The company went through several transitions over its 118-year history, each transition spawning a different type of sign. To help you date these gems of popular culture, here are a few guidelines.

The earliest signs (c. 1879–1885) were usually constructed of simple pine and hand-lettered by local artisans. They bear the phrase "5 and 10¢ store" or "5 & 10 CENT STORE" and either below that, above that, or before that, one would see the phrase, "F. W. Woolworth." Some were square, some rectangular, and some had rounded edges. Because Frank commissioned these signs to be made in the town he was presently infiltrating, there was no standard use of materials or lettering. These early signs are so rare that the odds of finding one intact are very low. If you do stumble upon one in good condition, then you can safely presume it is worth several thousand dollars.

During this period, Frank also went into partnership with other men (including his brother, Charles) the better to defray the cost of his overhead and expand into more cities. Therefore, there were also signs which read, "Woolworth Bros.," "Woolworth and McBrier," "Woolworth & Knox," etc. Frank Woolworth discontinued his practice of "partner-managers" around 1886, so most signs bearing two names would be dated before that time period.

Between 1886 and 1904, the same phrase—F. W. Woolworth "5 & 10¢ store"—still appeared on many mastheads, but Frank began to commission signs with slightly more elaborate designs, preferring an octagonal shape. Usually (but not always) these had a red background and gold lettering. It was during this period that the nickname "Red-Front" came into widespread use.

In 1905, Frank incorporated his growing empire and, in turn, the signs posted on his new stores read, "F. W. Woolworth & Co." This phraseology continued through 1913, until the great merger and a reincorporation ensued. Beginning in 1913, the new stores said: "F. W. Woolworth Co." The years between 1913–1915 were transitional, as one by one stores that once bore the name "McBrier," for instance, were all changed to "F. W. Woolworth Co." In at least one case, his merger-partner, Herbert Knox, insisted that *both* names appear on the masthead.

From the very beginning, variations on the theme started to surface. For example, some of the signs said: "5 & 10¢" while others said "5 and 10¢ + 15¢." In other cases, the word "and" was flanked by lines over and below, or the word "cent" was written out instead of using the ¢ symbol.

In the 1930s, the ten-cent price limit was lifted, so many new F. W. Woolworth Co. stores had signs which read: "5 & 10¢ store" or 5 & 10 and 25¢."

It is important to remember that the style of these signs varied greatly. There were numerous minor variations on the F. W. Woolworth theme, and the only thing that really remained constant (after 1885) was the use of the color red and the name "Woolworth." Even as late as 1980, Woolworth mastheads were not always uniform. To further complicate matters, there were some stores in rural and small towns that never changed their signs, regardless of how many years they were in business! Their original gold-and-red lettering of pre-World War I sometimes remained intact well into the 1960s.

After World War II, heavy plastic, veneered woods, and mixed metal and wood signs came into use. On most of the plastic signs (which were often illuminated from behind) the words "F. W. Woolworth Co. (or simply, "Woolworth") became the norm. Gone were the days when everything in the store sold for under a nickel or a dime, and therefore, the signs did not advertise as such. The signs became more streamlined throughout the 1970s and 1980s. During this period, some of the F. W. Woolworth mall stores bore *blue* lettering. Clearly, the styles of Woolworth signs varied, but as long as it says Woolworth's, Woolworth, or F. W. Woolworth, you are on the right track to find a piece of Americana.

For collectors, mastheads are the most popular, but indoor signs are also worth noting. Smaller reproductions of the masthead often hung inside the store, either on the walls or suspended from the ceiling.

Vintage store fixtures and furniture also fall into this category. Until the late 1950s,

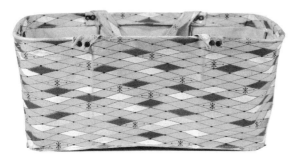

Canvas and plastic shopping baskets used by Woolworth's shoppers are popular and relatively affordable collectibles.

when self-service started to become the norm in Woolworth's, there were female employees (counter girls) stationed at individual counters throughout the store. Each girl had her own cash register and, in essence, her own five-and-dime domain. In the larger Woolworth's establishments, these counters were very elaborate. They were either mahogany or walnut (solid or veneered) and sometimes featured glass sliding storage shelves with brass fittings. These counters occasionally come up for sale, with prices beginning at $500.

The earliest manual cash registers, which replaced the overhead cable payment systems in 1900, are also desirable collectibles. The original registers were metal, painted gold or silver, and often featured detailed designs. One of the primary responsibilities of the Woolworth's counter girls was to keep these registers clean and polished, therefore, they often surface in specialty auctions in relatively good condition. When the Red-Fronts started to close down during the 1990s, the store managers also sold the fixtures, metal shelving, modern display counters, and anything else that wasn't bolted down. Customers walked out with all manner of Woolworth's mementos, many of them with the purpose of recycling the Woolworth's items into their own store establishments.

One of the most popular store items during the final day sales were Woolworth's shopping carryalls, which were hand-held canvas (and later, plastic) baskets. These were issued in a variety of styles and colors through the years, ranging from blue-and-green striped "collapsible" carryalls, to contemporary red plaid canvas. The individual store managers set the prices on these baskets, which ranged from $5 to $10. It is expected these

Five-and-Dime Items Tucked Away in Shoe Boxes or Attics Have Become Icons for Preserving the Woolworth Legacy.

LEFT: Lovelee Hair Net, c. 1920. RIGHT: "Famous First" ink blotter released by Davis Plywood Corp.

baskets, will begin to command $25 or more over the next few years. With rare exceptions, these baskets were time worn from so many years of use, but the customers who carried them outside on closing day didn't seem to mind. They knew they were purchasing a piece of Americana.

Advertising Memorabilia

The final Woolworth's category of specialty items is advertising memorabilia.

F. W. Woolworth Co. advertising memorabilia, like Woolworth's store signs, take on many different forms. One can readily find catalogs, magazine, and newspaper print ads, posters, and store signs featur-

Display for TopsAll watchbands, c. 1980.

ing particular products. An example of the latter would be the plastic sign for TopsAll Watchbands.

This Woolworth's ad commemorates the first Americans to reach the moon. Magazine and newspaper ads like this are becoming increasingly popular among collectors.

Some of the most colorful and nostalgic of advertising collectibles are the old F. W. Woolworth Christmas catalogs. These first appeared in the 1950s and contain pages of toys and household notions, complete with illustrations and original prices. These catalogs are a great source of research for dealers and collectors trying to determine the original price of that Mickey Mouse lamp for which they may have just paid two hundred dollars! The covers of these catalogs sometimes featured watercolor photos of famous Woolworth's stores. Catalogs start at $20 based on condition.

Pre-1950 magazine print ads for F. W. Woolworth are also hard to find. The company just did not invest much money in lavish magazine ads. A few ads have surfaced (dating as far back as 1915) in publications such as *Ladies Home Journal,* but by and large, the company did not begin to advertise extensively in magazines until the 1950s. Usually, the older ads focused on a particular line of products, such as Woolco cottons or yarns.

Newspaper ads and supplements are more commonplace than magazine ads. Individual store managers routinely advertised back-to-school sales, grand reopening sales, and holiday bargains. On occasion, you will also stumble across ads financed by the Woolworth Company itself, in order to commemorate a landmark event. In 1969, for example, they took out ads throughout the country thanking the first men on the moon. The value of magazine and print ads are difficult to estimate, as they range from as little as $2.00 per ad to $40 per ad.

Miscellaneous Memorabilia: The Heart of F. W. Woolworth Collectibles

There are countless F. W. Woolworth five-and-dime collectibles that do not actually fall into one broad category, but are worth mentioning just for their nostalgic or novelty value. A nickel coin wrapper bearing the Woolworth's name might not be worth as much as a vintage cast metal Woolworth's bank, but the wrapper means a lot to the manager who walked to the bank each night to make a deposit.

Due to the fact that the old five-and-dimes played such an important role in the lives of millions of former employees and patrons alike, individual items tucked away in hope chests or show boxes have special significance for casual collectors. The old Depression-era sales receipts from the year you somehow managed to buy all six children Christmas

gifts for under $2.00 . . . the empty bottle of Evening in Paris perfume you received from your first beau in the 1940s . . . the Lovelee Hair Net purchased for a dime which you thought was such a great deal because it was made of "real human hair" . . . the first tube of Tangee lipstick you purchased to go to the high school dance . . . Woolworth's penny weight cards, old photos taken in the photo machine . . . the instructions from Peerless Water Waver curlers . . . these are all examples of items that bring back memories. Some might even be worth money in the open market, but even if they aren't, one treasures them all the same.

F. W. Woolworth collectibles and memorabilia are all part of the domain of "five-and-dime infinity." When "time" finally ran out for the five-and-dimes, the products that were generated over its 118-year-old history took on both a financial and nostalgic appeal.

These, and other Woolworth's collectibles, are the fragments of the past that will help to keep the F. W. Woolworth Co. phenomena alive for decades to come.

"Remembering Woolworth's"

This bibliography is by no means a complete record of all the works and sources consulted while writing this book. It indicates the substance and range of reading upon which I have formed my ideas, and I intend it to serve as a convenience for those who wish to pursue further study of Frank Winfield Woolworth and the F. W. Woolworth Co. In addition to the books, periodicals, and Internet resources listed below, I also consulted numerous F. W. Woolworth Co. annual reports, company newsletters, interoffice correspondence dating as far back as 1890, and interviewed hundreds of former Woolworth's employees and patrons.

Books

Baker, Nina Brown. *Nickels and Dimes: The Story of F. W. Woolworth.* New York: Harcourt, Brace & World, 1954.

Brough, James. *The Woolworths.* New York: McGraw Hill, 1982.

Bruce, Addington H. *Above the Clouds and Old New York: An Historical Sketch of the Site and a Description of the Many Wonders of the Woolworth Building.* New York: F. W. Woolworth Co., 1913.

Cochran, Edwin A. *The Cathedral of Commerce: The Woolworth Building, New York.* New York: Broadway Park Place Co., 1917, 1921.

Comyns, Barbara. *Our Spoons Came from Woolworths.* New York: The Dial Press (Doubleday & Company, Inc.), 1983.

Dupre, Judith. *Skyscrapers.* New York: Black Dog & Leventhal Publishers, 1996.

Eldridge, Mona. *In Search of a Prince: My Life with Barbara Hutton.* London: Sidgwick & Jackson, 1988.

Glassner, Lester and Brownie Harris. *Dime-Store Days.* New York: Penguin Books, 1981.

Heymann, David C. *Poor Little Rich Girl: The Life and Legend of Barbara Hutton.* Ontario: Lyle Stuart, Inc., 1983.

Hurst, Fannie. *Five and Ten.* New York: Harper & Brothers, 1929.

Kirkwood, Robert C. *Newcomen Society: The Woolworth Story at Home and Abroad.* New York: Princeton University Press, 1960.

Lebhar, Godfrey M. *Chain Stores in America: 1859–1959.* New York: Chain Store Publishing, 1959.

Maher, James T. *The Twilight of Splendor.* Boston: Little, Brown and Company, 1975.

McBrier, Edwin Merton. *The Origin of the 5 and 10 Cent Store:* Part II, McBrier Genealogy. Privately printed, 1941.

McAtamnet, Hugh, Compiler. *Commemorative Book for the Dinner Given to Cass Gilbert by Frank W. Woolworth, April 24th, 1913.* New York: 1913.

Myers, Elisabeth P. *F. W. Woolworth: Five and Ten Boy.* Indianapolis: Bobbs Merrill, 1962.

Nash, Sunny. *Big Mama Didn't Shop at Woolworth's.* Texas: Texas A&M University Press, 1996.

Nichols, John P. *Skyline Queen and the Merchant Prince: The Woolworth Story.* New York: Trident Press, 1973.

Nichols, John P. *The Chain Store Tells Its Story.* New York: Institute of Distribution, Inc., 1940.

Randall, Monica. *The Mansions of Long Island's Gold Coast.* New York: Hastings House, 1979.

Winkler, John K. *Five and Ten: The Fabulous Life of F. W. Woolworth.* New York: Robert M. McBride & Company, 1940.

Wolff, Miles. *Lunch at the 5 & 10: The Story of the Greensboro Sit-Ins.* Chicago: Elephant Paperbacks, Ivan R. Dee Publisher, 1970, 1990.

Woolworth Co., F. W. *Fortieth Anniversary Souvenir: 1879–1919.* New York: F. W. Woolworth Co., 1919.

Woolworth Co., F. W. *50 Years of Woolworth: 1879–1929.* New York: F. W. Woolworth Co., 1929.

Woolworth Co., F. W. *Home Shopping Guide.* New York: F. W. Woolworth Co., 1929.

Woolworth Co., F. W. *60 Years of Woolworth: The Story of Everybody's Store.* New York: F. W. Woolworth Co., 1939.

Woolworth Co., F. W. *The Dinner Given to Cass Gilbert by Frank W. Woolworth: April 24, 1913.* New York: privately printed, 1913.

Woolworth Co., F. W. *Woolworth's First 75 Years: The Story of Everybody's Store: 1879–1954.* New York: F. W. Woolworth Co., 1954.

Articles

"Barbara Hutton Haugwitz-Reventlow Has Husband Trouble." *Life* (July 18, 1938): 20–23.

Berridge, John R. "Good 1d and 6d Pays Off in Britain for Woolworth Company." *Christian Science Monitor* (Apr. 30, 1959).

"Bit of Americana Bids Farewell: Store Lunch Counter Left to History Books." *Chicago Tribune* (Aug. 2, 1997).

Bryan, Jodell L. "From Vaudeville to the Silver Screen: Popular Entertainment in Lancaster." *Journal of the Lancaster Historical Society* (Fall 1997): Vol. 95, No. 4: 109–125.

Corbett, Patrick R. and DiPasqua, Aida. "Idea for store born in Utica, where locals will miss its presence." *Observer-Dispatch* (July 18, 1992):4A.

"Deaths of Firemen Here Largest Toll on Record." *The Charleston Gazette* (Mar. 6, 1949):1, 14.

Fargo, Helen. "History of the Woolworth Memorial United Methodist Church-Great Bend, NY." *4-Rivers Journal of the 4 River Valleys Historical Society* (July–Dec. 1995):1.

"F. W. Woolworth from Watertown to the World." *Museum Musings: Newsletter of the Jefferson County Historical Society* (Jan. 1998):1.

"F. W. Woolworth, Head of Chain of 1,038 Ten-Cent Stores, Dies." *The St. Louis Star* (Apr. 8, 1919):3.

"Lightning on Woolworth Tower." *New York Times* (June 21, 1913):1.

Maine, Kathern. "A Man of Vision." *Journal of the Lancaster Historical Society* (Fall 1997):Vol. 99, No. 33:130–140.

"Method of Escavating the Cellar of the Woolworth Building in New York." *Engineering Record* (Apr. 27, 1913):472–473.

Proeller, Marie. "Remembering the Five-and-Dime." *Country Living Magazine* (Sept. 1997):96.

Quick, Bob. "Woolworths on the Plaza closing shop." *The Sante Fe New Mexican* (July 18, 1997):A1, A6.

Schreiber, Paul. "Life After: How One Village is Coping." *New York Newsday* (Sept. 15, 1998):C10.

"State, City Officials Help Woolworth to Celebrate 80th Year." *Lancaster Intelligencer Journal* (June 20, 1959):4, 8.

Steinhauler, Jennifer. "A Highflier in an Uphill Battle: A Retail Star Has Yet to Win Respect for Woolworth's Successor." *New York Times* (July 12, 1998): Section 3:1,11.

Kirkwood, Robert C. "The Woolworth Story: 80 Years of Progress." *Christian Science Monitor* (Mar. 30, 1959).

Trapnell, Stephen. "Woolworth to Shut, Sell 400 Stores." *Lancaster Intelligencer Journal* (July 17, 1997):A-1.

"When Vaudeville Held the Boards on the 'Roof Garden' of the Woolworth Building." *Lancaster Sunday News* (May 17, 1931).

Wilkerson, Chuck. "In 1879 A Man Had a Notion and 118 Years Later, Nothing Left but Memories." *Diamond "W" Newsletter* (August 1998):1.

Wilkerson, Chuck. "Milestones of Distinction." *Diamond "W" Newsletter* (Oct/Nov 1998):1.

Winkler, John and Sparkes, Boyden. "Dime Store." *The Saturday Evening Post* (Feb. 24, 1940):22–23, 80, 82, 84–85.

"Woolworth Chain Plans Big Doings Here." *Lancaster Intelligencer Journal* (May 12, 1959):1, 15.

Yaeger, Lynn and Sietsema, Robert. "The Last Days of Woolworth's." *The Village Voice* (Aug. 12, 1997):16.

"$200 Loan to Woolworth May Have Changed Future." *Lancaster Intelligencer Journal* (May 16, 1959):4.

Internet Resources

Increase & Diffusion: A Smithsonian Web Magazine: "Sitting for Justice."

http://www.si.edu/i%2bd/sitins.v2.4.html

Peggy Trowbridge's Home Cooking Guide: "Lunch Counter Lingo."

http://homecooking.miningco.com/library/weekly/aa081897.htm

Woolworth's: Britain's Favourite Family Store.

http://www.kingfisher.co.uk/investor/woolworth_profile.htm

Woolworth Ltd. of Cyprus: The Department Stores.

http://www.windowoncyprus.com/woolwort.htm

Woolworths: Nostalgia in the 99¢ Bin

http://www.geocities.com/Athens/Ithaca/9326/index.html

The Woolworth Family Genealogy Web

http://www.thewoolworths.com/

INDEX

ABOUT THE AUTHOR

Karen Plunkett-Powell is the author of the nationally-acclaimed, *The Nancy Drew Scrapbook: 60 Years of America's Favorite Teenage Sleuth* and co-author of *Home Design from the Inside-Out: Feng Shui, Color Therapy and Self-Awareness*. She has published hundreds of magazine and newspaper articles, and four mainstage children's plays. Karen is also a freelance editor and a frequent speaker on the writer's conference circuit. You can write to the author at Remembering Woolworth's, P.O. Box 3128, Sea Bright, N.J. 07760.

PHOTO LISTING & CREDITS

The author gratefully acknowledges the use of images from the following sources. Great effort has been made to trace the proper copyright holders of the photographs herein, and/or to acknowledge the photographer of record. If there are any omissions we apologize, and will make appropriate acknowledgments in future printings.

Reprinted from ***American Weekly***: Part Two Title Page (Frank Woolworth and daughter, Switzerland, 1890)

Author's Collection: 14 (Stock Certificate), 127 (lunch ad, Cuban), 179 ("Blue Waltz" perfume), 216 ("Win Again in '69), 234 (Woolworth Building sketch by artist A.E. Poor)

Sandy Biggs, photographer: 231 (Woolworth Building powder set)

Reprinted from *Five and Ten Boy*, 1962, **Bobbs Merrill**: 20 (Gray Morrow illustration of Frank Woolworth and William Moore)

Charles Boyle, photographer: 129 (exterior, Woolworth's of Cyprus)

Veronique Daganaud, photographer: 232 (Woolworth Building bank)

Images courtesy of **Dorn's Photo**, Red Bank, N.J.: 3 (store interior, Red Bank, NJ), 141 (lunch counter, Red Bank, NJ, c. 1945), 150 (interior shot, candy and fudge counter)

Reprinted from ***Engineering Record***: 90 (escavation of Woolworth Building, c. 1911)

Mike Frankel, photographer: 1 (penny weight cards), 2 (placards), 6 (toothpaste), 115 (souvenir thimble), 168 (Lone Range lunch box), 170 (Christmas ornaments, top right), 198 (album cover), 209 ("Sea-Dog" fish tank toy), Part Four Title Page (Woolworth's store business hours sign), 227 (Hot Wheels LTD Edition set), 228 (Porcelain spoon rests; Herald Square ribbon; Woolco snaps), 229 (Barbie "Special Expressions"; Topps Baseball cards), 230 (Guy Lombardo record brush; Woolworth Co. yardstick, Woolworth Building Needle Book), 231 (Stereograph), 232 (Pewter salt & pepper shakers; pewter shoe), 233 (souvenir coins dated 1925, and 1988), 235 (menu from Kentucky Woolworth's), 238 (shopping basket; Lovely Hair Net; Famous Firsts ink blotter), 239 (Watchband sign)

Greensboro Daily News, 158 ("The Four Freshman" 1960), 159 (Frank Harris, 1960)

Images courtesy of **Lancaster Historical Society**: 74 (Woolworth Building, Queen St., Lancaster, early 1900s), 152 (Frank Woolworth and local dignitaries)

Stacey McDonald, photographer: 128 (Woolworth Ltd. Metro, Sydney, Australia)

Reprinted from ***The New Movie Magazine***, 1930: 191 (cover; Western Union ad)

Monica Randall collection: 37 (Winfield Hall estate, Glen Cove)

Arthur E. Scott, photographer: 12 ("Closing Forever" sign; "After 118 Years"...sign), 45 (commemorative plaque, Lancaster, Pa.), 52 (Woolworth's home on Lemon St, Lancaster, Pa.), 92 (stone caricatures of Frank Woolworth and Cass Gilbert), 131 ("Thank You For Shopping

Woolworth's sign), 134 (Woolworth memorial, Woodlawn, NY), 137 (interior, Shadow Lawn Estate, NJ), 156 ("Closed" sign over soda dispenser), 165 (booths), 167 (Welcome to America's Christmas Store ad),

Patricia Sinnott-Stott, photographer: 5 (exterior storefront, London)

Images courtesy of **Venator Group**, formerly F.W. Woolworth Co., New York: Frontis (Frank Woolworth portrait), Prologue Title Page (store interior, 34th St. NYC), 1 (milk shake; sandwich), 4 (waitress near stove), 6 (100th anniversary logo), 7 (pages from Home Shopping Guide, 1929; kitchen supplies, 1939), 10 (Woolco store; Kinney Shoes), 27 (Watertown, NY square), 38 (first 5¢ table), 43 (ladies' hair ribbon display), 54 (Charles Woolworth), 56 (Chart, Woolworth's First Decade), 64 (Group photo of executives, c. 1901), 67 (counter girls on break, c.1950s), 76 (William Moore; Founding Fathers, 1912), 77 (Chart: Stock information, c. 1911); 84 (Woolworth Building Tower; Woolworth Building etching), 87 (Pre-American Revolution map), 88 (Cass Gilbert), 92 (Woolworth Building mini-hospital; pool room), 95 (Empire Room); 97 (Cass Gilbert illustration of Grand Arcade, c. 1912), 103 (Seymour Knox; Earle Charlton), 104 (doll display, Quebec store, c. 1960), 111 (fishing gear ad), 112 (exterior, Woolworth's, Blackpool, England), 116 (Interior, Breman, Germany store), 123 (Interior, lunch counter, Havana, Cuba, c. 1955), 137 (Hubert T. Parson), Part Three Title Page (Interior, Woolworth's store, NY), 143 (busy lunch counter scene, midwest, c. 1939; couple in restaurant, Virginia, c. 1979; Chuck Wagon Food Court, Denver, Co.), 145 (Fountain and Lunch Department ad, c. 1939), 147 (Schraffts Candy ad), 153 (Pick-A-Balloon Game" flyer), 154 (Lunch counter menu, c. 1929; window display, dairy promotion; interior lunch counter, turkey promotion), 171 (Christmas ornaments and wrap paper ad), 171 (toy ad), 172 (Nativity scene ad), 175 (Easter supplies ad; Valentine's Day ad), 181 ("For School" products ad, "Back to School" supplies ad, 1939), 182 (Woolco, Gretna, La), 182 ("Plastic Ensembles" ad), 183 ("Lay Away Plan" ad), 185 (Tournament of Roses Parade) 187 (Woolworth News, Summer/Fall 1994), 200 (interior family scene); 202 (MacGregor cologne ad), 203 (Honolulu, Hawaii storefront), 206 ("Palm Beach" ad), 208 (interior, Woolworth's, Denver, Co.), 210 ("Hartz Mountain" bird food ads), 217 (Manager teaching "Learner"), 221 (Counter Girls, Detroit, MI), 232 (Counter Girls' strike, 1937), 234 (cover: Fortieth Anniversary Souvenir booklet), 239 ("What A Thrill" ad, 1969), 240 ("Time is Running Out" flyer),

Courtesy of **Chuck Wilkerson**: 215 (Brochure for Diamond "W" Newsletter)

John D. Yeck, photographer: 12 (family storefront scene, New Mexico)

The original sources for following historical images are unknown: Part One Title Page (Frank & Charles Woolworth, c. 1866), 21 (Jasper & Elizabeth Woolworth; John & Fannie Woolworth; Henry and Kezia McBrier; Woolworth & McBrier storefront), 24 (exterior, Champion, NY family home), 29 (postcard, Watertown, NY Moore's 5&10), 31 (William Moore), 35 (Jennie Creighton-Woolworth), 44 (postcard, Roof Garden & Vaudeville House, Lancaster, Pa), 48 (exterior, 170 North Queen St. store, Lancaster), 49 (First convention of five-and-ten syndicate), 53 (Edna, Jessy & Helena Woolworth), 54 (Woolworth Bros. Storefront c, 1881), 57 (Wedding of Seymour Knox w/Frank & Charles Woolworth), 58 (Edwin M. McBrier, c. 1888), 61 (postcard, interior of a Woolworth store, c. 1910), 69 (postcard, Powell St., San Francisco), 75 (postcard, a main street, Clearwater, Fla.), 80 (The Woolworths at Palm Beach, c. 1913), 136 (Hutton family photo, train station, Paris), 192 (cast photo, "Girl From Woolworth's", c. 1929), 200 (postcard, Northampton St, Easton, Pa.), 207 (postcard, Laramie, WI), 214 (postcard, Woolworth Building, Jacksonville, Fla)

==========

Lyrics from "Love at the Five and Dime" (pg. 1) courtesy of Nanci Griffith

Poem entitled "The Smells of Woolworth" (pg.202) courtesy of Elizabeth Larrabee